STAR HEALING

YOUR SUN SIGN, YOUR HEALTH & YOUR SUCCESS

David Lawson

with Jennifer Griffiths

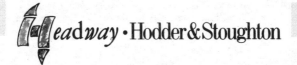

Headway · Hodder & Stoughton

Cataloguing in Publication Data is available from the British Library

ISBN 0 340 606 46 0

First published 1994
Impression number   10 9 8 7 6 5 4 3 2 1
Year   1999 1998 1997 1996 1995 1994

Typeset by Wearset, Boldon, Tyne and Wear.

Printed in Great Britain for Hodder & Stoughton Educational, a division of Hodder
Headline Plc, 338 Euston Road, London NW1 3BH by Cox & Wyman Ltd, Reading.

Contents

CONTENTS

Biographies

David Lawson is an English healer, writer and course leader. Together with partner Justin Carson he travels the world teaching self-healing techniques, hands-on healing, psychic development and spiritual growth.

Sometimes he just stops to enjoy the view.

His work includes *Money and Your Life – A Prosperity Playbook* (with Justin Carson) and the audiotaped visualisations *I See Myself in Perfect Health*, Vols. I and II, all published by Healing Workshops Press.

David and Justin are authorised worldwide facilitators of courses based on *You Can Heal Your Life* by Louise L. Hay. For details of these and other forthcoming events please write to:

Healing Workshops
PO Box 1678
London NW5 4EW
UK.

Jennifer Griffiths became a personal astrologer after graduating from the polytechnic of North London with a BA degree in Classical Civilisations and Film Studies. Her work focuses on personal growth, self-healing and the journey of the soul.

Acknowledgements

I would like to thank the following people for their support and belief in this project:

Susan Mears (my agent), Rowena Gaunt (my commissioning editor), Chris Halls, Sue Hart, Andrew Swaffer, Steve Eddy, Mina Haeri, Sunny Halevi, Lilian and Eric Lawson, Anne and Alex Carson, Millie Drummond, Theresa and Anna at the Portofino Hotel, Nerja. The Delicious Kitty Campion and all of my friends, family, clients and guides.

Special thanks to Louise L. Hay for her inspiration and encouragement and also to my partner Justin Carson whose practical support, ideas, good humour and rapid typing skills helped to make *Star Healing* a reality.

David Lawson,
Órgiva, Spain
January 1994

Foreword

Astrology was always meant to be a deeply spiritual study. The Magi in the bible were astrologers. That is how they knew where to find Jesus: they followed the stars. Today, modern astrologers no longer talk about malevolent planets but see the good and the lessons in every configuration.

David Lawson goes a step further in *Star Healing*; he takes you deep within your Sun sign personality to find your hidden treasures.

Astrology is just another way of explaining life. It is not fortune-telling as much as it is a deep study of your own being. I believe that we choose our astrological charts before we are born, just as we choose our life lessons before we come into the world.

In this wonderful book David Lawson takes you on a journey that provides you with the tools to master your Sun sign and change your life for the better. It is a book to study for the rest of your life. Each time you read it you will continue to explore the depths of yourself. I highly recommend it.

Louise L. Hay,
8 October 1993

A Personal Note

The path for our spiritual growth can come to us from countless sources, although all routes will lead us towards a similar destination.

Once we have discovered the joyous possibilities of thinking and acting positively and being loving and non-judgemental, whatever circumstances we find ourselves in, our life's journey will have brought us to a point where, if we choose not to fight the process, our lives can begin to flow in harmony with the divine. This is true regardless of our birth sign.

Astrology, used well, is a marvellous tool to help us focus on those things that we want to create, and to help us to disengage from those life events, character traits and behaviour patterns that we wish to leave behind.

David Lawson is a marvellous teacher and wonderful healer who, throughout the years, has helped many people discover their potential by helping them to understand their true worth and overcome the negative programming that we were all brought up with. This approach has helped people to revitalise their lives in new and exciting ways, building on their inherent strengths and abilities and giving them the confidence to use them.

David is approachable and has a real commitment to the needs of others. He is readily available, with an open ear and, perhaps more importantly, an open heart.

It has been a wonderful experience co-leading courses and workshops with David – from our weekends in Hands-On Healing and Spiritual Growth, to the wonderful 'You Can

Heal Your Life' workshops based on Louise Hay's seminal book of the same name. Indeed Louise has been a constant presence and inspiration in our lives and work since we first met her in 1989.

As you will see from reading this book, David has the rare gift of helping people to appreciate their own being as well as their life purpose. I recall the end of a Healer Training and Spiritual Growth course in Dublin when we asked participants to comment on what they had gained from the experience. One wonderful lady who had been casually dressed the whole weekend exclaimed, 'I'm discovering that I'm one hell of a nun!' Great praise indeed that this woman, like so many others, could continue to learn her uniqueness in the constantly positive atmosphere that David Lawson generates.

Justin Carson

This book is dedicated to three very special people: my friends Francesca Montaldi (Aquarius) and Rebecca Davis (Aquarius) who were there when I needed them most and my partner Justin Carson (Gemini) whose life and work inspires mine. With Love, David.

Introduction

WELCOME TO *STAR HEALING*

Thank you for choosing this book. We wish you joy, fun and healing in reading it and in using the ideas that appeal to you.

Star Healing – Your Sun Sign, Your Health and Your Success is an astrology book with a difference. It takes a fresh look at Sun sign astrology and explores the trends within each of the twelve signs of the zodiac towards spiritual growth, material success, physical health, intimate relationships and emotional expression.

Astrology can be used as a positive tool for self-exploration. By focusing on the special qualities of our own Sun sign we can all find inspiration to help us to heal and enhance the special relationship that we have with ourselves. *Star Healing* bridges the gap between a knowledge of your own Sun sign and the practical ideas and self-healing techniques that can help you to develop your special, inborn gifts.

Each astrological sign has its own tendencies for self-discovery that can be utilised to maintain a psychological, emotional and physical balance. When you begin to look at your astrological personality positively then you may find yourself undergoing some magical changes of attitude.

In *Star Healing* we do not talk about the positive or negative qualities of each Sun sign because we do not see any constructive, healing value in making those judgements. We describe the characteristics and tendencies of each sign as positively as we can, offering suggestions for how you can

1

work with the special energy of your sign for self-healing and balance. When you place your attention on your strengths rather than on your weaknesses then you automatically expand your ability to grow in strength.

Our 'suggestions' include the use of specially tailored positive thought techniques and visual meditations for each sign. We have also added some ideas about complementary therapies, forms of physical exercise or creative pursuits that you may enjoy experimenting with. Please be free to use the ideas that feel right for you and discard those that do not suit you. You are the person who knows what is best for your body, mind and emotions.

The suggestions in this book are intended to complement medical treatment rather than replace it. We would be delighted to think of anyone using this book as a tool to aid or inspire their healing process but please get plenty of advice from medical and complementary practitioners and make an informed choice about the appropriate courses of treatment for your needs.

Any form of healing, whether physical, mental, emotional or spiritual, can be assisted by learning to understand yourself better and thinking positively about yourself, your life and any treatments or therapies that you use.

HOW TO USE THIS BOOK

It is easy to identify yourself with one of the twelve Sun signs described in this book. All you need to do is check which sign relates to your date of birth and then begin to play with the ideas or meditations in that chapter. You probably already know your Sun sign from the general forecasts in newspapers and magazines that give us all so much fun. If not, we have included a table for you to check your sign below.

Aries – fire – cardinal – 22 March – 21 April.
Taurus – earth – fixed – 22 April – 22 May.
Gemini – air – mutable – 23 May – 22 June.
Cancer – water – cardinal – 23 June – 23 July.
Leo – fire – fixed – 24 July – 23 August.
Virgo – earth – mutable – 24 August – 23 September.
Libra – air – cardinal – 24 September – 22 October.
Scorpio – water – fixed – 23 October – 22 November.
Sagittarius – fire – mutable – 23 November – 22 December.
Capricorn – earth – cardinal – 23 December – 20 January.
Aquarius – air – fixed – 21 January – 20 February.
Pisces – water – mutable – 21 February – 21 March.

If in addition you choose to read about the other eleven Sun signs (and we hope you do) you may find some suggestions that could also benefit and inspire you in some way. Our choice to link certain therapies or positive thoughts to certain Sun signs does not exclude them from being of benefit to anyone else. Just because, for example, rebirthing is an ideal therapy for the transformational drives of Scorpio, it does not mean that it would not suit a person born in Leo or Libra. Please use and enjoy anything that appeals to you from any part of this book.

We are all influenced by the special combination of astrological signs and planets at certain positions in our birth chart. The characteristics in each chapter are specifically written to describe Sun signs and the tendencies that the Sun highlights within each sign of the zodiac. However, they may also be a helpful introduction to the qualities to be found in other areas of your chart. Allow your instincts to draw you to any chapter or area of the book that would benefit you; you will probably find that in using your intuition in this way you are expressing some part of your basic astrological make-up and bringing healing to that aspect of yourself too.

WHAT IS A SUN SIGN?

Your Sun sign is the sign of the zodiac through which the Sun appeared to be travelling at the time of your birth. It is only one aspect of your overall astrological personality but it is generally considered to be the most important one.

The movements of the Sun, the Moon and the planets – Mercury, Venus, Mars, Jupiter, Saturn, Uranus, Neptune and Pluto – through the heavens are documented. Their positions at the moment of your birth and relative to your birthplace form the basis of your birth chart. These and many other factors are taken into consideration when an astrologer gives you a reading of the characteristics or psychological profile that you were born with. In addition, this information gives the blueprint from which future trends can be evaluated or forecast.

The general position of the Sun at the time of birth is perhaps the easiest area of astrology for the lay person to assess for themselves. However, you may have noticed that magazines and books vary slightly in the dates they give for the beginning and end of each Sun sign. This is because there are slight variations from year to year, and so all tables of dates are approximate, including the one that we have chosen for this book.

If you are unsure of your Sun sign then the best way to

check is by visiting an astrologer and having your full birth chart drawn up properly. There are also businesses that calculate and print up your birth chart by computer and some of these are good value for money, although for a proper reading the work of a personal astrologer would be best. That aside, if you are born two to three days either side of the changeover from one Sun sign to another you may benefit from using the ideas and suggestions in both of the corresponding chapters of this book; both could give you valuable insights into your personality. It is also possible that you will find yourself particularly drawn to other chapters that reflect some other strong characteristic of your birth chart.

We are all a mixture of many astrological trends. The Sun sign chapters we have written describe astrological types that may relate quite powerfully to how you see yourself but there may well be passages that do not relate. You are an individual formed from many astrological influences, including your environment, your education and your underlying spiritual purpose.

THE INFLUENCE OF THE SUN

The Sun in our astrological chart is a guiding creative force, a special inner light that illuminates our path through life. The Sun may inspire us with spiritual purpose, helping us to integrate the many facets of our personality and direct them towards our highest potential as we meet the adventures and challenges of our lives.

Developing a strong awareness of our Sun sign can help us to attune to our own inner wisdom and insights. The position of the Sun in our chart endows us with the special qualities of our self-expression and can awaken our creative gifts and abilities. The Sun can be said to highlight our particular radiance of joy, vitality, health and happiness. Knowledge of our Sun sign can help us to heal ourselves, find a greater meaning to our lives and view ourselves with positivity and love.

We hope that *Star Healing* will help you to discover aspects of your creative potential and the gift of expansion in your life and awareness. A willingness to embrace your Sun sign and to utilise its special qualities can awaken the Sun in your heart.

ELEMENTS AND QUALITIES

The twelve Sun signs are divided up according to the four elements and the three 'qualities'. The signs may share elements and qualities with each other but they each have their own unique expression of these fundamental motivating forces. The element and quality of our Sun sign will direct our inner motivation and provide special keys to our process of healing or personal development.

The elements are the four elements of life: *Fire*, *Earth*, *Air* and *Water*. The power of the elements has long been used to aid spiritual, physical, mental and emotional healing.

Fire is the element of the spirit. The fire signs are Aries, Leo and Sagittarius.

Earth is the element of the body. The earth signs are Taurus, Virgo and Capricorn.

Air is the element of the mind. The air signs are Gemini, Libra and Aquarius.

Water is the element of the emotions. The water signs are Cancer, Scorpio and Pisces.

There are three astrological qualities that express the fundamental nature of the signs: *Cardinal*, *Fixed* and *Mutable*. These qualities are key to the expression of our life purpose and our inner drives.

Cardinal signs initiate and instigate. They are Aries, Cancer, Libra and Capricorn.

Fixed signs stabilise and contain. They are Taurus, Leo, Scorpio and Aquarius.

Mutable signs develop and change. They are Gemini, Virgo, Sagittarius and Pisces.

The descriptions of each of the Sun signs in this book expand upon and utilise the healing nature of the elements and astrological qualities. Each sign can only ever be said to be of one element and one quality. However, in *Star Healing* we have begun each chapter with an exploration of the essential elemental nature of each sign and then taken that sign into the realms of each of the other elements. In this way we have described the tendencies and the unique healing potential of the Sun signs when involved in the realms of spirit, passion and creativity (*Fire*), engaged in the world of business, success and material manifestation (*Earth*), inspired by the realms of the intellect, logic and higher vision (*Air*) or touched by the world of romantic love, emotional expression and intuition (*Water*).

THE POWER OF POSITIVE THOUGHT

The use of positive thought techniques for health and well-being is not a new concept. The power of words and of positive visual images has been known for centuries. In recent times successful self-help books have catered for a growing desire that many people have to learn more about the power of the mind and become more aware of their inner strengths, so that they can take control of their own healing process.

Complementary therapies have successfully used will-power and imagery alongside physical, herbal or auric healing skills. Some areas of standard medical practice are beginning to recognise the value of using positive thought to aid or accelerate healing, and businesses are increasingly training their staff to think for success.

Star Healing is probably unique in combining these techniques with Sun sign astrology, placing a strong emphasis on fun and creative positive images for each astrological sign. Many of these ideas are linked to the spiritual journey or life purpose of each sign and are designed to bring out their strengths and special qualities.

WHAT ARE AFFIRMATIONS?

Positive affirmations are bold, bright, positively focused statements or ideas that can be used to transform mental attitudes and aid physical, emotional or spiritual healing. An affirmation is simply a tool that can retrain the mind to think in more positive, constructive and life-enhancing ways. 'I see myself in perfect health' and 'I now create a healthy mind and body' are two examples of positive affirmations.

Our thoughts, beliefs and attitudes directly affect our experience. Positive, joyful thoughts are likely to create positive, joyful experiences. Negative, limiting or rigidly held beliefs can adversely affect our emotional state, our ability to create fulfilling relationships and our physical health.

Many people are aware of the concept of the self-fulfilling

prophecy and the idea that our thoughts affect the life experiences and feelings that we create. Our minds are powerful. What we think affects the way we feel about ourselves today and forms the reality of tomorrow. We are more likely be happy, healthy and prosperous if we are willing to believe that these experiences are available to us.

Regular use of positive affirmations can enhance any treatments, exercise programmes, healthy diets or therapies that we are using. What is more, the rhythms and discipline of positivity can help us to deal with and transcend the challenges of life while extending the bliss and pleasures of the good times. Affirmations are simple to use and will work for anybody who is willing to persist with them and who is open to new, brighter expectations and patterns of thought.

Many people think quite positively for much of the time but there can be areas of old, restrictive or fearful thought that are deeply held or unconscious. These thoughts are often learned, along with some positive ones, very early on in life. The beliefs, attitudes and moods of our parents or parent figures, were colouring our view of the world from day one and as we grew up, we were also influenced by the beliefs and behaviour of brothers, sisters, grandparents, teachers and other children at school. Wider patterns of belief came to us from our religion, our community and the media.

Affirmations are used to replace old, learned patterns of thought that no longer serve us, with new, positive ones that do. By affirming positively, we alter our beliefs to support our needs and desires, changing our reality accordingly.

9

SOME GUIDELINES FOR USING AFFIRMATIONS

Star Healing contains many positive affirmations that have been specially tailored for each astrological sign. They have been created to balance and enhance the personality traits and energies of the signs, opening positive channels of thought that may help with health, success, emotional expression and spiritual growth.

Here are some guidelines and suggestions for using affirmations:

★ Affirmations can be written, typed, spoken aloud, sung, chanted and said to yourself in the mirror as well as being repeated over and over in your mind. Many people find that they benefit from filling their homes with affirmational thoughts, perhaps writing or painting them out in bright colours and pasting them on the bathroom mirror, the fridge, on the doors or anywhere else where they will be constantly visible. Be creative and choose ways to use them that work best for you.

★ Affirmations are wonderful when they are used in conjunction with meditation or physical exercise. Choosing one or two affirmations that are easy to remember and repeating them silently to yourself in your mind with the rhythm of your breath or in time to the repetition of a familiar exercise can help them to become second nature. You may even repeat affirmations in your mind as you walk, pacing them out with every step.

★ Affirmations can be easily recorded for you to listen to while you are meditating, relaxing, having a bath, pottering around your home, travelling to work or at any other time. You could make a tape by getting a trusted friend or family member to speak your chosen series of positive thoughts into a tape recorder. Ask them to include your name from time to time so that it is as personally tailored to you as possible. Even more powerful would be a recording of your own voice speaking the affirmations; again put your own name into some of the positive statements. For example, 'I, David, am passionate about my ideas.' Or 'David, you are always motivated and inspired.' You may choose to build up a collection of tapes to use over and over again.

★ Although it is wonderful to set aside some special time every day or every couple of days to focus on your affirmations, you do not have to view them as yet another task to fit into your busy schedule. Perhaps the best way to use them is to make them an integral part of your life. You could affirm on your way to and from work, while you are cooking the dinner, while you are doing the housework or going through your morning routine. Perhaps the best times to do affirmations include those last few minutes at night just before you go to sleep and those first few minutes in the morning when you are still waking up. These are times when your mind is receptive and when you can influence your night's rest or the mood of your day ahead. After a time you may wake up with the positive thoughts already there in your mind repeating themselves with brightness and clarity to welcome you to the day.

★ Some of the best affirmations to use are those that run contrary to your current beliefs or differ greatly from what is presently real and true for you. For example, if you are sick then it may seem strange to affirm, 'I am always in perfect health.' However, this will probably be one of the best positive statements for you to practise. You still need to recognise what is happening to your body and make appropriate choices about treatments, but while you are doing this the affirmation will support your healing process and enhance whatever treatments you have chosen.

★ The more you use affirmations, the more they can work for you. Sometimes it is good to have a few favourite affirmations that you will always remember wherever you are while frequently introducing your mind to new ones that address a particular need. You can never have too many positive thoughts but when you are first introducing your mind to them it is perhaps better to have a few that you will be able to memorise and use than an endless list that can be easily forgotten.

★ Affirmations are meant to be fun. Play with them, experiment with them and find ways to use them that are entertaining for you.

CREATING YOUR OWN AFFIRMATIONS

After using the affirmations that we have devised for you in this book you may wish to experiment with creating some of your own. Here are some general guidelines to help you.

★ Affirmations need to be phrased in the present tense. For example, 'I now create . . .' (present simple tense) or 'I am always . . .' (present continuous tense). If you affirm for something as if it is already true for you then your mind can more readily make the changes that will alter your experience of life. However, if you affirm that something is *going* to happen or that it *will* happen then you are creating it in the future, and that is where it will stay, constantly out of reach. 'In three weeks I will be . . .' will always stay three weeks away.

★ Affirmations often work best when they are relatively short and easy to remember.

★ In most cases affirmations need to be positively focused on your desired outcome rather than focused on the situations or conditions that you want to release. For example 'I am healthy and relaxed' is a much more effective affirmation than 'I am never sick or tense.' The latter will keep your attention unduly focused on the negative outcome, continuing to make it a reality in your life.

★ Your negative or limiting thoughts are the raw material for creating positive affirmations. Each negative thought contains the foundation for positive change and growth. 'I will never be free of back pain' can become 'My back is free, healthy and comfortable.'

★ For anyone wishing to explore the use of affirmations, positive thought techniques and other aspects of self-healing there are many excellent books available. Perhaps the most widely loved of these is *You Can Heal Your Life*, by Louise L. Hay, published by Eden Grove Editions.

HOW TO USE VISUALISATION

Visualisation is the use of mental images to create the experiences that we choose to have in our lives. Using the power of our minds we can daydream away stress, create calm and peace, prevent illness, promote good health, speed up the recuperative process and in many cases aid the healing of all areas of our lives.

Many have already discovered that the power of creative daydreams has a miraculous effect on their home environment, their career, their finances and their relationships. To change your world you begin by changing the way that you picture it; the rest follows naturally.

Visualisation and all positive thought techniques work directly on the most important relationship of all, the relationship we have with ourselves. How else can we create health and love in our lives if we don't see ourselves as healthy and lovable and deserving of these things?

Star Healing takes you on a voyage of images for each sign, highlighting the essential nature of the signs and sowing seeds for the imagination. The use of visualisation is a powerful way of accessing innate abilities and providing a key to positive changes.

The ideal environment for meditation or visualisation exercises is somewhere safe, quiet, warm and comfortable. Minimise distractions by unplugging telephones and ensuring that other people will not disturb you. Use music in the background if it helps you to relax but make sure that it is calming and melodic and without lyrics that would fight for your attention.

Either sit with your back properly supported, making sure that your feet are firmly planted on the floor, or lie down on your back in a comfortable position. It is preferable to keep your arms and legs, hands and feet uncrossed; keeping your body open and receptive. Remember to breathe deeply and slowly throughout your visualisation and ensure that your body will be warm as you relax.

Once you are familiar with the images and techniques suggested, you may wish to practise them in many situations – for example sitting on a bus. However, the above scenario is the easiest. They are not to be used while driving a car or in any other situation where you need all of your concentration.

It is not important to follow every detail of the visualisation exercises exactly; it would not be very relaxing for you to feel that you have to work hard to get all of the details correct and in the right order. Just read them through a couple of times to familiarise yourself with their essence before settling down and trusting your mind to take care of the images perfectly for you. If it helps, then make a tape-recording of your voice guiding you through the visualisations or positive thoughts. Alternatively you could get a friend to talk you through them.

Some people have a natural ability to think in pictures while with others it comes with practice. Regardless of how your mind works, your intention is much more important than your capacity to get strong visual images. Just holding the concept, or the idea of the picture in your mind is enough for these techniques to work for you.

Giving your mind the freedom to play is more beneficial than trying hard to be absolutely accurate. Remember that the more you play with the visualisations, the easier they become. Please feel free to adapt any of the images; after a while you may find that your imagination automatically extends and enhances them.

Healing with Fire

TURNING ON THE LIGHTS WITH THE FIRE SIGNS

Fire is the element of the spirit. It is positive, passionate, forward-looking and visionary. The people born into the element of fire are optimistic, energetic, creative and strong.

The three fire signs are:

ARIES – CARDINAL FIRE
22 MARCH – 21 APRIL

KEY QUALITIES:
INITIATING, ENTHUSIASTIC, DYNAMIC, ENERGETIC,
IMPULSIVE, COURAGEOUS.

LEO – FIXED FIRE
24 JULY – 23 AUGUST

KEY QUALITIES:
CREATIVE, CHARISMATIC, BOLD, SHINING, NOBLE,
DRAMATIC.

SAGITTARIUS – MUTABLE FIRE
23 NOVEMBER – 22 DECEMBER

KEY QUALITIES:
ADVENTUROUS, OUTGOING, PHILOSOPHICAL, OPTIMISTIC,
EXPANSIVE, SPIRITUAL.

CHAPTER ONE

ARIES

22 March - 21 April

CARDINAL FIRE

Aries is the spontaneous first spark of the astrological cycle; a spark that ignites the fires of conception and birth. Arien people are active, energetic and volatile by nature, born to instigate new projects and jump into life's adventure. For Aries each new moment contains an opportunity; they love the excitement of new risks, great challenges and spontaneous bursts of activity.

Being the first sign of the zodiac, Aries has a pure, forceful energy and an innocent thirst for exploration. Many Ariens are quite childlike in nature. They are uncluttered by complications or negative expectations and are able to achieve things that other people would not even attempt. Like children, Ariens are often unaware that what they are doing is supposed to be impossible and so they succeed because they expect to.

Picture a spring scene with new shoots bursting into life from plants and seeds that up until now have lain dormant. The miracle of new life and new growth comes with an impelling Arien sense of purpose, raw and powerful. A seed doesn't know that germinating and growing is an incredible task; it just does it because it is motivated by light and pre-programmed within its cellular structure. In the same way, the Arien is motivated by the light of the moment and fired into activity.

The symbol for Aries is the ram. The glyph or pictogram for this sign depicts the two horns of the ram curving outwards from a central point of initial impulse (♈). The ram was a powerful figure in Greek mythology as well as being revered in ancient Egypt, Sumer and Babylon.

Arien people are often seen to be the leaders of the astrological flock, having the energy, drive and impulsiveness to carry other people as well as themselves into new realms of experience. Their impulsiveness is both heroic and foolhardy, inspired and rash. Ariens do not look before they leap; and this is, on the whole, a positive and healthy tendency. Whether we are Arien or not, if we could predict the outcome of each new step, we would probably talk ourselves out of some of the most advancing actions of our lives. It is the Arien purpose to advance, regardless of outcome.

The ruler of Aries is the fiery planet Mars. In mythology Mars was the god of courage, action, strength and energy. Thus Mars endows Aries with active capability and skill, driving Ariens to sharpen their minds and hone their sense of purpose. The influence of this planet supplies them with boundless energy for their adventures. For most Ariens, the key to self-healing lies in harnessing this energy.

Ariens are dominant, fiery people with extraordinary grit and determination. They take a direct approach to life, moving headlong into the excitements and surprises of each new day. Whatever their age, Ariens never seem to lose their capacity to greet life head on. This can keep them youthful, interesting and vibrant right into their later years.

ARIES IN ITS ELEMENT

The element of fire conceived its child Aries with passion and brilliant intensity. Aries is perhaps the most archetypically fiery of the three fire signs; it expresses fire in its raw state through fundamental impulses and a creative urgency. Like fire itself Ariens can move through life with speed, spontaneity and shimmering brilliance.

The influence of Aries' ruling planet, Mars can give Ariens an extraordinary amount of physical energy, spiritual drive and fiery determination. It is how individual Ariens handle this that will make the difference between health and disharmony or success and frustration.

Ariens can sometimes feel overwhelmed by their drives and impulses. It is essential that they find suitable outlets for them. When unable to channel their energy, they can display restlessness, impatience and even downright irritation.

An Arien who has learned to direct these powers will radiate a glowing contentment, warmth and generosity, and a positive sense of personal satisfaction. Ariens can often best serve themselves by coming to the aid of other people. They are sometimes inspired by heroic acts and can find great satisfaction in becoming a hero or heroine for other people. In most cases this does not mean plunging into dangerous situations, although many Ariens do enjoy taking risks; it is more likely that this heroism will be displayed through impulsive acts of kindness.

Ariens find peace through action. They have too much will and wilfulness to be comfortable with passivity. Later in life some Ariens may discover the ability to contemplate and find comfort in stillness, but only for short periods of time. Even octogenarians can fidget like children if they have an excess of fire energy and nowhere to direct it.

Just like the fire from which they are born, Ariens are essentially free. They relish their freedom and independence and resist any controlling outside influence. Arien children will push and push at parental boundaries, always demanding to have their own way. Ultimately they cannot be contained and will break through whatever restrictions are imposed on them. Interestingly, they are often happiest with strong parental figures who are willing to stand up to them and against whom they can feel safe to push and rebel.

Arien energy is akin to the raw fuel of creativity; it is the initial thrust that pushes new projects into life. Arien people are forever starting new schemes, providing the force and vitality required for creative or business ventures to get off the ground. Aries people motivate themselves and others with a great deal of fiery enthusiasm, fun and guile.

ARIEN ZONES OF THE BODY

Aries rules the head, cerebral system and the adrenal glands. Head and facial massage or facial treatments of all kinds may be beneficial for Arien people whose general mood and health can be enhanced by some liberal pampering in this area of the body. Even a trip to the hairdresser can be uplifting and relaxing for Ariens, many of whom feel clearer and lighter after a haircut or new styling.

Ariens would do well to take special care of their physical senses, perhaps getting their eyes tested regularly and doing eye exercises to keep their vision strong. Care also needs to be taken with the ears; Ariens will benefit physically and psychologically by avoiding continuous loud noise despite the fact that some may enjoy the stimulation of amplified music.

The mouth is another area that benefits from positive attention. Oral hygiene, essential for us all, is particularly important for Aries.

The head acts as a good barometer by which Ariens can check their overall stress levels. Too much pressure may be experienced as muscular tension of the face, jaw and scalp. Muscular tightness or headaches would indicate to Ariens that they need to stop what they are doing for a while, or at least slow down. The headstrong passions of Aries are wonderful for making things happen in the world but Ariens do need to be aware of when they are pushing themselves too hard and put on the brakes before they get overtired or run down.

Ariens need to find a healthy balance between stimulation and relaxation. Too much activity and they can overdraw on their seemingly limitless reserves of energy, running on their nerves rather than drawing from their normal fiery glow. Too little activity and they can become listless, bored and emotionally turbulent. Both scenarios can be stressful and create muscular tension throughout the body.

The adrenal glands control the production and flow of the hormone adrenalin around the body. We all need a certain amount of adrenalin to keep us healthy, active and motivated, fuelled up to respond to the challenges of life. However, too much of this natural chemical can deplete the immune system and be generally debilitating. Ariens are particularly sensitive to adrenal secretions and benefit from regulating their stress levels. Physical or mental overwork can flood the body with excess adrenalin and affect the overall health or balance.

Many Ariens are blessed with a naturally healthy constitution and their innate, positive energy helps to keep them in good health. If, in addition to this, they learn to listen to their body and respond accordingly, then they are more likely to remain on the path of well-being and happiness. The best preventative treatment consists of learning to take care of your needs when they first present themselves rather than waiting for the tensions to build up.

EXERCISE AND THERAPIES

Most Ariens love physical activity of all kinds. They enjoy competition and often rise to an opportunity to test their skill, strength and stamina. Active Ariens enjoy team games like football, hockey, baseball or netball. They often keep up the energy and enthusiasm when team mates become dispirited or start to flag.

More solitary activities for Ariens could include cycling or running and athletic pursuits like pole-vaulting, high-jumping or long-jumping. Ariens need regular outlets for their flammable, impulsive energy and so it is worth them exploring sports centres and gymnasiums to find a range of physical activities that they will enjoy.

Ariens can find physical, mental and emotional harmony through many of the martial arts that are now taught internationally. Karate particularly may help them to channel their energies effectively and allow them to become more focused and confident. More passive forms of oriental exercise or martial arts such as Tai Chi or Chi Kung may help to make Ariens more contemplative.

Aries people respond well to massage of all kinds; that is, if they can sit or lie down for long enough to allow someone to massage them. Foot reflexology, more associated with Pisces, can help to ground and balance Ariens, settling them down when they become overly focused in their heads and suffer from too much nervous energy. The feet act as a map of the entire body with points corresponding to particular organs and glands. Massage of the toes will help to relieve tension in and around the area of the head.

Ariens tend to be keen to be in the driving seat of their own self-healing or fitness programme and many will want to develop skills or techniques that they can use on themselves. For this reason Do-In may be a good discipline to learn. Do-In is a form of the oriental massage, Shiatsu. Unlike Shiatsu, which requires the involvement of a therapist, it is intended as a system of energetic stimulation that people can practise on themselves by exercising and massaging pressure points around the body.

ARIEN INSPIRATION AND CREATIVITY

Aries people are born to create, create, create! It is as if they abhor a void and have to fill each waking moment with new activities, all charged up with their special blend of energy and enthusiasm. Eternal optimists, Ariens frequently launch themselves into ambitious projects, willing to attempt the impossible when other people withdraw defeated. In doing this, sometimes with a blinkered force of will, Aries is able to create things that would otherwise never come into existence.

Ariens are wonderful at instigating creative ventures but they need to learn how to take care of the details and follow things through so that they can be assured of lasting success. Refusing to take no for an answer, Ariens can turn their hands to creating anything. They are often more interested in the process of creating something new than with the finished product. Ariens need to have regular creative expression to stay healthy and happy, so it is important for them to find a career that allows them to express at least some of this creative urge. Many Ariens will also be drawn to numerous creative hobbies and handicrafts to keep them entertained in their spare time.

Through its ruling planet Mars, Aries is often connected to metal and various forms of metalwork. Mars is particularly linked to iron and steel, so practical Ariens may find themselves developing an interest in wrought iron work, metal sculpture, the production of fine cutlery and beautiful jewellery. The Mars influence can be seen, too, in the use of cutting implements for carpentry, wood sculpture and dressmaking. Some Ariens may even be drawn to working in wool although not all will have the patience for knitting, weaving or tapestry.

Ariens are often most inspired by heroic deeds both real and mythical. They themselves love to be the hero or heroine who rushes in to rescue a person in need from some drama of life and they will often draw inspiration from news stories of courageous daring. Children and adults alike will love fairy stories or legends that harken back to times of chivalry with knights in armour slaying dragons or Greek gods embarking on impossible quests.

One such Arien story is the tale of the Greek hero Jason who encountered danger and excitement in his quest for the Golden Fleece. Perhaps this myth conveys two archetypal aspects of Aries. Jason himself represents the pioneering adventurer that shines brightly from within all Arien souls and the fleece, too, is the embodiment of Aries. It is the golden, glittering prize that Ariens can find in harnessing their creative energy and mastering their passionate drives.

Certainly for Ariens who have become a little dispirited or who feel that they have lost their way there is nothing like a good heroic yarn to remind them of the adventure of their own life.

Fire Affirmations for Aries

I am glowing with health and boundless energy.

Life is always full of new adventures for me to enjoy.

I love the adventure of my personal development.

My head is healthy, clear and light.

I am the hero/heroine of my own glorious life.

My adrenalin flow is healthy, balanced and perfect for my needs.

I always have the perfect outlet for my bright creativity.

My life is inspired by positivity, energy and success.

Each moment of my life is a glorious awakening.

I am always youthful and alive with joy.

Fire Visualisation: Birth of the Ram

Breathe and relax. As you do, picture a spring scene with a field full of fresh green grass decorated with clusters of yellow and orange crocuses. The air is clean and alive; all is filled with a sense of newness and wonder.

Imagine a single, brilliant shaft of sunshine coming

down to create an intense pool of light at the centre of the field and as it does picture a fiery spark of golden energy shooting out from the earth at this spot. See this spark of golden energy take form as a newborn lamb, perfect and beautiful.

Imagine yourself becoming one with this lamb; see yourself with the body of a lamb, adapting rapidly to the new world and getting ready to spring and leap with youthful vitality. Feel this youthful vitality zinging through your veins; your very being becoming imbued with a limitless spontaneity and zest for life.

Feel yourself as this lamb maturing into a young ram. Imagine your muscles becoming stronger and more supple. Your body is full of strength, power and passion. Your mind is charged with a positive force of will that celebrates the joy of being alive. Each part of your body and mind exudes health and energy.

Imagine all of these qualities filling your human body and mind too. You are easily able to access and unleash youthful vitality, strength and positive power from within. See yourself filled with spontaneous joy and surrounded by sparks of creativity.

THE RISING SAP OF ARIEN WATERS

Fiery people, including those with their Sun in Aries, do not readily understand or feel comfortable with the element of water. Fire and water are both elements that deal with powerful forces of creativity and sensuality but they operate in entirely different ways. Fire is bold, passionate, spontaneous and immediate, while water is deeply mysterious, subtle, feminine and enchanting.

Arien people can best experience the element of water through their ruling planet Mars. Mars is also the ruler of the water sign Scorpio and its planetary influence brings a potent sexuality and fierce drive to both of these otherwise unrelated signs. Arien people can be highly motivated by their sexuality; it is by sexual attraction and sexual expression that many Ariens move into their hearts and explore themselves emotionally.

Spring has traditionally been the time when young men's thoughts have turned to love and maidens have yearned for passionate suitors. Poets throughout the ages have thrilled to the theme of the sexual and emotional sap beginning to rise after the long winter slumber, perhaps for very good reason. The awakening of new life brings with it the stirring of passions and emotional needs; the desire for love and excitement is rekindled. Aries is the Sun sign of spring and Arien people of all ages can find themselves fired up and glowing with an attractive potency that can last the year round.

LOVE AND ROMANCE

Ariens make bold and generous lovers who are often willing to initiate romantic or sexual encounters. Sometimes they can get carried away by their enthusiasm and steamroller the object of their desire into a romantic involvement, an emotional commitment, marriage or sometimes just into bed. This is not to say that Ariens have no sensitivity – many do. It is just that their passions often drive them with an intense energy that has to find an immediate direction or outlet.

Arien passions can be filled with warmth and love for the other person, fired with a chivalrous romanticism that may be both innocent and rash. Prospective partners who need a little more time to warm to the idea of a relationship and who need more subtlety in their love life may be tempted to dash off in the opposite direction. However, as many Ariens have discovered, the direct approach to love can work wonders on many occasions.

For some Ariens a degree of risk or uncertainty can add spice to their ardour. Some may even prefer lovers or potential marriage partners who are a little distant; the thrill of the chase can be more valued than the romantic or domestic bliss to follow. Ariens love the opportunity to display heroic boldness and persistent determination in their pursuit of a mate. Romance can even be inspired by fairytale images of courtly love, imbued with shining ideals and the quest for a glittering prize.

Many Ariens yearn for marriage or long-term involvement only to find themselves unprepared for a mature, ongoing relationship when it arrives. Ariens like relationships but do not always take the time to make a balanced assessment of a prospective partner before plunging into a commitment. If you do not look before you leap you cannot always be assured of a safe landing.

Ariens are more likely to form healthy relationships if they consider all the possibilities before making rash commitments. It helps if they take the time to develop a level of companionship that allows for a more subtle exchange of ideas and energies. They need to ensure that there is a mutual interest between them and their partner, and that the other person is not just getting carried away by a rush of Arien enthusiasm. Perhaps more simply, Ariens just need time to take a good look.

The ideal partner for an Arien will be someone who is able to balance out the Arien passions with some cool logic and a more level approach to life while also being able to enjoy the warmth that Aries loves to radiate in their direction. Aries likes to have a partner who can be fired up to a passionate pitch but they like to be the one who gets things simmering, not the other way round.

Once Ariens have chosen the right partner they can be fiercely loyal, highly protective and very loving. Some Ariens, however, may enjoy injecting a little creative conflict into the union from time to time as a way of keeping things exciting and making sure that passions remain aroused. It is worth remembering though that the most powerful experiences of love often come at times of subtlety and not at times of high drama.

The glittering prize of love that many Ariens seek can often be found in the quietest, simplest moments, devoid of rapid action, busy-ness and noise. Those Ariens willing to slow down enough to allow themselves to experience their emotions are the ones whose heroic voyage of discovery brings them to the golden fleece.

Water Affirmations for Aries

My emotions are vital, exciting and alive.

I love and appreciate my sexuality.

All of my relationships bring me joy.

My passion motivates me to health and happiness.

My anger is safe, healing and transformational.

I create the perfect balance of stillness and activity.

Water Visualisation: The Sun's reflection

Find a quiet, comfortable spot where you can be still for a while. Breathe and relax and, as you do, imagine yourself sitting by a lake looking at a glorious sunset. The light is bright red and orange as the sun gently drops towards the horizon. Even on its descent it radiates a reassuring warmth and aliveness that you allow to soak in to every pore of your body.

Imagine the rich radiations of the sun sending healing energy to all of your powerful emotions. Imagine any areas of anger or frustration within you becoming balanced and attuned so that you can harness these feelings for creativity or motivation. In your thoughts feel the sun's rays awakening the fun and pleasure of your passions, joys and sexuality. Feel yourself able to express all of these feelings safely and harmoniously.

As the sun reaches the horizon and begins to drop below, visualise it filling the lake before you with its red and orange lights. As you look at the lake see that the reflection of the sun within it is as beautiful as the sun itself, only a little different. The radiations of light on the water shimmer with mystery, subtlety and wonder. In places there is stillness and calm. Elsewhere the ripples distort the red and orange into playful patterns.

Imagine that the light bouncing off the water brings

31

healing energy to all of your gentle emotions; highlighting areas of joy, wistful sadness, tender sensitivity, vulnerability and empathy. The light strengthens them and makes it safe and healthy for you to express them and release them, making your life richer, happier and more beautiful.

Allow yourself a few moments of stillness with your thoughts and feelings before you complete this meditation.

THE EARTHLY QUESTS OF ARIES

The energy of Aries is so fast-moving and youthful that bringing it down to earth and learning how to channel it in practical ways can take commitment. Arien people need to find a purpose for their passions and an outlet for their force of will; otherwise they can become frenzied and frustrated.

The element of earth, with its worldly concerns and stability, can sometimes seem to be too slow or dull to offer Aries satisfaction. Most Ariens prefer to be caught up in a lusty spontaneity that takes them from one flurry of activity to another. However, it is through the fertility of the earth that Aries needs to express itself in order to find the purpose it craves. Greater satisfaction ultimately comes with activity that has a tangible direction.

The energy of Aries, when properly applied, can be like an explosion that unearths buried treasure or a forest fire that clears away the old, dead wood, to make way for new life and new growth. Arien people have a special talent for starting exciting new projects that can bring themselves and others warmth, fulfilment, prosperity and joy. Ariens will often manage to get things moving when others have failed. Sometimes a direct, forceful approach without analysis, subtlety or sentimentality is the only way.

PARTNERSHIPS, BUSINESS AND SUCCESS

Some Ariens enjoy the cut and thrust of the business world. Many need to have a good dose of competition to keep them on their toes, loving to have colleagues, bosses and competitors who push them in some way. Although Arien people can be brilliantly self-motivating, there is nothing quite like external challenge or constraint to add brilliance to their operating power.

Ariens love to take risks. Tell an Arien that a task is impossible or dangerous and they will be flexing their muscles ready to take a run at it before you can intervene. They are also very goal-orientated and can become quite restless without a glittering prize to pursue. To keep Ariens healthily occupied and so on their toes, it helps to have an ongoing series of challenges set out ahead of them, each one more attractive and more stretching than the last.

Ariens whose work involves selling or promoting products and ideas love to conquer new markets. The Arien person in a company or team delights in being the pioneer who breaks new ground and expands the creative or financial possibilities. They also like to feel that they are in the driving seat of any operation, and to some extent they often are.

The ideal colleague or business partner for an Arien will be someone who can keep the momentum going and take care of all the details that will ensure a successful ending to any enterprise. In addition it helps to be able to withstand the frenzied excitement of Arien energy; enjoying the enthusiasm that working with an Arien can bring while managing to stay level and calm in the wake of the latest spontaneous explosion of inspiration. When Ariens have all systems fired up and ready to run they usually expect everyone else around them to be geared up and ready too.

Ariens can be brilliant achievers because they are so single-minded; once set on a goal, very little will distract them. An Arien who wants something from other people will conjure up charm, persuasiveness, guile, assertiveness and, in some cases, sheer brute force to help them get exactly what they want. Few people bother to argue with an Aries – they are much too good at it.

The Arien time of year heralds increased activity and a need for higher energy levels. An Arien in a work or business setting brings the injections of energy needed to deal with times of crisis, sudden expansion and increased speed. For Arien people this means that they are often in demand and frequently appreciated.

However, many Ariens need to learn how to adapt to the quieter moments at work. It is perhaps worth them remembering that these times are also an important part of life's adventure. They are moments when experiences can be digested and previous successes enjoyed. The best way of relaxing into them is to find suitable outlets for unused energy during leisure time, through sports or creative hobbies.

On the whole it does not serve Aries to become too earthbound and caught up in the day-to-day practicalities of life and work. To be healthy and happy, they need careers and lifestyles that keep them on the move, spontaneous and free. However, success for Aries is inextricably linked with the urge to take formless possibilities and turn them into tangible expressions of creativity; this is like smelting raw metal and forming it into a sharp cutting edge. For the ram to be able to charge into action, it needs to start with its feet on the ground and pay some attention to detail along the way.

Earth Affirmations for Aries

My passionate energy yields prosperous rewards.

I always have goals that keep me motivated and lively.

My actions bring tangible, prosperous results.

My life is both stable and forward-moving.

I value everything I do.

My career is both stimulating and fertile.

Earth Visualisation: Spring Awakening

Breathe and relax. As you do, imagine yourself sitting by a plot of rich, fertile earth. It is the end of winter and the ground is still hard and icy, its fertility held in suspended animation waiting for the spring to come. Somewhere just below the surface of the ground there are seeds ready to be activated into life. All they need is the warmth and light that will trigger their potential to grow.

Imagine that you are so full of fiery Arien energy that every part of you begins to glow with deep orange, red and golden light. Visualise your head so full of positive thoughts, wonderful inspirations and successful ideas that it begins to glow brighter and brighter; radiating out brilliant beams of energy in all directions.

Imagine your heart so full of positive, passionate, joyous feelings that it, too, sends out warm beams of brilliance in all directions. See every part of you glowing with light that gently warms through the earth around you as if you were a miniature sunshine bringing the awakening messages of spring.

Picture your plot of earth thawing out and becoming moist. The mixture of warmth and moisture stirs the seeds into life and beneath the soil they begin to crack; see the first tentative shoots begin to emerge, green and lush. In your mind's eye see yourself radiating even more light from your limitless supply of creative power.

Drinking in the brilliance of your light see the shoots rapidly grow into fully mature plants and trees. As they develop see some with the most beautiful flowers and others bearing delicious fruit. Still more are growing golden coins, banknotes and anything else that may represent prosperity or material opportunities for you at this time. You easily continue to radiate more and more light and your garden of riches rewards you with every gift you can imagine from physical health to increased financial rewards or wonderful inner feelings.

When you complete this visualisation write down or record any ideas that you had for health, success or prosperity in your life at this time. Also make a note of any practical steps that you may need to take to help you achieve this. Perhaps you could return to this garden in a future visualisation so that you can continue growing your dreams from your radiant light.

THE AIR OF BRIGHT, NEW INSPIRATIONS

The element of air is a very comfortable playmate for the Arien soul. Air rules the mind, the higher awareness and the intellect. Many Arien people are highly intellectual, delighting in any opportunity to use or demonstrate their brain-power. They love to spend their lives in a realm of bright new ideas where many exciting things are possible.

Ariens are mentally agile; they are very quick-thinking and incredibly quick-witted. Their humour often springs from a clever play on words or ideas; rapidly delivered and brilliantly executed. Some may enjoy puzzles, mental teasers or word games that will challenge them to come up with fast answers and inspired solutions.

The Arien mind can sometimes be so fast that it overlooks important details, such as the possible snags or even potential advantages of a project or subject of mental enquiry. Aries enthusiasm may lead them ahead of themselves. The Arien mind may be vibrant and brilliant but some Ariens do need to learn to be more calculating, reflective or philosophical.

However, even at speed Aries has a keen mental edge that can bring sharp, clear discernment to any situation. Ariens can often cut through any amount of woolliness or hot air. Unless, of course the hot air is of their own making. The Arien mind goes straight to the point and is a cocktail of three distinct qualities: intelligence, innocence and impatience.

Aries perhaps best experiences the element of air and the realms of the mind through its opposite Sun sign, the air sign of Libra. The Libran influence can give Ariens a sense of higher aesthetics, balanced judgement, beauty and harmony. Ariens who allow themselves to move from their raw passions into their intellect do have the capacity to develop a rich and balanced wisdom as they mature.

Some Ariens may love the intellectual study of art and creativity, enjoying art galleries, museums, lectures on art appreciation or books on art history. Other Ariens may find that their minds are quite attuned to legal matters, having a talent for assessing contracts and agreements or perhaps just having a sense of justice and fair play. All interests will be scrutinised by that fierce and fiery Arien intelligence.

Air Affirmations for Aries

My mind is filled with positive thoughts.

I think my way into healthy new experiences.

I always have ideas that inspire me into positive action.

I explore the innovative brilliance of my mind.

I allow my mind and my life to find a healthy balance.

My thoughts are passionate, joyful, inspirational and strong.

Air Visualisation: The Higher Currents

Breathe and relax, taking in full, even lungfulls of air. Allow yourself to listen to the sound and the rhythm of your breath for a while as you settle into a comfortable stillness.

Imagine yourself standing in the basket of a beautiful hot air balloon. The balloon, which is almost fully inflated, is brightly coloured and shining in the early morning sunshine. Visualise yourself cutting the ropes that tie you to the ground and begin to rise smoothly upwards. You feel perfectly safe and completely in control of this healing journey.

Picture yourself able to generate and radiate fiery, passionate energy that warms the air around you to inflate the balloon further, lifting you higher with grace and speed. As you rise, imagine the ground receding beneath you. The earth becomes a pretty patchwork of fields, buildings and trees. Imagine all worries, fears and tensions dropping away from your mind and body. All burdens dissolve away from you.

Once you are in flight allow yourself to surrender to the air currents; surrendering in your thoughts to the guidance of your higher mind or higher awareness. Voyaging above the ground in your imagination, it is easy for you to allow yourself to free-float in the realms of fresh, inspired, healing thoughts.

Imagine the air currents bringing you an overview of your life and giving you a balanced perspective of your health, career, relationships and creativity. Perhaps as you look down from your balloon you see different aspects of your life below you in the distance and you are able to gain new insights into how you can heal your life at this time.

What do you need to do for your physical, mental or emotional health? What changes would you like to make in your work? How could you improve your relationships? Just allow your mind to drift and allow this journey through air to bring you a sense of peace and perhaps some new inspirations.

When you are ready, allow the balloon to bring you gently back to earth. Imagine yourself finding a soft and comfortable landing in positive, beautiful, healthy surroundings.

When you are complete you may choose to write down or record any ideas or inspirations that you had.

THE SPIRITUAL PURPOSE OF ARIES

The spiritual purpose of Aries includes learning how to channel and handle large quantities of energy. All of us, Arien or not, need to learn about directing our physical, emotional, mental and spiritual energies effectively into our relationships, creativity or careers. Sitting on our passions or inspirations and not using them can cause frustration, disease or disharmony.

For Arien people there is usually an almost inexhaustible supply of raw energy and drive that has to be given full expression through a wide variety of physical, emotional or creative outlets. Being an Arien is an exciting opportunity to rush at life headlong, enjoying the wonder of each new moment and finding exhilaration in life's challenges, large or small.

Some Arien children seem to have an excess of energy. They dash from one activity to another, not quite sure what to do first and wanting to do everything at once. Arien adults too can be like this, needing to let off steam and demanding instant results from everything they do.

As they mature and develop Ariens learn how to harness their energy, in many cases to great effect. Successful and healthy Ariens discover how to bring a sharpness and clarity of mind to bear on one activity at a time. They keep themselves focused for long enough to allow their energetic attentions to have the powerful impact that they desire, bringing new projects to life.

It really helps Ariens to have an underlying sense of purpose to everything that they do. The purpose can be anything from the desire to provide for their family, to a wish to create something beautiful for other people to enjoy or a passion to create a practical service that will benefit others. The purpose does not have to be large or significant although many Ariens do like to be doing something that makes a statement in the world.

For us all, Arien or not, having a purpose and a series of goals to work towards can keep us healthy, interesting and alive. If you do not feel that you currently have a purpose for yourself then it may be valuable to create one. All you need to do is choose what you would like your current purpose to be and begin directing your positive thoughts and energy towards it. If it doesn't work for you then you can change it; nothing is irreversible. Goals and purposes are meant to be used and outgrown, making way for something even more wonderful.

Ariens are discovering the creative adventure of life. Finding out how the world works and learning about the impact that they can have on the world and the other people around them. Areas of disharmony, times of illness, lethargy or erratic imbalance can often be eased or transformed by rediscovering the joy and adventure within each new moment. Positive, healing change often starts with a change of attitude.

THE ARIEN GIFT TO THE WORLD

Ariens motivate us all to clear away the past, get up on our feet and face the adventure of life. Without the energy of Aries in the world many new paths would not have been forged and many wonderful new ideas or schemes would not have been created. Aries teaches us all to get passionate or angry enough about our lives to do something constructive with them.

Arien people can be found in professions that require strength of will, positivity, aggression and physical or mental vitality. Ariens make wonderful leaders or bosses of organisations, movements and projects. They are the enterprising crusaders, the pioneers and the motivators of the zodiac.

Ariens can be drawn to politics, journalism, engineering, mechanics and jobs that allow them to fight good causes or correct injustices. Some Ariens make excellent professional sportsmen and women. Many are drawn to creative professions of all kinds. Ariens with an interest in healing may choose to specialise in surgery or dentistry. Those that teach may concentrate on teaching personal or business motivational skills.

Aries brings us new life and new growth, reawakening drives and impulses long forgotten and awakening all that is totally new and fresh. Like the bright light of springtime it encourages us all to wake up to the innumerable possibilities of life and create, create, create! Arien people bring us all healing with their boisterous, adventurous spirit, initiating us into the joy and wonder of being alive.

CHAPTER TWO

LEO

24 July - 23 August

FIXED FIRE

Leo is sunshine itself. Larger than life, bold, brash and warm, filling the world with its golden radiations. If you imagine our own sun as the source of a huge spotlight shining, centre stage, into the world then the star performer standing in that pool of brilliance would be the Leonine soul.

Leos are the outrageously theatrical extroverts of the zodiac who cast themselves in the lead role of their own life drama. They are often compelling people who demand attention and in some cases they are absolutely fixed on getting it. They can be quite noble in their bearing and convey an image of proud self-assurance.

The symbol for Leo is the powerful Lion, leader of the pride or family. As Leo is a male sign the Lion is usually depicted with sturdy masculinity and a full mane of golden hair that streams out like the radiations of the sun. He is an archetypal male figure: the proud father, strong husband, extroverted actor, powerful leader and monarch.

Both women and men of this sign can display these confident, assertive, fiery qualities, despite their inner feelings or hidden sensitivities. The qualities of Leo are much more concerned with outward masculine traits and external appearances than with receptivity or contemplation. The brilliance of the Leonine personality often masks the subtleties, softness or vulnerabilities that the people born of Leo can also have.

A Leo person walking into a room can have the same effect as a bright light being turned on. Other people wake up and pay attention. They are often compelling personalities who draw the eye and demand to be noticed, even on the rare occasions when they attempt to make a quiet entrance. Of course, some would say that Leo does not know how to do anything quietly.

The glyph or shorthand notation for Leo can be likened to a lion's tail (♌). The line is also similar to one half of a heart shape. The heart is an important part of the Leonine symbology, depicting Leo as a central figure in all arenas of life. Leo can be the heart of the family, the heart of a social gathering or the central person in creative and artistic projects.

The ruler of Leo is our own Sun. The Sun's influence endows Leo with illumination, clarity, warmth and the ability to give or sustain life. Like the Sun, Leonine people are compellingly attractive; they often bring a feeling of well-being, excitement and healing to others. The sunshine of Leo can wake up the world to positivity, creativity and fun.

The Sun can bring to Leo a strength of inner purpose that is as brilliant as the outer radiance of the Leonine personality. Through the Sun Leo discovers the path to vitality, health, happiness and joy. Beyond the clouds of delusion and fear the Sun shines as a core of self-actualisation for us all. It is just there to be uncovered.

LEO IN ITS ELEMENT

The element of fire becomes golden and shining when it enters the regal domain of Leo. The fires of Leo are the focused lights of the creative force. The spontaneous eruptions of the fire element are harnessed into tangible forms of beauty by the strength that Leo possesses. All Leos have an innate capacity for creativity that can be powerfully channelled in ways that are bound to have an impact on other people.

Leo can be said to be doubly creative. Leonine people have a unique ability to initiate imaginative projects and they often feel themselves to be the central creative force from which many subsidiary projects are activated. They can be the inspirational core of the family, workplace or community who switches on the inner light of creativity for everyone else.

As well as having the power of initiation and inspiration, Leos also have the ability to shine new light on anything that has already been created, giving it a focus that allows other people to appreciate it more fully. One example might be the performer whose interpretation of a song turns it into a hit for the first time. When Leo lends their personality to a project it can take on a completely new level of majesty and excitement.

Leo is certainly one of the actors of the zodiac but unlike the watery theatrical types, Pisces and Cancer, Leos tend to project their own personality to the world. They are too extrovert to remain hidden behind clever mimicry and characterisation. All Leos, regardless of profession, have a tendency towards theatricality in their life and work, using their own personality as a tool for creativity, inspiration and influence.

The Leonine personality is highly seductive. Leo can influence other people with directness and passion or with a more subtle approach that can be quite mesmerising. In most cases Leos project such a strong belief in themselves that other people easily fall into line and comply with their wishes. This is not to say that Leos always believe in themselves. Sometimes they do and sometimes they just give that impression, regardless of how they feel inside.

In many cases Leos are quite shy people, but you would rarely guess it. We are all so easily dazzled by Leo's outer brilliance that we are generally unable to see beyond to any timidity or uncertainty. The only clue to spotting Leo's moments of self-doubt is to notice when their behaviour has become just a little too confident or when Leo is trying particularly hard to keep up the sunny image. The healthiest Leos are often those who are willing to be seen as vulnerable on occasion; vulnerability can also be a strength.

The fire of Leo is very cheering, and Leos themselves are always cheered and motivated by their own warmth. Leonine fire stirs those around them to positivity and bravery; Leos themselves often fix upon a positive outlook or lifestyle. They can find a set of beliefs or a role in life that works well for them and stand firm in that position regardless of the outcome. Leos present a cheerful certainty in an ever-changing world.

Like all fire signs, Leo is fascinated by the future and its possibilities. Their view of the future often includes a vision of themselves becoming an increasingly important central focus for their family, community, sphere of business or social group. Leos often see themselves as the heroes or heroines of a wonderful fairytale. Perhaps they are the lost prince or princess who returns to claim their destiny, and preside as crowned monarch over their domain.

LEONINE ZONES OF THE BODY

Leo rules the heart and the dorsal region of the back. Back and chest massage of all kinds will be beneficial for Leo, as will aerobic exercise that keeps the heart functioning well and provides general toning. For Leo these areas of the body provide an excellent gauge for general health and well-being.

Medicine has always relied upon the heart rate to indicate the state of health, its rhythm and regularity being a key to the physical, mental and emotional state. For Leo, it can be an extraordinarily powerful key to self-awareness and self-healing. Anyone whose stresses have caused their heart to race can consciously breathe deeply, relax and focus on their heart rate decreasing as a way of regaining psychological and physiological normality.

Leos would benefit from using the natural rhythms of the heart as a tool for meditation. Focusing on the feeling or inner sound of the heart beating can be an effective way of stilling the mind and putting Leo back in touch with their own natural impulses. The internal sounds of the breath and the heart act as a guide for Leo to return to the centre of their being, physically, mentally and emotionally.

Most forms of exercise are beneficial for the heart. When exercising it helps to listen to the heart too; a jog, a swim or an aerobics dance class needs to be strenuous enough to quicken the pulse significantly but it is important to take regular breaks to allow the heart to return to a more stable pace. Exercising while remaining sensitive to the body's rhythms is the best way to build up stamina and train the system to adjust to changes in activity.

Tension in the chest area or the back would be a good indication for Leo that they need to stop whatever physical, mental or emotional activity they are engaged in and slow down for a while. Leo sometimes carries emotional hurts on their back or on their chest. Perhaps a chance to stop and talk through emotional disagreements or just to have a good cry is the best way to discharge this kind of tension.

EXERCISE AND THERAPIES

Leo would probably benefit more than most signs of the zodiac from visiting a health farm for a programme of exercise and therapy. Leo will benefit even more from the many regimes on offer if they visit a spa that really concentrates on pampering its clients. Leo responds so well to royal treatment that their interest in their health can be positively stimulated and encouraged.

The postural therapy of Alexander technique is excellent for Leo. The body movements and the spine are gently re-educated to act and rest in a healthy, neutral position. Frequently performed actions such as getting up from a horizontal position, sitting down, standing up or picking up objects can be improved by gently reminding the body of its innate healthy posture. This not only improves the back by reducing bad habits that may jar the spine but may also have benefits for the nervous system, the circulation, the throat and the voice.

Yoga is wonderful for Leos, providing them with exercises that strengthen the back and create greater flexibility throughout the body. Leo always benefits from anything that will keep them flexible and supple. Many yoga exercises regulate the heart rate and aid circulation while opening or expanding the chest area. Yoga can bring Leos a feeling of peace, well-being and universal love.

Leos often derive childlike pleasure from participating in or watching sports and games of all kinds. All spectator sports that involve and entertain large numbers of people have a measure of Leonine influence. Active Leos enjoy being the star player who commands the attention of spectators with their larger than life persona. Leo could be the tennis star, the cricketing personality or the golf pro. They may also be drawn to squash, football or the French pastime, *boules*. Some may even burn up excess energy through stage fighting or modern-day jousting displays.

Any exercise programme for Leo would be wonderful when taken in the early morning sunshine; many Leos love to stretch and work out in the light. Some Leos may also like to dance in the sunshine or in the brilliant glare of a spotlight. Leo could find fun and healthy exercise while disco dancing or moving to the excitement of Caribbean rhythms. Some Leos like ballroom dancing, complete with the glamour, the sequins and the mirrored balls that reflect the light onto the dance floor.

Perhaps Leo would benefit from acting out and resolving dilemmas, family roles and inner conflicts through drama therapy. Group or individual therapy sessions provide the opportunity to role-play life dramas as a way of making sense of childhood influences and life choices. Injustices or imposed limitations can often be healed in this way. Leo would respond well to the combined theatricality and practicality of this approach.

The best therapy for Leo is often a good holiday. Leos love to be the centre of family holidays or outings, particularly those that include fun and games in the sunshine and a regal dose of luxurious living. However, it is important that Leo remembers to take time out from being the hub of social activity to enjoy some peace and quiet. The greatest luxury of all is uninterrupted rest and relaxation.

LEONINE INSPIRATION AND CREATIVITY

Doubly creative, Leos delight in expressing themselves in numerous ways for their own enjoyment and to entertain and inspire others. Leo loves all creative forms that involve the use of light. Some may produce stained glass windows or hanging panels that burst into life when the sunshine pours through them. Others may work in glass, paper or fabric to produce lanterns that transform electric light or candlelight into brightly coloured patterns.

The Leonine soul can particularly enjoy the light of a candle flame, perhaps because on some level it reminds them of the beautiful, loving radiations of their own Leonine heart. For this reason some Leos may be drawn to candle-making and the creation of displays that involve candles, from the top of a birthday cake, to an altar for meditation or prayer.

Mirrors can provide a source of inspiration and fascination for Leo. Some may express their creativity by framing, hanging or arranging mirrors around their homes; dressmakers may enjoy working with sequins, mirrored beading or mirrored buttons as well as shiny reflective fabrics that will catch the light and shimmer seductively.

Leos who are interested in jewellery or metalwork may find they have a natural aptitude for working in gold. Gold is the metal of Leo. Its soft, sunny reflective quality holds a fascination for us all. Leonine jewellers are likely to produce bold, chunky adornments rather than fine, intricate pieces.

Leonine artists often love to concentrate on conveying the

radiance and movement of light. Some may be fascinated by the depiction of light on reflective surfaces such as water, metals or mirrors. They are also interested in the reflective quality of human skin. Leonine artists working in paint usually prefer bold, colourful strokes and large canvases rather than fine detail and muted subtlety.

There is perhaps no end to the creative potential that Leo can draw from and no creative medium that is closed to them. Some Leos spend their lives exploring one creative form after another, drawing inspiration and pleasure from each. To say that Leo can derive great healing from the creative process is an understatement; creativity is the essence of the Leonine soul.

Leos are inspired by the magical qualities of children and many Leos express their creativity through the raising, teaching or guidance of children. Leo is the sign of the zodiac associated with fatherhood; both women and men of this sign can have a paternal influence over other people. They are often seen as the charismatic parent or older relative in the family, regardless of their physical age. They may also feel responsible for the care and protection of everyone else around them even when there is no need for them to be.

Perhaps above everything, Leonine creativity is theatrical expression in all of its glory. The theatre can be quite magnetic for many Leos who love to watch bold, dramatic performances of all kinds. Some will nurture a fantasy of being up there in the spotlight and some will even choose acting or theatre arts as their profession or their cherished hobby. Whether they enjoy the theatre or not, all Leos cast themselves in the heroic, starring role of their own life drama and they play to the crowd with charisma and style.

Fire Affirmations for Leo

I grow in strength, beauty and brilliance every day.

I am glowing with health, love, power and wisdom.

I shine love and well-being to the world.

I radiate courage and charisma.

My heart is healthy and shining with love.

My back is strong, healthy and flexible.

My creativity is brilliant, powerful and inspired.

My life is filled with golden moments of pleasure.

I act with confidence, clarity and wise judgement.

I centre myself in glorious vitality.

Fire Visualisation: The Lion's Mane

Find a quiet, comfortable place and relax, preferably lying down or sitting with your back properly supported and your body open.

Imagine a huge, golden lion with a mane that streams out from his majestic head like the fiery emanations of the sun. Know that the lion is completely safe and friendly. Picture yourself approaching him to stroke his warm, tawny back and feel the sturdy form of his body.

See yourself placing your hands into his rich, golden mane and imagine a tingle of bright energy rippling through your hands, up your arms and around your body.

Visualise yourself being able to collect pure healing light from his mane; he emanates an unlimited supply of energy for you to use and benefit from.

Picture yourself collecting balls of light from the lion's mane that you are able to pick up with your hands and place directly into your heart, your chest or any other part of your body that needs healing, regeneration or a boost of positivity at this time. Imagine yourself placing light into your mind to boost your powers of positive thought and inspiration too.

When you feel complete thank your lion for his healing energy and know that you can return to this image whenever you choose.

THE EARTHLY KINGDOM OF LEO

The element of earth provides challenges and rich spoils for the Leonine soul to explore. Earth represents the material pleasures that Leo is compelled to discover and gain sovereignty over; a little like a king or queen expanding the boundaries of their earthly kingdom.

For Leo, the challenge of earth often comes with learning to slow down enough to ensure a full and fertile delivery of practical, creative and financial projects. Earth demands patience, tangible actions and attention to detail. Leos are so good at making big, bold, exciting things happen by pure strength of will and charisma that they may not know how to take care of the smaller practical details that are often needed to ensure lasting worldly success.

Many Leos carry an air of positive expectancy and are as keen to see what the next moment will bring as children at a birthday party. However, Leo being a fixed sign, they do have the ability to command themselves to stay presently focused when they choose and this can help with the creation of material wealth and the manifestation of prosperity.

Leo often expects the world to provide for their material needs. This does not mean that they are not willing to put energy or commitment into achieving or attaining what they desire; often their strength of commitment is second to none. It is just that many Leos convey an air of self-assurance and a belief that prosperity is their God-given right. To some extent this is true but it is important for many Leos to let go of some of their fixed ideas of where money, creative opportunities, health or success may be coming from.

Leo needs to remember that we live in a vast universe with infinite possibilities available to each one of us. Leonine positive thought, strength of character, will-power and childlike wonder teamed with a willingness to take care of details and follow through ideas in a conscientious way can work like a magic charm. Financial success, creative opportunities, the keys to health and the pleasures of being alive can come from many sources and in unlimited ways. More than anything we need to be open and willing to receive it all!

PARTNERSHIPS, BUSINESS AND SUCCESS

Leo can be found at the heart of many businesses, partnerships or projects. Leo is often the hub of an organisation around which other partners, employees or colleagues revolve. They provide a central focus for the work or creativity of others; their presence helps other people to act and respond with inspiration or enthusiasm.

In many companies, Leo is the boss, presiding over junior partners or employees with an air of regal nobility and grace. Leo makes an excellent leader because she or he often refuses to be bound by limitations and restrictive vision. Their imagination and their strong, self-willed, charismatic presence galvanises others into taking action, giving confidence and purpose to every member of the team.

Leo's desire to be the sovereign of their life and career means that some Leos prefer to remain independent in their work, and many are self-employed. However, this rarely means working in isolation from other people. They nearly always act as the guiding light for others, whether clients, sub-contractors, students or other freelancers.

Perhaps the healthiest Leos are those who are so secure within themselves and within their inspirational, guiding role that they can relinquish that role from time to time. Many Leos need to learn flexibility. The best bosses, leaders and teachers are those who are strong enough to be fixed upon achievement, while remaining flexible enough to allow the skills of others to be the guiding light when that is for the greater good of the company or organisation. Professionally and personally, Leo always benefits from listening to advice and stepping aside for anyone with expertise and inspiration to share.

Leos often establish a career in which they can be the star and make all the big, bold decisions while others work behind the scenes taking care of details. Leo usually needs to have colleagues, partners or employees who can be down to earth and practical when they cannot. When you are so focused on the greater goal, it is important to have people to work with who are able to see and take the necessary practical steps along the way to ensure attainment.

To be the leader, the boss or the creative genius takes courage, commitment and a good dose of cheek. It also helps to have a strong sense of your own ego, and a desire to put yourself forward and exert your will. The materially successful Leo will have all of this while learning to have some humility too. When you are willing to roll up your sleeves and deal with the practicalities of life, even if they sometimes seem a little mundane, then you can begin to understand the roles and needs of other people around you. Good leadership comes with a willingness to be part of the team.

Many Leos find success in their lives because they expect it; in some cases they simply do not envisage any alternative. Leos often find success as breadwinners, providers, creative pioneers, teachers and entertainers purely because they have an inbuilt belief that it is necessary for them to do so. What is more, the Leonine vision of the future is often so strong that they become magnetic to the achievement of their goals.

Success for Leo rarely means financial success alone. Money is often seen as a means to an end; it is viewed as being a valuable and important commodity but it is not the full measure of glorious achievement for Leo. Many Leos enjoy the luxury and comfort that money can bring but most feel the need to be financially solvent so that they can provide for the people they love. The golden reward that many Leos seek is recognition.

For Leos to be fully successful they need to acknowledge their own achievements. Some are so keen to rush onwards to the next creative or material endeavour that they do not always give themselves enough time to enjoy what they have already achieved. Leo or not, we all need to enjoy our successes and feel good about ourselves for our many achievements large or small.

Earth Affirmations for Leo

I recognise all of my achievements and successes.

I provide for myself and others with prosperity and joy.

I value myself and I value the contributions of other people.

I am gloriously healthy, prosperous and alive.

When I am successful, everyone wins.

I am passionate, patient, committed and receptive.

Earth Visualisation: The Sunflower Field

Make yourself comfortable, breathe deeply and relax.

Imagine yourself standing in a field full of sunflowers; row upon row of these magnificent blooms are growing around you for as far as you can see in all directions. Picture the sun coming out, full and golden, sending its beams to warm the land and nurture these special plants.

As you look, you see the heads of these golden yellow flowers following the path of the sun across the sky and drinking in the abundance of light and energy that the sun provides. Notice that the stems, leaves and petals of the plants are growing rapidly in strength, beauty and glorious colour. Feel yourself absorbing the regenerating expansive properties of the sunshine too.

Picture yourself placing your hands on one of the large yellow flowers and imagine it dissolving into a mass of golden coins that you are able to collect in your palms. Place this golden prosperity into your pockets and do the same with another flower and another, collecting financial success and golden opportunities. Repeat this image as many times as you choose, holding the idea that you are expanding your ability to attract whatever material or creative opportunities you need.

Next, see yourself reaching to touch a flower, and this time picture it dissolving into the pure golden light of healing and prosperity. Visualise the light flowing directly into your heart to make you more and more magnetic to success, recognition, health and peace. Do this with another flower and another, seeing this prosperous light moving into every cell of your body; giving you the ability to radiate joy and attract whatever you desire.

Return to this image whenever you choose to boost your power of prosperity and expand into new opportunities for healing. When you complete you may also choose to write down or record any creative, healing or financial ideas that you had.

THE AIRS AND GRACES OF LEO

The element of air is a comfortable consort for fiery Leo. Leos love the realms of the mind that are ruled by the air; they enjoy exercising their mental skills and demonstrating the powers of their intellect in passionate discussion or debate. Many Leos are bright, mentally active people who need regular mental stimulation to help them feel as healthy and alive as they can be.

Leos best experience the element of air through their opposite Sun sign, the air sign of Aquarius. Through Aquarius, Leo can develop original thought, bold, revolutionary ideas and the ability to experiment with new approaches to life. Leonine thought can often be strongly reactionary or strongly radical; either way, Leo's opinions are held and expressed in a manner that often has a powerful, revolutionary impact on others.

The ability to think big and impress other people with charismatic, intellectual debate can make Leos excellent politicians or political activists. Some Leos become the figureheads of campaigning or charitable movements that stir people into new thought and positive action. While remaining open to new ideas, Leos often become fixed upon the beliefs that they choose for themselves and this allows them to enter all arenas of discussion with an air of confidence and conviction. However, a little flexibility of thought would help Leo to discard any beliefs that have become outmoded or naive.

Leo has the ability to see the larger picture, and this can be useful in providing a perspective on life's daily dramas. This larger vision can allow Leo to feel the inspirational breezes of the higher mind and give them an interest in esoteric philosophies, spiritual growth or psychic abilities. Leo has an extraordinary potential to transform intellectual understanding into a greater awareness that is held by a passionate and expansive heart.

Air Affirmations for Leo

I expand the power and the majesty of my intellect.

My thoughts are filled with humour, lightness, strength and purpose.

My mind is both flexible and strong.

I inspire myself with healthy, passionate, creative thoughts.

My ideals create positivity within my world.

I expand into the brilliance of my higher mind.

Air Visualisation: Kite of Inspiration

Breathe and relax, taking a few moments to notice the movements of air through your nostrils or in and out of your lungs.

Imagine yourself standing at the top of a hill on a mild but breezy summer's day. The sun is shining brightly while the wind rushes playfully around you to ruffle your hair and clothing.

Picture yourself with a heart-shaped kite made of a shiny golden material. The kite has a tail of golden streamers that shimmer in the sunlight. See yourself launching the kite into the wind with ease and instant success, letting out the strings so that the air can carry your heart of gold high and free.

As the kite rises higher, dancing in the wind, imagine it being able to catch the freshness of the air; it is capable of collecting new thoughts, original ideas and magical inspirations. Imagine the special healing energy of the air travelling from the kite, down the strings and into your hands where it is able to enter your body and your mind. You may picture this energy moving down to you like golden, electrical ripples of joy.

Imagine the new ideas and inspirations from the air displacing and dissolving old, outmoded thoughts and beliefs from your mind. Any old, negative or limited thinking is replaced with new positive, healthy beliefs and insights. Picture the kite bringing you wisdom, spiritual awareness, fun images and practical ideas for your self-healing process.

Even if you do not instantly receive new ideas and images, see them becoming clear in your mind during the next few days; expanding your mental abilities and your higher awareness.

When you complete this visualisation you may choose to write down or record any ideas that you had.

THE WATERY REFLECTIONS OF LEO

The emotional and intuitive realms of water provide Leo with a deep well of experience to drink from and to see themselves reflected in. Some Leos can be highly emotional but many prefer to channel their feelings directly into creative or passionate action rather than allow themselves to be saturated with sentimentality and prolonged displays of tearfulness.

A willingness to explore the emotional depths can bring fiery Leo to an awareness of their innate powers of perception, feminine receptivity or psychic gifts. The elements of water and fire do not readily combine but when they do they bring forth a creative intensity, a spiritual zeal and a richness of expression that is a wonder to behold.

LOVE AND ROMANCE

Leo is often a highly glamorous, romantic and attractive figure. Their charismatic, shining persona often seduces others even when they themselves are not interested in attracting a mate. In addition, the confident exterior that many Leos have makes them easy to notice and easy to fall for.

When they are aware of the romantic interest they are creating, Leo can enjoy the adulation. Even Leos who feel or feign embarrassment in flirtatious situations or at times of great romantic intrigue may be secretly pleased with the effect that they are having on others. In some cases the romantic or sexual interest of another person can be a powerful turn-on in itself. Leos usually notice and enjoy the effect they have on would-be admirers.

Certainly Leos like the idea of being a romantic or sexual siren. Their strong desire to be loved can sometimes lead them to engage actively in flirtations or sexual conquests, particularly when they are first exploring their sexuality. However, for many Leos it is the fantasy of having a series of affairs rather than the reality that appeals and most are happier with long-term, committed relationships.

Once committed, most Leos are loyal to their partners, making bold displays of affection or exercising feelings that are powerful and sincere. Leo brings sunshine, warmth and excitement to the object of their desire, often protecting and cherishing their partner. In return Leo expects to be exclusively adored. In many cases this relationship works well but it would be healthy for Leo to accept that their partner may have a need for independence.

Many Leos in long-term relationships are faithful and trusting and they expect their partners to be faithful too. Some Leos refuse to believe that their relationships can be anything other than honest or straightforward and in many cases their confidence is borne out. Leo does need to learn to take care of the small details of a relationship; not taking themselves or their partner for granted. Generous Leo may make big-hearted demonstrations of love but sometimes it is the ability to notice and respond to the subtle needs of a lover that can make the difference.

The ideal partner for Leo will be someone who can balance the big dreams or creative brilliance of the Leonine soul with some earthly stability and realism. If in addition this person is able to provide Leo with regular doses of intellectual stimulation and is willing to engage in the demonstration of mutual adoration, then Leo will be in heaven.

The healthiest relationships for Leo are those that support them in being as big and bold as they like to be while helping them to keep their feet firmly on the ground. They need to be encouraged to be part of a team, and not just a star in their own right. Leo needs to learn to step to one side occasionally so that their partner can also take a starring role in social or family events. Fortunately, Leos are so big-hearted and so committed to their relationships that they are willing to learn a bit of give and take as the years go by and their love expands.

Water Affirmations for Leo

I reflect upon my deeper emotions with safety and with joy.

I express the full range of my feelings, passions and creativity.

My relationships shine with adoration and flow with affection.

My love opens hearts and brings forth waves of joy.

I charismatically attract the love and care that I need.

My life is filled with emotional support and loving awareness.

Water Visualisation: Reflection of Love

Breathe and relax, picturing yourself standing at the edge of a huge lake. The sun is directly overhead sending bright beams of light to warm and bounce off the surface of the water. See yourself watching the ripples of the water playfully distort the reflected sunlight into a myriad of patterns and shapes.

As you gaze into the depths, visualise the ripples dissolving into stillness to be replaced by your own clear and focused reflection, surrounded by an aura of light. See how your image has become magnified; it stretches out, larger than life, across the lake.

See how beautiful, special and unique you are. The reflected image shows you in full health and glowing with love and joy. As you look, it is easy for you to love and accept yourself fully. Imagine your reflection becoming healthier, happier and filled with more love in every moment.

When you are ready, picture yourself putting your hands into the lake to break the image. Imagine the special healing energy of your reflection flowing up your arms and into your heart, filling your mind and emotions with all of that health, happiness and love. See yourself becoming your reflection, emotionally, physically, mentally and spiritually flowing with health. Thank the lake for its healing properties and return to this image whenever you choose.

THE SPIRITUAL PURPOSE OF LEO

The spiritual purpose of Leo includes the challenge of learning to receive love, acceptance, adoration and the caring attentions of other people. The energy of love is infinite and readily available for any of us who have learned to accept it. When Leos expand their hearts to receive the love that is available for them they instantly increase their ability to radiate love and acceptance for other people.

Leo is also learning about the largeness of life. There is always more to know, more to explore, more to love and more to enjoy. Leo is constantly expanding to discover the infinite possibilities that the world provides, growing into greater glory, aliveness and wonder.

Leo is compelled to be at the centre of things, finding most fulfilment through starring in their own life story. Leos are rarely invisible; they are meant to be seen and noticed by other people. In most cases it is right that they take a key role within their family, their community, their business life or social world.

Leo's spiritual purpose is also concerned with leadership. By providing leadership and guidance for other people many Leos are learning to lead or guide themselves along their path of greatest joy, finding their way to spiritual strength and well-being.

In some cases the guiding light of Leo can be quite a religious one. Many Leos are drawn to religious practices or systems of belief that provide them with a fixed code of morality to live by and a set of spiritual aspirations to inspire their future vision. As Leos mature they often feel a greater and greater need for some kind of spiritual or religious devotion.

Perhaps the spiritual purpose of Leo also includes an ever-expanding capacity to have fun. As Leos grow older they need to take the time to rediscover their own inner child, remembering to see the world as a child would see it – with wonder, excitement and a healthy dose of love. For Leo the greatest healing often comes with a return to their childlike nature, rediscovering the healing power of laughter, spontaneity and freedom of spirit.

LEO'S GIFT TO THE WORLD

We all need the creative brilliance of Leo to inspire us and to lead us to develop greatness within our lives. Leo people are like miniature suns that bring healing warmth, energy and a powerful sense of well-being to others. Leo's positivity, strength and fixity of purpose guides us towards a glorious future.

Leos can be spiritual leaders, politicians or captains of industry. They make excellent chairmen or women, organisers, managers, overseers and directors. Their leadership skills may inspire them to become teachers, particularly of children. Leos can be found in many situations that allow them to work with and guide children of all ages.

Certainly Leos are drawn to every kind of role or profession that allows them to express their immense creativity. Leos can be actors, film stars, singers, jewellers or lighting engineers and designers. Those who are physically active may choose to star as professional sportsmen or sportswomen.

The gift of Leo is also one of luxury and well-being. Leo opens the heart and creates within us the feeling of a warm summer's day when everything is shimmering with light and all is well in the world. Leonine people can fill us with optimism, lightness, stability and fun.

CHAPTER THREE

SAGITTARIUS

23 November - 22 December

MUTABLE FIRE

The sign of Sagittarius brings with it a rush of bright, positive energy that delights in expanding outwards towards new horizons, often in all directions at once. Sagittarians are active, outgoing people, dramatic in nature and often in appearance. Their sights are set on future opportunities and they are inspired by distant travel, both in the physical sense and in the form of mental journeys.

Sagittarius is symbolised by the mythical centaur. From the waist upwards the centaur's body was that of a strong man; below that it took the form of a powerful horse, muscular and elegant.

If you are a Sagittarian then you carry with you a presence of noble strength that comes from your own unique blend of higher reason and instinctual animal nature. Sagittarians are predominantly extroverted and sociable but there is always some elusive quality; mysterious sensibilities that remain hidden and unavailable for others to grasp.

The glyph or symbol for Sagittarius is an arrow (♐), which symbolises the Sagittarian need for goals, targets and the motivating force of a desirable future. Centaurs were famed as skilled archers, able to fire arrows with accuracy even while travelling at speed. The arrow can be likened to the spirit of Sagittarius shooting its awareness into the future while galloping off in the pursuit of new adventures.

The rulers of Sagittarius are the planet Jupiter and the planetoid Chiron. Jupiter is the planet of expansion; it has the power to open up the spiritual side of human nature and its influence constantly motivates Sagittarians to expand into new realms of spiritual awareness. In doing so it also encourages them to explore the expansiveness of the physical world.

The planetoid Chiron was named after the noble centaur of mythology. Chiron was a highly civilised philosopher with a knowledge of life, nature and human behaviour gleaned from experience and study. Yet he was also a wild and savage beast filled with animal drives and passions. Sagittarians are able to harness and combine all that physical passion with higher wisdom – a potent cocktail of intuition and reason.

Chiron was the ruler or priest of his tribe of centaurs with a special gift for teaching. He was said to be the teacher of many heroic figures, including Jason, who voyaged in search of the Golden Fleece. Though fearing Chiron's animal nature, many kings sent their sons to him to be schooled in the noble arts of combat and the skills of philosophical thought and wise government. The combined influence of Jupiter and Chiron endows many Sagittarians with special gifts for leadership, wisdom and the guidance of others.

SAGITTARIUS IN ITS ELEMENT

The element of fire fuels and is fuelled by the Sagittarian soul. Sagittarian fire can be likened to the deep orange lights of a sunrise on a distant horizon. The light plays magically over far-flung lands and charts a course across the daytime sky before disappearing over the edge of the world to explore the unknown wonders beyond. For mental and emotional health, Sagittarians need to maintain a bright vision of the future and a curiosity about other worlds or possibilities that are just over the next horizon.

Sagittarius is often linked to the rising sun, and the energy of this sign demonstrates new awakenings and new freedom. The presence of a Sagittarian can be like a new day dawning, bringing with it many new possibilities and a liberation from negativity or depression. Most Sagittarians are essentially optimistic and their bright presence can shine the light of expansion to inspire many.

Sagittarian fire brings with it divine magic and encouragement. Healthy Sagittarians will easily motivate and inspire themselves; they have a 'life is for living' attitude, seldom sitting and waiting for life to come to them. Sagittarius is usually to be found at large in the world actively seeking the next adventure.

Most people with a strong Sagittarian energy will love all journeys and the farther afield they travel, the happier they will be. They see life as a wonderful journey to be undertaken with enthusiasm and positivity. Those Sagittarians who do not travel may in some cases feel that they are missing out on something. At the very least they would benefit from getting out and about and having a good social life.

Sagittarians who have chosen a home or work environment that is too claustrophobic and restrictive may need to escape to open spaces to facilitate healing. Sagittarians do not stay as healthy or robust as they might be if they choose lifestyles that keep them cooped up indoors. They need to expand beyond the immediate environment. A good burst of natural light, a regular change of scene and some space to move freely will be a magical tonic in most cases, providing a psychological, emotional and spiritual boost that may even aid physical healing.

Sagittarians have a divine fire burning in the heart, a strong spiritual or religious drive that motivates even the Sagittarian atheist. This divine fire can be expressed through a fundamental devotion to any belief system, cause or project.

Many Sagittarians choose a vocation that they can religiously pursue or a philosophy to which they can dedicate their lives. Perhaps the healthiest Sagittarians will be those who have a clear focus for their passionate enthusiasm. When they lose touch with the core of their inspiration or simply lose faith, their characteristic reaction is to cast around in many directions at once for a new goal to rekindle their divine spark.

SAGITTARIAN ZONES OF THE BODY

Sagittarius rules the hips and thighs. Many Sagittarians store a great deal of energy in these parts of the body. For reasons of health and balance this energy needs to be constantly released and utilised. The comfort and strength of the hips and thighs can act as a good barometer for general levels of health, well-being and relaxation.

Sagittarians need to keep moving. A sedentary lifestyle could see Sagittarius putting on weight in the region of the hips, thighs and buttocks. Many Sagittarians are drawn to physical exercise as a safe and productive means of releasing their natural energy, and this is to be encouraged. Even naturally lean Sagittarians may hold tensions in the muscles or bones of the hips and thighs that could be released through appropriate activity. However, in many cases Sagittarians will be strong and flexible in these areas. Some will have a look of physical power that is not unlike the horse part of the centaur, poised to gallop great distances.

Physical activity always needs to be tailored to the age, general health and the physical condition of the individual; with Sagittarians it is also best linked to some kind of mental stimulation. Sagittarians often thrive on sports or games that allow them to learn new skills or use clever tactics.

Sagittarians who have received over-protective parenting in childhood and have had their natural tendencies towards physical activity or exploration too strongly curtailed could appear to be holding a level of frustration in their lower limbs. There could be an air of discomfort with the self or a feeling of not being fully comfortable within the body.

In these cases the natural Sagittarian inclination towards sporting activities could be harnessed for physical and psychological release. Even less sporty Sagittarians can find release through walking or by using the stairs rather than the lift. When the hips and thighs are regularly exercised for flexibility as well as strength, then the whole body will benefit and the mind will become more peaceful.

EXERCISE AND THERAPIES

A Sagittarian receiving a full body massage would do well to ask their massage therapist to concentrate on their hips, thighs and buttocks. Deep massage work in these areas can magically release tension from other areas of the body too. In particular, tension of the upper spine or shoulders can often stem from the hips and lower back.

Sagittarius's ruling planet Jupiter rules the bloodstream and particularly the arterial system. Sagittarians may benefit from hydrotherapy that stimulates the circulatory system through sensible use of steam rooms, saunas, cold pools or showers, although extremes of heat and cold are to be avoided.

Similarly, sitz baths, where one alternates between sitting in fairly hot water while one's feet are in cold water and then sitting in cold water while the feet are in warm water, would stimulate the circulation. Again, extreme heat is to be avoided and anyone with a tendency towards high blood pressure would need to consult their doctor before doing this.

Acupuncture, which focuses on the subtle forms of circulation or energetic meridians that run throughout and around the body, could also be of benefit to Sagittarius. The penetration of the body by small needles, not unlike the arrows of Sagittarius, stimulates or releases blocks in these energetic meridians, helping to bring the whole person, mind, body, spirit and emotions, into a healthy balance.

It is interesting to note that many acupuncturists may disapprove of the hydrotherapy suggested above, as the treatments stem from different ideologies. Sagittarians often enjoy this kind of philosophical diversity as a means to explore their many routes to healing, relaxation and balance. They tend to be strong-minded individuals who like to be informed and given a choice.

Herbal medicines of all kinds could suit Sagittarius. In Greek mythology centaurs were known to have an empathic understanding of healing herbs. Chinese herbalism is often used very effectively with acupuncture and Western herbal traditions, too, could well be of benefit. Both homoeopathic remedies and Bach flower essences contain very small quantities of herbal or mineral extracts that help by stimulating the body's natural capacity for self-healing.

Perhaps Sagittarius's best form of therapy comes through sporting activity of all kinds. Sagittarius often seeks speed and physical power, so horse-riding would be highly beneficial, particularly since it exercises the hips and thighs. Some may even enjoy polo, show-jumping or other equine sports and events. In the winter, activities like ice-skating and skiing would be fun, combining speed with balance and a good use of leg muscles.

Particularly animated Sagittarians may enjoy hang-gliding, parachuting and athletic pursuits that involve leaping through the air such as the long jump, the high jump and pole-vaulting. Throwing the javelin is also Sagittarian; spears as well as arrows are traditionally associated with Sagittarius, being the ruler of hunting and weapons of the air.

Sagittarian children and adults alike will enjoy games or sports that allow them to act out their tendency to aim and pursue; archery is an obvious example but darts and fairground games like the rifle range or the coconut shy may also be entertaining. Certainly a touch of frivolity from time to time would be therapeutic and enlivening.

SAGITTARIAN INSPIRATION AND CREATIVITY

See yourself as a majestic centaur shooting with a bow and arrow towards distant goals and you may be able to feel that essential Sagittarian quality of ambition. Sagittarius delights in setting off in pursuit of those arrows and making many new and unexpected discoveries along the way. The arrows of course are aspirations, dreams, ideals and visions; the goals are the new horizons of philosophical, spiritual or material expansion.

Inspiration can come to Sagittarius through foreign travel, an interest in future trends and through games of chance. Sagittarians love the thrill of the unknown and are excited by chance encounters as they journey through life. Coincidences, synchronicity that brings unexpected opportunities or lucky encounters, delight and inspire Sagittarians, who are often seen as the lucky gamblers of the zodiac. Of course there will be many who do not believe in coincidences, choosing to see all fortunate experiences as part of their positive destiny – and perhaps they are right!

Many Sagittarians fulfil their need for distant journeying through the intellect, the imagination, the higher mind and the inner vision. Sagittarius is the sign of higher education, teaching and philosophy. Education provides Sagittarius with a constantly widening world of goals and objectives. There is always something new to learn, and Sagittarius continually awakens to the excitement of learning.

Sagittarians are often inspirational for others and as such can make wonderful teachers. Sagittarius will often come to a new understanding of a subject through acting as a teacher or a guide for another person. The expression, 'We teach best what we most need to learn' is highly pertinent for Sagittarians; many would benefit from listening to and acting upon their own advice. The most successful Sagittarians are often those willing to become the spiritual teacher for themselves by taking the time to attune to their own inner wisdom and patiently guiding themselves to a state of inner peace.

Sagittarians frequently choose to bring healing to themselves or to their lives by helping other people. The centaur Chiron was known as the wounded healer, healing the wounds of others in his search to find healing for his own wounds. Sagittarians are often drawn to the compassionate aid of other people who have similar physical, emotional or psychic traumas to their own. They may even start up self-help groups or offer support and advice to anyone who is dealing with illnesses or traumas that they have already tackled in their own lives. By helping others they are able to put their personal situation into perspective, coming to terms with the past and bringing their attention firmly forward onto the glorious opportunities of the future.

The wounded healer is a commonly occurring figure in many ancient cultures. This is one aspect of the Shaman, Medicine Man or Woman, Witch Doctor or Sage. In many traditions these healers would bring assistance to others through the journeying of the higher mind, visions of the future and the teaching of wise philosophies. Many of these qualities or skills can be attributed to Sagittarius.

Shamanic practices can tell us much about the nature of Sagittarian creativity. In numerous folk traditions around the world, medicine people would practise their healing arts through highly ritualised forms of dance, theatre, music, body painting and other visual or sensual expressions. Sagittarian creativity often comes from acting out or externalising feelings in a way that can provide a safe release for other people as well as for themselves.

Sagittarians who are drawn to perform can do so with a great deal of humour and wit. They can often combine skills in mimicry and linguistics with a fine repertoire of stories to entertain others in a variety of social settings. Most often Sagittarians will entertain at ritual events, being a good after-dinner speaker at weddings, and at annual functions of professional or scholastic bodies.

Sagittarians have an excellent ability to convey and

illustrate the feeling of their experiences and they can be wonderful comedians who combine very clever intellectual humour with corny puns. Sagittarians instinctively know how to use humour as a healing gift; they are able to express and exorcise areas of pain through laughter. Often their stories can take the form of travellers' tales that transport the listener through vivid images, wonder and suspense with a few perfectly timed, witty lines thrown in to break the tension.

Fire Affirmations for Sagittarius

I fuel my divine spark with healing power.

I am filled with light and energy.

I am glowing with positivity.

Bright visions inspire and heal me.

I expand into greater awareness.

I am filled with positive anticipation.

My destiny is bright, my journey is sweet.

I travel light and free.

My aim is true, my goals are shining and my vision is clear.

My body is light, flexible and strong.

Fire Visualisation: Becoming the Centaur

Breathe and relax and as you do visualise yourself standing beside a beautiful horse. The horse is large, elegant,
muscular and powerful. Pat and stroke it and discover
that it is friendly and calm. Feel safe enough to put your
arms around its neck and hug the horse. Know that you
have a deep understanding of each other.

Next, see yourself easily mounting this majestic steed.
Although it is unsaddled and unbridled you find that
you are perfectly comfortable and balanced up there.
Hold on to the mane or the neck as your horse begins to
walk forwards. Discover that you know perfectly how to
ride and that you are completely safe.

As the two of you begin to move, imagine that you
feel the rhythms or vibrations of pure fiery energy rippling up through the horse's body and into your own. As
the horse speeds up into a trot and then into a gallop
feel those vibrations quicken and feel the rush of air on
your face.

As you journey imagine yourself absorbing the
strength and power of the horse. Imagine your body
becoming stronger, fitter, healthier, more alive and filled
with energy. See your body and the body of the horse
begin to merge, becoming one noble, magnificent being.
Feel the thrill of life rushing through you as you gallop
towards distant horizons.

Be aware of your body, mind and spirit coming into
full alignment, then picture yourself decreasing speed
and gently coming to a point of stillness. See your body
detach from that of the horse and as you dismount feel

yourself taking with you all of that health, strength and power.

Hug the horse and thank it for all of its gifts. Imagine the feeling of fiery energy glowing within your human body as you walk away.

CHARGING THROUGH AIR

The element of air is the realm of the intellect and the higher mind and Sagittarius is usually very comfortable with the greater planes of mental awareness. Internally and externally Sagittarius longs for, plays with and celebrates air. Internally air fuels the Sagittarian realms of higher education, philosophy, teaching, wisdom, visions of the future and higher consciousness. Externally air represents the physical need for freedom, open spaces, sport and travel.

If you watch a horse galloping, you will see that at speed this majestic beast barely seems to touch the ground. Horses in motion are a beautiful expression of physical power and grace, appearing to travel great distances with lightness and ease. Horses have often been said to fly like the wind and the horse part of the mythical centaur is no exception to this. The human half of the centaur is already within the realms of reason or higher consciousness and at times of speed the centaur's animal nature can also be drawn up to journey on the higher currents of thought.

On a physical level Sagittarius enjoys the element of air as a means of travel and sport. Sagittarians often appreciate aeroplanes, not necessarily for the experience of air travel itself, nor for the technological achievements of flight but for providing the means to reach distant lands, exotic cultures and new adventures.

The element of air represents continual change, flexibility and spontaneity for Sagittarius. As the archer, Sagittarius delights in shooting arrows through the air and watching them speed off into the distance, before galloping off in pursuit. This is Sagittarius formulating ideas before sending them out into the world to see where they land. For Sagittarius each new idea is an exciting new goal to be pursued.

Part of the gift and the challenge of Sagittarius is learning how to harness all of that Sagittarian mental or spiritual energy and give it a clear direction. The realm of ideas is the magical world of all that is not yet in form; there are so many seductive possibilities that it could be all too easy to become overly involved in mental fantasy and not allow the ideas to become real. In some cultures the arrow is a symbol for direction; in others it symbolises truth. For Sagittarians to stay healthy they need to remain true to themselves, cutting through any self-delusion and formulating clear goals.

Air Affirmations for Sagittarius

I think my way to health.

I teach myself direction and purpose.

My mental journeys bring harmony and health.

I set off in the pursuit of wisdom.

I activate my higher goals.

Knowledge brings me healing.

Air Visualisation: Heavenly Flight

Breathe deeply and relax, taking a few moments to observe your breath moving in and out of your lungs; filling them fully and gently with air and releasing that air slowly.

Picture yourself as the mythical winged horse Pegasus, beautiful and elegant. Your expansive wings stretching out to swoop and glide as you fly through the heavens. Imagine the freedom of the flight as you reach out your wings and allow yourself to be supported by the higher currents of the universe.

Breathe deeply, imagining each in-breath bringing you new ideas, new goals, new inspirations, and new knowledge to learn and to teach. Every out-breath releases all that is old and complete from your mind and your life. See yourself letting go of beliefs or thoughts that no longer serve you as you journey through the higher realms.

The more you breathe, the more you fill yourself with positive, healthy thoughts and cleanse yourself of limitations, restrictions and negative self-opinions. Imagine your breath becoming visible, tangible and real. See the in-breath as shimmering white starlight that fills you with blissful serenity and ecstatic joy. See the out-breath as dark smoke that safely releases any fear, worry or disease from your body, leaving you feeling calm and tranquil.

Continue this image for a while and notice any special thoughts or inspirations that come to your mind. When you complete this visualisation you may choose to write down or record any ideas that you had.

TRAVELLING THROUGH WATER

A journey through the element of water provides Sagittarius with interesting and necessary areas of expansion but brings with it many challenges. Water rules the emotions; many Sagittarians are more comfortable with the pursuit of their intellectual, material or spiritual aims than with the expression of their feelings. This is not because Sagittarians do not feel anything; on the contrary many of them are highly sensitive. It is perhaps because of their wish to remain positive that they do not always believe that it is appropriate to let their sensitivities show.

Sagittarius often appears to be elusive or mysterious. This is partly because Sagittarian people are so busy enjoying the many adventures of life that they tend not to stay in one place for too long. In some cases, the other reason for this elusiveness is that they would prefer to keep their feelings private. In company, Sagittarians generally prefer to be seen for their bright, optimistic, lucky selves rather than admit their vulnerability to others.

Even Sagittarians who have strongly aspected emotional tendencies within their wider astrological personality can be known to give themselves little space to express their emotions with others, preferring the safety of solitude to shed a few tears. Sagittarians may need to learn to love and accept their emotions more and not to judge themselves harshly for being human and sensitive.

LOVE AND ROMANCE

For Sagittarians to stay healthy and balanced it is important for them to develop loving relationships that allow them to have a degree of freedom. In love Sagittarius needs to discover the compromise between honouring their own desire for independence, or for the pursuit of external goals, and nurturing some level of emotional involvement that will provide a base of tenderness and companionship to which they can return.

Sagittarians are often happier with the pursuit of love than with developing long-term, committed relationships. Sagittarius loves the stimulation of fascinating new encounters or the challenge of winning over a new heart. Because of the Sagittarian tendency to journey to distant parts of the world or distant areas of the mind, Sagittarians will often choose to focus their desires on lovers who seem exotic in some way. Sagittarians often pursue romantic contacts with foreigners or with people who have a cultural or religious background that is different from their own.

The ideal partner for Sagittarians who choose to stay married or involved in a long-term relationship would be a person who allows them plenty of freedom, without clinging. A Sagittarian's partner needs to be prepared to uproot and venture forth with Sagittarius as a travelling companion on some occasions and be left behind on others. This would best suit someone who also desires freedom and who has their own goals to pursue.

Married Sagittarians can sometimes maintain their freedom through the imagination, mental journeys or the expansion of the higher mind. This is to be encouraged as to do otherwise would dampen the very nature of Sagittarius. However, Sagittarians would do well to remember that emotional contact with others can free the soul as much as mental or physical space.

Sagittarians who fully embrace their emotional side often

feel a greater freedom or expansiveness than those who deny or ignore their feelings. Many Sagittarians create restrictive relationships purely because they believe that commitment automatically means restriction. Sagittarians who change their expectations can break this negative self-fulfilling prophecy and attract lovers or partners who give them the relationship they need.

Water Affirmations for Sagittarius

It is safe for me to be vulnerable.

I travel to the centre of my heart.

I experience the freedom of my feelings.

The pursuit of love brings me all that I desire.

I now create the loving partnership of my dreams.

Love expands my horizons.

Water Visualisation: Exploring

Allow yourself to be comfortable, breathe and relax.

Imagine that you can walk on water and picture yourself travelling across the surface of a bright blue ocean. See and feel the water supporting you from below as you step forward. With each step that you take the water remains solid and firm beneath you, although it appears to be fluid.

In your mind's eye see yourself picking up speed and starting to run. Imagine your body being supple, energetic, strong, healthy and flexible as you speed across the water, feeling free and alive. In your thoughts, know yourself to be fully supported by your emotions, healed and safe.

Next, visualise yourself slowing down again and imagine yourself walking down into the water; you are supported firmly as you descend. Picture this to be just like walking down a set of steps, each step lowering you safely into the waves. You are comfortable and able to breathe fully.

As you become submerged imagine yourself transforming into a beautiful sea-horse. Picture yourself as this sea-horse riding the currents and exploring this underwater world. Take yourself on a magical journey through this realm of sensation, colour and form and as you do this explore your inner emotional state. It may help you to ask yourself these questions:

Where in my body am I holding tension?

What emotions do I need to feel?

What emotions could I express?

Where am I hurt or wounded?

Where in my body, mind or spirit am I carrying joy?

What do I feel in my heart?

What is my heart's desire?

Imagine your sea-horse self showing you ways to express your emotions through creativity or artistic pursuits.

When you feel complete, picture yourself swimming

to the surface of the water and taking human form once again as you begin to step upwards. The water becomes solid again beneath your feet to support you. Picture any old or surplus emotional energy dropping away safely and peacefully from your body, leaving you feeling tranquil and calm.

On completing this visualisation you may choose to write down or record any creative ideas or healing inspirations that you had. Please note that as this visualisation is fairly involved it may help you to record your voice guiding you through it or get a friend to read it to you. Alternatively, you could practise it in stages until you are familiar with the images.

EARTHLY PURSUITS

The element of earth rules the material world and provides a valuable key for the long-term healing and fulfilment of the Sagittarian soul. Being fiery in nature, Sagittarius isn't always comfortable with this element. Earth requires the creativity, expansion and inspiration of Sagittarius to become grounded and real. Sagittarius is challenged to have an impact on the physical or financial realms; bringing higher awareness into matter.

Sagittarius is the harmonising and synthesising of opposite forces, human consciousness and animal drives, divine purpose and that purpose brought into form. With all that creative spiritual fire it is no wonder that Sagittarians can sometimes be so restless and unsure of what to do with themselves or their talents.

Sagittarians can harness their special energy through the earth, through physicality and appropriate, tangible action. This is why they often need to be so physically active. Movement, exercise and sport are good ways to ground that restlessness and achieve balance and inner harmony. When there is a fire in your soul you just want to run, jump and dance!

PARTNERSHIPS, BUSINESS AND SUCCESS

Another way of grounding or 'making real' Sagittarian energy is through a career or vocation. Sagittarius often carries the highest aims of all of the signs of the zodiac, needing to set goals and pursue them in order to feel fulfilled and happy. Some Sagittarians are highly ambitious and will set their sights on rapid promotion and creative advancement.

Sagittarius will be a motivating force in any business partnership or team, monitoring long-term projections and goals and inspiring others to keep moving towards them. Sagittarius can be a reassuring presence in the company or department, filling the workplace with warmth, brightness and healing. Sagittarius can also bring out the highest aspirations in junior colleagues, trainees or employees, providing a sense of purpose, excitement and stimulation.

Many Sagittarians will be self-employed, preferring to be a law unto themselves than get bogged down in corporate politics or departmental restrictions. Some will be drawn to professional roles that give them the opportunity to be outdoors or to travel great distances. Sagittarius is more likely to be the travelling representative or the field worker than to be office-bound.

Sagittarian business people are often on the look out to find ways that their business can expand. Sagittarius is the sign of luck and many Sagittarians have stories of their lucky breaks; some have an uncanny knack of being in the right place at the right time for their career or business to take off. Good fortune can bring many creative opportunities to them and in turn they often bless their workplace and colleagues with good fortune too.

Sagittarians may find themselves redefining their notions of success quite frequently as they move through life. Each new goal or set of goals will bring some shift of perspective, no matter how small. Many Sagittarians will experience more than their fair share of larger shifts of consciousness, too, as they travel within the world and within themselves.

In general, younger Sagittarians will focus on material aims and the attainment of financial success. As they develop, Sagittarians will become more and more fascinated with the creative process itself. They will explore the joy of creation, whether of money, a healthy physique, art, or an inspirational project.

As life progresses, the fascination with material aims and the creative process transmutes into greater and greater spiritual aspiration. Many Sagittarians will desire to be close to God. Physical activities, earthly pursuits and even material gain will be seen as vehicles for spiritual learning and attainment.

Earth Affirmations for Sagittarius

I now embody my glorious future.

My aspirations bring me material and spiritual rewards.

My work is a shining adventure.

My direction is always clear.

My body is healthy and filled with energy.

I create wealth and wisdom with equal ease.

Earth Visualisation: Arrows of Fortune

Breathe and relax. As you do, picture yourself as a Sagittarian archer priming your bow with a golden arrow. See the arrow glint in the sunlight as you draw back the string. Imagine the arrow becoming imbued with a goal, idea or aspiration that you have as you shoot it into the air. See your arrow, together with your goal or aspiration, gaining momentum as it whizzes through the atmosphere and see it slow down and fall to earth, landing accurately in some rich, fertile soil.

Imagine the arrow taking root in the earth and see it begin to grow. You could see it becoming a plant or tree with beautiful flowers or leaves. Alternatively you could visualise it transforming into a symbol or object of your achievement like a new house, a pile of money, a blossoming relationship or something beautiful that symbolises your health or spiritual development. Repeat this visualisation for each creative idea, aspiration or goal that you have.

See yourself travel to touch or feel each of these symbols or images of physical health and material success. As you connect with each one imagine them becoming a reality within your body or within your life. You are magnetic to the achievement of your goals; health and success manifests for you wherever you go.

When you complete this visualisation you may choose to write down or record any ideas that you have for practical action at this time. Think about how you can best aid your healing process, your career and your creative advancement and take the necessary steps over the next few days or weeks to help make your visualisation become a tangible reality.

THE SPIRITUAL PURPOSE OF SAGITTARIUS

The energy of Sagittarius is both mature and spontaneous. Of all the signs with expansive, fiery qualities, Sagittarius is the most free-flowing and free-thinking. Sagittarian people have a wealth of potential for tapping their divine energies and channelling them into self-healing, the liberation of the soul and the healing of others.

Sagittarians are learning to handle an ever-expanding awareness. It is as if their inner and outer horizons are continually being stretched, giving them a constantly increasing spiritual picture of the world and of themselves. The challenge for Sagittarians is to remember that they are both human and divinely inspired so that they can give this awareness some kind of clear direction.

Sagittarians can sometimes be like a horse that has been stabled too long and has just been let out into a field. Naturally, it wants to gallop everywhere at once to burn off pent up energy and test out or even stretch the boundaries of this newfound freedom. In the astrological cycle, Sagittarius follows Scorpio, which is the Sun sign associated with the act of going into the darkness to heal, transform and bring hidden aspects of the self to the light. Sagittarius is that light with its discovery of new freedoms and the adventure of life.

The purpose of Sagittarius is to find a clear focus for all of that liberated energy so that it may be used for greater self-healing and for the healing of the world. The secret to this is to remember that one will automatically facilitate the other. As we heal ourselves we heal the world. As we heal the world through teaching, love, spirituality, peace or positivity we activate those qualities within ourselves.

The centaur Chiron gave up his immortality to help another being and in doing so he discovered his special gifts and his divine purpose. By acknowledging their own mortality, humanness and vulnerability, Sagittarians can bring all their wisdom and inspiration to bear on their own advancement. In addition they will find that they have a positive impact on those around them. Sagittarians celebrate the joy of being alive, finding wholeness within themselves and pointing the way towards positive future possibilities for us all.

THE SAGITTARIAN GIFT TO THE WORLD

Sagittarius reminds us of our limitless nature and of the potential that we all have to create a glorious future for ourselves. We need the wise teachings of Sagittarius to help us to heal and to know that the power of healing comes from within; it just needs to be harnessed and given direction.

As well as being drawn into roles and professions that involve the teaching or guidance of others, Sagittarians may choose a career in sport or physical fitness. Sagittarius can be found amongst schoolteachers, lecturers or professors, sportspeople and personal exercise trainers. They may also be philosophers, lawyers, travel guides, explorers or priests.

Sagittarius shows us that there is always more to learn, new places to go, new things to see and do. If we curl up in a ball and resist the challenge then we are only half alive; if, on the other hand, we rise to the challenge, then the world delights in supporting us and personal expansion can be ours.

Above all, Sagittarian optimism teaches the world to discover the playful adventure within each new moment. In doing so we learn how to extend ourselves into a oneness with God, the universe and all living things.

Healing with Earth

BACK TO THE ROOTS WITH THE EARTH SIGNS

Earth is the element of the body and of the material world. It is stable, structured, physical and presently focused. The people born into the element of earth are reliable, thorough, materially adept and practical.

The three Earth signs are:

TAURUS – FIXED EARTH
22 APRIL – 22 MAY

KEY QUALITIES:
SENSUAL, PROSPEROUS, STABLE, LUXURY-LOVING, TACTILE, PHYSICAL.

VIRGO – MUTABLE EARTH
24 AUGUST – 23 SEPTEMBER

KEY QUALITIES:
HEALING, RELIABLE, PURE, INDUSTRIOUS, ANALYTICAL, PRECISE.

CAPRICORN – CARDINAL EARTH
23 DECEMBER – 20 JANUARY

KEY QUALITIES:
PIONEERING, PERSISTENT, STRUCTURED, AMBITIOUS, SUCCESSFUL, ORGANISED.

CHAPTER FOUR

TAURUS

22 April - 22 May

FIXED EARTH

Taurus is the sign of the zodiac that revels in the sensuality and the comforts of the material world. The people born into this sign are tactile, lovable, affectionate and strong; they exude a luxurious quality of certainty and steadfastness within a world of change. Perhaps this is why they often have a stabilising effect on everyone and everything around them.

Picture in your mind the pretty blossoms, warmth and fertility of late spring or early summer and you may already find yourself relaxing into a feeling of well-being that is inextricably linked to Taurus. Taurus brings with it rich assurances and conventional pleasures that seduce us all into the fun and frolics that material resources can provide. With Taurus comes the feeling that the good times are here to stay.

The symbol for Taurus is the bull – strong, lustful and sturdy; a very male image for what is essentially a female sign. In fact Taurus can be seen as both bull and cow; both genders representing the rich femininity and abundant splendours of the earth. Taurus is the sign of nature's prosperity, providing us all with sustenance, harmony and enrichment.

Taurean people are good-natured, generous and warm. Slow to anger, they are straightforward and generally accepting of other people. They are excellent at creating financial and emotional security for themselves and for the people they love. They are often strongly orientated towards the family or the herd of familiar souls with which they surround themselves.

The glyph, or shorthand notation for Taurus is like the head of a bull or cow with a large curved horn on top (♉). This is perhaps similar to the curved horns of cattle to be found in the Eastern countries where astrology originated. This glyph could also be described as a crescent moon above a full moon representing the potent femininity of this sign.

Taureans are steady, determined and productive. They like to be able to build things in their lives that are going to last and sustain them over a long period of time. Their careers, relationships and environments are created to provide them with long-term security, certainty and support. On the whole, Taureans shun change in favour of constancy and a reliable familiarity.

The ruling planet of Taurus is Venus, named after the goddess of love. The influence of Venus imbues Taurus with a love of beauty, aesthetics and romance. Venus also contributes to the strong sexuality of Taureans, making them seductive, flirtatious and often very attractive to other people. In Taurus, Venus is not abstract or ethereal; its influence is as tangible and juicy as a ripe peach.

Venus brings to Taurus a creativity that is very often channelled into the acquisition of material things. Taureans love to make money and spend it in pursuit of the good life. Even less financially adept Taureans seem to have a talent for creating a degree of material comfort that can verge on the luxurious. Many Taureans appear to be magnets for material success, although they are generally willing to apply energy and commitment to acquiring it.

TAURUS IN ITS ELEMENT

The element of earth provides a rich and opulent playground for its sensual child Taurus. The earth abounds in the material splendours that Taureans love to revel in. Life for Taurus is about creating or manifesting physical pleasures to be sampled and enjoyed.

Many Taureans love to acquire possessions; they enjoy having a warm, comfortable home filled with beautiful things. A Taurean home is often rich with colours and textures. They may have beautiful pictures on the wall and warm, soft furnishings, thick rugs or padded sofas to curl up into. The wardrobes of male and female Taureans alike are often filled with smart, comfortable clothes. This may include designer suits and expensive fashion items, but you will rarely find anything too way out or wacky.

Some Taureans really enjoy talking about money, and are often fascinated by the process of making it. They like to talk about stocks and shares, property, investment opportunities and numerous money making schemes. Taureans love to discuss business in social situations, enjoying business lunches or cocktail parties where they can make valuable contacts. They also take pleasure in discussing ways of spending or enjoying money; they are often equally comfortable with making it and using it.

Taureans who shun the trappings of materialism may express their earthiness by going back to nature, growing vegetables and experiencing the good life by being close to living things. However, even these Taureans may be attached to comfort and security and may find themselves enthusiastically planning ways of increasing their productivity and marketing their skills. Inevitably some will find themselves drawn back to the world of commerce and physical comfort.

Many Taureans like to eat, drink and be merry. Taurus has a famous love of food, often choosing to dine well and enjoying the opportunity to entertain. Taureans like other people to share in their sensual pleasures and may enjoy creating lavish dinner parties at home or taking their friends out to expensive restaurants when funds allow.

It may benefit Taurus to dine simply sometimes to compensate for their tastes in rich food and rich living. Over-indulgence can affect the general health and well-being of the Taurean soul. Fortunately many Taureans have a physical constitution that can handle occasional excesses, but it is best to keep the consumption in check. Too much rich food affects the weight, digestion and overall toxicity of the body, but small doses of indulgence can boost the morale or heal the Taurean spirit.

Like all earth signs, Taureans derive great benefit from being with plants, animals, nature spirits and the elemental world. Pottering around in a garden, going for long walks or tending to the needs of pets and livestock can provide Taurus with a healthy antidote to overindulgence. Being close to the earth restores Taureans to their natural stability.

Taureans often have a plodding, rhythmic pace to their lives. They achieve what they set out to do with certainty and good grace, following through projects with a timing that ensures tangible results. Like the earth itself, Taureans know that everything has its season, with all things developing in their rightful time. Taureans make their lives work by staying grounded and being fixed on the tasks or pleasures of the present.

TAUREAN ZONES OF THE BODY

Taurus rules the neck and throat as well as influencing the thyroid gland and the ears. General health and well-being could be reflected in the freedom or comfort of the neck area. Any tension may well be felt in the muscles and bones of the neck even if the tension or imbalance stems from some other part of the body.

The stiffness or flexibility of the neck area can be a good barometer for anxieties, mental rigidity or general emotional well-being. Things that are left unsaid or emotions that are not fully expressed can be held in this part of the body, sometimes contributing to sore throats or laryngitis. Rigidity of thought can also create tensions or trapped energy that can be held in the neck or the throat.

Neck exercises of all kinds will benefit Taureans and they may feel greatly relieved by massage of the neck and shoulders. Gentle neck rolls performed daily can help to dispel the build-up of stress. Care needs to be taken not to force the head and neck around, but rather to let the weight of the head bring it forwards onto the chest and then softly roll it to the side, the back, the other side, and around to the front again in a gentle arc, circling first one way and then the other.

Taureans may also benefit from voice work, singing lessons or any other opportunity to extend the range or expression of the voice. Singing, whether in the bath or in a choir, can bring pleasure, stress release and a greater flexibility of mental and emotional attitudes. Voice work and singing are particularly recommended for any Taureans who were told that they couldn't sing or who feel awkward about their voice in any way.

Taurus often loves music, enjoying its fun and sensuality. Listening to music of all kinds will be good, but care must be taken to avoid jarring, discordant sounds and any music that is too loud. Taureans have a tendency towards sensitive hearing and a general sensitivity to sounds or vibrations of all kinds. Being in a workplace, for instance, where there is a constant bombardment of jarring noise, may adversely affect the mood and the overall health or well-being of a Taurean.

The thyroid gland is associated with the rate of physical growth. It releases a hormone into the body that helps to regulate the size and shape that we will become. For Taurus, the concept of growth is an important one. Taureans may need to moderate their food consumption as well as keeping generally active so that they burn up the calories.

As well as being aware of physical growth Taurus may benefit from an awareness of their mental, emotional and spiritual growth. Taureans who are actively developing themselves through ongoing education, mature relationships and spiritual study are more likely to stay in balance or harmony with themselves and with the world.

EXERCISE AND THERAPIES

Taureans respond well to the healing vibrations and the colours of flowers. Sick or sad Taureans often brighten up when given gifts of flowers or flowering plants. What is more, they tend to respond well to flower essences of all kinds, including Bach flower remedies. Taureans who are interested in healing may be drawn to work with these remedies as practitioners.

Taureans are very influenced by the power of physical

touch and may derive special benefit from tactile forms of healing or therapy. As well as massage and gentle stroking of bruised or tense areas of the body, hands-on healing that places emphasis on physical contact often produces great relief. Emotionally Taureans very often respond well to being hugged and cuddled. Taurean children and adults alike can be nursed back to health with a good dose of physical affection.

Sporting Taureans may enjoy contact sports like rugby, American football and some forms of acrobatics. Martial arts can be good for Taurus, promoting physical discipline, strength and grace. Judo may be particularly favoured. Some Taureans may like weight-training or body-building although it is wise not to overdo rigid, masculine forms of exercise.

Taureans love to be pampered, perhaps with mud baths, warm herbal wraps, saunas, facials, manicures and the occasional week on a health farm or spa. They often receive a healing boost of morale from having their hair done or buying new clothes. With Taurus a bit of luxury, care and attention can work wonders.

Perhaps of all the Sun signs, Taurus is the one that can derive the greatest fun and healing from dance, from Disco to Ballroom, from Tango to Tap. Taureans respond particularly well to the earthy rhythms of Latin music. The thrill of Salsa or Samba may provide exercise, flexibility and a good dose of entertainment for them. While dancing, Taurus can lose themselves in rhythm, sensual expression and movement.

PARTNERSHIPS, BUSINESS AND SUCCESS

Taureans are generally good with money – attracting it, handling it, accounting for it and spending it. Within any company or partnership the Taurean may well be the financial director, the accounts person or the person who turns the creative inspirations of others into hard cash. Taurus has a genius for financial creativity that can transform money-making into an art form.

On the whole, Taureans prefer secure jobs with long-term prospects for promotion, financial advancement and the pleasant rhythms of regular social contact with colleagues or clients. They are attracted to jobs that provide them with perks like company cars or the opportunity to earn bonuses for extra productivity and commitment. As bosses or employees alike, they are usually honest, trustworthy and reliable.

Some Taureans are occasionally tempted away from their secure post by a 'get rich quick' scheme. Taureans do love to be seduced by glamour and golden opportunities. Most, however, like to find themselves a good long-term source of regular income. They are happy to develop and build their prosperity at a pace that ensures success.

Many Taureans like to choose jobs that place them in beautiful locations. These can be situations of natural beauty or well-designed interiors. Taureans can be found around gardens, farms, galleries, boutiques, design consultancies or smart hotels. Beauty and aesthetics are perhaps more important for Taurean health than many realise. Environmental stress can be a big cause of disharmony and illness. Taureans who do not work in a congenial location may consider changing jobs or putting some energy into making their surroundings more pleasing to the eye and easier on the soul.

Taureans are generally friendly, easy-going people to work with. They are usually patient and understanding with the people around them and they enjoy being part of a team. The social side of work is often important for Taureans and some may choose to socialise regularly with colleagues outside working hours. It is not unheard of for Taurean business partners to go on holiday together, although they will be sure to leave someone reliable 'holding the fort'.

Taureans often enjoy working with other Taureans or, at the very least, people of another earth sign. However, Taurus will benefit from an alliance with a partner or colleague who is able to handle the promotions, publicity and the communications of the business. They may also need the input of someone who has a flair for creativity and invention.

Taurus is willing to put energy and commitment into work; believing that a job worth doing is worth doing well. Taureans are keen to put in the extra hours if it is going to mean financial security, promotion or the ability to afford a bit of luxury. They are willing to pay their way and do their fair share; they are often very generous with their earnings.

Taurean business very often revolves around property, possessions or lifestyle. They like to provide services, products or expertise that help to make the lives of other people more comfortable, pleasant and luxurious. Taurus has a strong sense of the splendours of the earth and they like to see everyone else having the joy and benefit of the material world.

Some Taureans may have a special flair for property; the sale of it, the design of it, the building of it or perhaps interior design. They tend to be good home-makers, enjoying the comforts of a safe, attractive environment. They also like to provide their families and friends with a hub of material security to return to or visit. Taureans take a pride in their home and they generously love to have other people enjoying it too.

Earth Affirmations for Taurus

Beauty, prosperity and joy are everywhere for me.

I am physically healthy and secure.

I am always in secure and harmonious locations.

My throat is clear, open and healthy.

I enjoy the sensuality of my body.

My body functions beautifully in health and grace.

I stretch and grow into new awareness and greater pleasures.

Making money is easy, enjoyable and fun.

I am enriched by each new moment of my life.

My life is filled with fun and affection.

Earth Visualisation: The Golden Bull

Breathe and relax, and as you do imagine yourself looking at a beautiful golden bull, youthful, stocky and elegant. This is a mystical beast whose skin shimmers in the sunlight of day and is luminous in the darkest of nights.

This bull is a special guide who helps you to find prosperity, peace of mind and physical well-being. Although he is wild, you are safe in his presence as he takes you on a special healing journey.

Imagine your Golden Bull guiding you through your sensual world of needs, aspirations and desires. The bull shows you images of the material things that you need or desire at this time. Picture everything physical or financial that you would like to create in your life right now and imagine yourself becoming magnetic to those creations.

Be guided to images of the relationships that you would like to heal, transform or attract into your life. The Golden Bull shows you the faces of the people to whom you need to send loving thoughts at this time. Imagine yourself becoming magnetised to positive, loving, healthy relationships.

Finally, allow the bull to show you the areas of physical, mental or emotional healing that you need in your life right now. See yourself becoming magnetic to the treatments, therapies or love and care that you need to make a positive difference to your health and wellbeing.

When you complete, you may choose to write down or record any ideas that you had for prosperity, relationships or personal healing. Thank your Golden Bull for his guidance.

THE FIERY SENSUALITY OF TAURUS

The element of fire can be both challenging and attractive for Taurus. The challenge comes when the inspirational spontaneity of fire confronts the security and stability of Taurean energy. Fire is fast-moving and focused on future possibilities, whereas the earthiness of Taurus likes to stay with what is present, safe and real.

The attraction that Taureans can have to the fire element comes from the Taurean desire to have or possess everything that is beautiful, shining and sensually alive. Taureans love the creativity of fire, from the quality of light in an exquisite painting to the warmth of the sunshine that seduces the flowers into opening their petals.

Fire can lend Taurus a positive opportunism or the motivation to acquire or create something new. Taureans often wish to develop some area of themselves or their lives that will bring an exotic lightness to their solidity and strength. All that glistens may not be gold, but glittering aspirations can motivate learning and healing on all levels.

Perhaps Taureans best experience the element of fire through the expression of their sexuality. Taurean sexuality is more likely to be sensuous than lusty but there is a full-blooded quality to it that can awaken some fiery passion. Even the most passive and peace-loving Taureans tend to have a little gleam of fire in the eye and potentially, a larger fire down below.

TAUREAN INSPIRATION AND CREATIVITY

Taurus is a beautifully creative sign, its creativity usually coming with slow, organic development rather than in bursts. Taureans are artistically versatile people who are willing to develop their skills over a long period of time so that their harnessed talents can express greater and greater beauty.

Being a highly tactile sign, Taurus loves to work with creative media that reflect the sensuality of touch. Many Taureans love working with fabrics and some may choose to be dressmakers, fashion designers or weavers. Others are drawn to the use of rich fabrics in upholstery, interior design or collage; they may even turn their hands to textile design itself. Those that create in this way will often love the smell, colour and warmth of fabric as well as its overall feel.

Some Taureans may choose to be cooks as they enjoy the satisfaction and fulfilment that good food can bring. They can take pleasure in eating and preparing good solid meals, often going in for rich sauces and colourful presentation. Taurus enjoys the art of food; they love to prepare dishes that people can eat with their eyes and their soul as well as stimulating the stomach and the taste buds.

Taureans may be fired up to create pottery or sculpture. Some can reach quite blissful meditative states whilst shaping and moulding raw clay into objects of formed beauty. It is as if the sensuality of Taurus' ruling planet Venus combines with the Taurean earthiness to produce something magical. The magic comes with the process of creativity as well as with the end results. Taurus can also have a good eye for the colouring of glazes or the decoration of pots and sculptures.

In addition to all of their other talents Taureans are often wonderful musicians. Many love to give and receive pleasure by playing musical instruments at social events. Even Taureans who do not consider themselves to be musical may find that they are drawn to the sound of live music; anything from Rock to Baroque, Opera to Orchestral. Perhaps it is music that can most readily awaken some fire in the rich earth of Taurus: fire to make them sing, dance and be merry.

Fire Affirmations for Taurus

My natural beauty is always highlighted and enhanced.

My life is filled with enthusiasm and joy.

I have a lightness of touch and a strength of purpose.

I enjoy the warmth and the richness of my sexuality.

Health shines out from every pore of my body.

I revel in lightness, laughter, harmony and healing.

Fire Visualisation: The Stones of Light

Make yourself comfortable and relax. Breathe deeply and as you do imagine yourself walking along a dry river bed at the end of a hot summer's day. As you walk you notice the sculptural beauty of the rocks and stones beneath your feet and of the larger boulders at the side of the river bed. The vegetation around them is lush and green and the air is clear as the atmosphere cools.

With the sun sending its final golden beams to exquisitely illuminate this magical place, imagine yourself stopping and fixing your attention firmly on one particularly beautiful boulder or large stone. See how special it is, crafted by wind and water into smooth rippling curves. It seems to be like a huge, friendly being with its own special personality; a gentle, compassionate giant.

Picture yourself placing your hands on this stone, feeling the warmth and energy that it has absorbed from the day's sunshine. Imagine yourself soaking up some of this warmth and feel your body relaxing as you do, all tensions dropping away. Perhaps you see yourself moving closer to rest on the stone or to hug it. Visualise your rock beginning to glow with the light that it has accumulated from the sun; radiating it into every part of your body and filling you with vitality and creative power.

The light from the rock begins to shine brighter, awakening the very cells of your body to healthy, passionate expression and a feeling of well-being and lightness. Imagine a particularly powerful radiation of light shining into your throat and neck and see it moving to fill and surround this part of you. In your throat the light awakens and energises your full creative voice and vocal expression. Imagine yourself able to express your thoughts, feelings, inspirations and intuition clearly, brightly and with joy.

The beautiful light emanating from the stone awakens your innate creativity and fills you with a glow of health and energy. See this light growing brighter and brighter within you in each new moment and imagine your shining image awakening other people to health and creativity too. As you look around you, you discover that all of the other stones are shining brightly too, sending you their beams of brilliance.

Return to this image whenever you need to boost your health, energy and creative inspiration. The creativity is within you; the light just wakes it up.

THE AIR OF HEIGHTENED AWARENESS

The element of air encompasses the realms of logic, the mind and beyond to the higher mind and the spheres of heightened awareness. For Taureans, logic is often equated with realism, and anything beyond the current definition of what is real can be considered to be too illusory or too mystical to be valid. Taureans often voice a desire to have things black and white, nothing too abstract or metaphysical. However, even these realists have the capacity to stretch their awareness into the fast-moving realms of air. They just need to stick their neck out a little to catch the breezes.

Many Taureans will only become involved in intellectual or esoteric ventures if they are of obvious practical use. Taureans have their fair share of brain power; it is just that their intelligence becomes fixed on present action or activity rather than on concepts or future possibilities. If they undertake a course of study, it is usually because of the practical or financial benefits. Taureans who opt for a university degree are most likely to choose a subject that will make them more employable at the end of the course.

Perhaps the exception to this is the Taurean student who is drawn to the arts. The Taurean love of beauty and aesthetics can cause them to put practicalities to one side occasionally, but not completely. The Taurean fashion student is often the one who is having his or her designs made up for sale so that they can supplement their grant. The art history student is the one who is keeping one eye on the abstract concepts and the other on the potential jobs in museums or galleries, perhaps as a stepping stone to something more commercial.

Taureans best experience the realms of air through their ruling planet Venus, which is also the planetary ruler of the air sign Libra. A willingness to stretch the mind beyond solid, tangible realities can take Taurus from their earthy, sensual world of beauty to a conceptual one filled with infinite possibilities. Abstract romanticism and seductive new ideas are all available in this heady atmosphere.

The higher vision of Taurus is often one of peace and harmony. They may love to be told of real-life situations where people lay down their weapons or their grievances in favour of a peaceful settlement and a loving acceptance of others. We can all benefit from the Taurean tendency to be fixed upon brotherhood, sisterhood, love and tranquillity.

Air Affirmations for Taurus

I am fixed on present joys and I am open to new possibilities.

I enjoy the beautiful realms of my imagination.

My ideas bring me tangible rewards.

I fix upon the ideas that best serve my health.

My mind is filled with peace, health and stability.

I heal my thoughts with acceptance and compassion.

Air Visualisation: Magic Carpet Ride

Breathe and relax, concentrating for a few minutes on the flow of air moving in and out of your lungs. Imagine the air bringing with it a sense of peace and harmony for you to enjoy.

Picture yourself sitting or lying on a beautiful carpet, rich in colour and design. The fabric of this carpet feels warm and sensuous. See yourself settling into the luxury of its padded softness. You feel completely comfortable and safe.

Knowing that you are completely stable and secure, imagine yourself asking the carpet to rise up off the floor and visualise it doing just that. Currents of air rush in to support and pad the carpet from underneath as it moves upwards a few feet. In your thought imagine yourself practising with the carpet; directing it up and down, back and forth, side to side.

When you are ready, picture greater currents of air collecting beneath you and let them take you up and away, any obstacles dissolving immediately to allow you to travel high and free. Imagine all worries or fears dropping away from you; feel yourself growing lighter and lighter as you travel in style on your magic carpet.

Take yourself on a healing journey of peaceful ideas and rich images. Visualise yourself looking down on your life from your higher viewpoint. You are able to see all of your relationships with greater clarity; seeing your career, home life, health and well-being with new ideas and greater compassion. From this vantage point it is easy for you to put your life into perspective.

The currents of air continue to bring you new ideas, new solutions, increased wisdom and peace of mind. Imagine any mental or physical tension dropping away from you as you glide.

When you have completed this visualisation you may choose to write down or record any ideas that you had.

TAURUS AT THE WATERING HOLE

The element of water rules the emotions, the sensations and the intuition. For Taurus, water generally means one thing, and that is love. Taureans are often fascinated by love; their hearts can be fixed on how to receive more of it, give more of it and create more of it in the world around them. It is often through this fixation on love that Taureans experience a fuller range of emotional expression despite their practical, no-nonsense approach to life.

The realms of water are generally quite comfortable for Taureans, although they do like their emotional lives to have some safe boundaries. Taurean people can be highly compassionate, finding it easy to empathise with other people who are in an emotional state. However, they do tend to feel that there needs to be a good reason for extremes of feeling or upset and they can have limited patience for anyone who loses themselves too often in boundless irrationality.

In situations of great joy, deep sadness or emotional uncertainty, Taurus can be an excellent person to have around. They are often able to provide strength and stability for others without either denying their own feelings or losing themselves in the depths of them. They can convey a comforting self-assurance and a sense of peace that is quite settling for all concerned.

LOVE AND ROMANCE

Taureans are usually very affectionate lovers who enjoy cuddles and physical contact. Many enjoy sex, but gentle, caring, physical companionship that is non-sexual is often given equal, if not greater, importance. Physically demonstrative relationships help Taureans to feel safe and secure; in turn being cuddled by a Taurus is often a calming experience that brings strength and stability.

The Taurean ideal is of enduring family relationships that

get better and better over the years. Taurus may frequently make conventional choices about relationships, often preferring a stable marriage partner to a series of affairs. However, the Taurean love of beauty and romance can leave them open to the occasional flirtation, although this is usually kept in check by their overriding desire for a stable home. Taurean loyalty and good sense in matters of the heart usually prevent them from getting carried away.

Highly romantic in their approach to life, Taureans may sometimes give the impression that they will give everything for love. This is, however, rarely true. Certainly, love is an overriding motivational force for most Taureans but it is usually equated with material stability and the fulfilment of practical needs. Taurus is not the type to give up a good job to elope with a penniless artist. The exception to this will be the Taurean whose own material resources are already very secure.

Taureans tend to enjoy the symbology of love. Many will adore weddings with all of the paraphernalia that goes with them, from lavish dresses to wedding cake. Some Taureans can place great emphasis on having tokens of love like an engagement ring or a Valentine's Day card; they are equally concerned with providing romantic gifts as with receiving them. Some may even shed a tear at the simplest acts or tokens of sentimentality and this can be quite healing as it provides for safe emotional release.

Healthy relationships for Taurus will not only focus on stability and romance but will also bring some added passion for life or a touch of adventure. Taureans need lovers who balance their ordered view of the world with a little excitement. Perhaps nothing too exciting though: the stability of the Taurean world is too important to allow for anything or anyone that would introduce too much uncertainty.

The ideal partner for a Taurus is someone willing to build an enduring relationship based on solid demonstrations of love, romance and material security. In the way of old-fashioned marriage, Taureans often see a union as an economic bond as much as a romantic one. They value the importance of marriage and long-term partnerships as agreements that make provision for the needs of all concerned; they are contracts that ensure mutual care and fulfilment on all levels.

Taureans are as concerned with what they can provide for lovers, partners or children as they are with what they can receive for themselves. In many cases their own ability to contribute is of greater importance to them. As the provider, material or otherwise, Taurus has numerous ways of demonstrating their love. Taurus could be the traditional husband or father finding joy and purpose in earning money for his family. Taurus could also be the woman or man who is equally comfortable with being the breadwinner or the nurturing home-maker, doing whatever is required to keep the family unit as well provided for as possible.

Water Affirmations for Taurus

My life flows with love and stability.

My willingness to love builds more love in the world for me to enjoy.

I am fluid and flexible; strong and secure.

I easily and safely let off steam.

My emotional and romantic needs are well provided for.

I enjoy the healthy sensuality and sexuality of my body and emotions.

Water Visualisation: Summer Rains

Breathe and relax. Imagine yourself as a tree, perhaps a sturdy oak or a strong elm. Picture yourself with your roots firmly set into the ground and your trunk and branches growing strongly up towards the light. You are stable, set well in to the rich earth and fixed in beauty for the world to admire.

Visualise your tree-self being gently watered by mild, summer rain. The clean, shimmering droplets of water splash off your bark, shining your leaves and softening the earth around your roots. Imagine yourself drinking in the refreshing water through your root system and up into your trunk. The water is healing and allows you to regenerate and grow.

In your life, imagine the water to be the soft nurturing emotions of love, joy and pleasure. See yourself gently watered with the loving companionship and compassion of others and the blissful well-being of your own higher soul. It is as if you are always magnetic to healing emotions and pleasures; you always grow in strength, elegance, stability and beauty.

Return to the tree image whenever you need to reconnect with your own gentle emotions or when you would like to make yourself more available to the receiving of love from others.

THE SPIRITUAL PURPOSE OF TAURUS

The spiritual purpose of Taurus includes the fun and
enjoyment of living in the physical world. Taureans are
learning about the pleasures of physical life in all its forms,
from the joys of nature to the man-made creations of the
modern world, and perhaps most of all, the loving
companionship of family and friends.

Taurus takes pleasure in all that is presently available.
Taureans can therefore find great satisfaction and healing in
placing their attention firmly on their current activities.
Many spiritual philosophies or disciplines talk of staying in
the present moment rather than getting caught up in the
illusions of the past or the distractions of the future. For many
Taureans this is a natural state of being and for many more it
offers an excellent way to peace or stability.

For some Taureans the path of spiritual growth may be
inextricably linked to the discovery of a fundamental life
purpose. Taurus thrives when there is a basic purpose to life
and it helps when that underlying drive or motivation is easy
to understand. A purpose can be anything from providing for
a family to getting rich or to creating something beautiful
that other people will enjoy. The actual enrichment and
growth comes with the expression of the goal or desire rather
than with its ultimate attainment.

Each Taurean soul needs to be useful. Taureans love to do
things that have a lasting effect on the world and on the
people that they care about. They often need to create
something of value and worth that proves their abilities or
their love. Many Taureans choose to build solid and
permanent structures within their careers or families that will
continue after they have moved on, continuing to fulfil a

valuable purpose for others.

Perhaps above all, Taureans are learning about the concept of certainty. In a world that is constantly changing and evolving, Taureans are often concerned with creating stability in their own lives and providing an anchor of certainty for the people they love. Taureans like the world to be fixed and reliable. Invariably it is not, but their desire to make it so brings strength and beauty to others. Perhaps the healthiest Taureans are those who understand that the only certainty in the world is love.

THE TAUREAN GIFT TO THE WORLD

Taurus reminds us all of the physical pleasures that we are in the world to enjoy and the fun and sharing we can experience in the process of being alive. The energy of Taurus can be likened to the feeling of well-being that many people experience in late spring and early summer when the earth is filled with green freshness. It is like waking up on the first morning of a peaceful holiday shared with people you love.

Taureans are drawn to professions that express the material, artistic or financial aspects of life. They are often to be found in positions of trust and responsibility. Taureans can be builders, architects, surveyors, farmers, bankers or industrialists. Some may be civil servants, economists, accountants or auctioneers. Many will choose jobs that are solid and reliable for themselves and that provide a needed service for others.

The creativity of Taurus can extend into many different careers or professional roles. Taureans can be excellent singers or musicians, fashion designers or interior designers, sculptors, chefs, cooks, painters or jewellers. Interests and abilities in healing may be expressed through all forms of massage and some forms of counselling. Some Taureans make very good Bach flower practitioners.

Taurus brings a simple message of happiness and love that profoundly connects us to the gifts of life. More than anything else, Taurus reminds us that we live in a sensual world to be touched, tasted, ingested and experienced to the full in each new moment. We are surrounded by beauty that just begs to be noticed and enjoyed.

CHAPTER FIVE

VIRGO

24 August - 23 September

MUTABLE EARTH

Virgo is the earth sign of fertility and purity. Within all living things there is an innate fertile or creative potential. Every animal and every plant is precisely programmed to reproduce in order to keep its species alive. This is the energy of Virgo: precise coding that ensures the survival and creative development of all life. That coding has a purity of purpose that is both potent and innocent, sexual and chaste.

Picture in your mind the golden beauty of a field of wheat ready to be harvested. The plants are rich and vital, full of the energy that comes from the four elements acting upon each other to provide the building blocks for growth. The individual grains can be ground into flour to provide nourishment for many, and yet each one is precise, perfectly formed and encoded with all the information needed to create a whole new plant if returned to the earth. Life reproduces itself with mathematical precision.

Virgoan people contain all of that potency and sexual energy as well as being imbued with a precision of purpose that is coolly innocent. Virgo is a female sign; both women and men born at this time of year can express extraordinary feminine or receptive powers. Some may be archetypically virginal and celibate while others are compellingly sexual or earth-motherish. All convey a quiet strength. Virgo rules the harvests and is concerned with reaping the abundance of the earth while leaving the soil clean and empty, prepared for the potential of new growth.

The symbol for Virgo is of the virginal maiden, as yet untouched by life and by manhood, leaving her in a raw, innocent state. However, she is often depicted holding the ear of corn that shows her fertile potential. Inevitably she will become the mother, surrendering her innocence to fulfil her creative purpose. In doing so she will evolve into a new state of purity – that of fullness and fulfilment. The glyph or shorthand notation for Virgo is like a maternal 'M' with an extra arch or tail at the end (♍).

Men and women of this sign can seem distant and untouchable, the seeds of their life's purpose held deep inside. They can emanate a strong sense of purpose even if they are not consciously aware of it. It is as if they, too, are precisely programmed to fulfil certain tasks, create specific things and bring their lives to a point of fertile harvest. As Virgoans mature they can often become more available to others, both physically and emotionally, relaxing or opening out like a flower coming to full bloom.

The ruling planet of Virgo is Mercury. In mythology Mercury was the messenger of the gods who transported heavenly messages to the earth to enrich and inspire the lives of mortals. In Virgo, Mercury brings messages that have a practical application. Virgoan people are often inspired by ideas that they can enjoy putting into action and making into something real and tangible within the world.

For Virgo, Mercury finds the bridge between the intellectual and the practical. Virgos are clear-thinking and clear-acting with minds that are highly analytical and sharp. Their ability to evaluate and organise is second to none. They are able to assess the needs of others with great precision and act upon those needs effectively.

VIRGO IN ITS ELEMENT

The element of earth supports and is supported by Virgo. This sign is both the champion and the healer of the earth. Virgo people bring stability, careful tending and a devotional service to the planet, manifesting their high ideals in ways that make a tangible difference to the environment and to the well-being of us all. In return, the element of earth gives Virgos the vehicle through which to express their highest purpose, goals and aspirations.

Virgo learns the most through physical action. This can be the action of cataloguing or measuring their environment, making money, developing a career, learning to reorganise and reformulate their own lives or taking care of the lives of others in some way. Virgo takes delight in seeing their ideals and their presence making a physical difference to the world around them. For Virgo, to heal is to make real.

Virgos have amazing organisational skills. They are able to set up and administrate events of all kinds with detailed precision. Some are scrupulously clean and ordered and any environment that they move through is likely to reflect this in some way. Virgoans like to keep everything functioning perfectly and running smoothly.

Virgos' excellent administrative skills are aided by their ability to be detached and single-minded. They can be willing to take a hands-on approach to life even to the point of rolling up their sleeves and getting their hands dirty on occasion, despite the Virgoan love of cleanliness. Then, having done so, they are able to step back to assess the situation.

Virgo also displays an extraordinary mixture of pride and humility that aids them in being effective and diligent workers. They take great pride in the detail of their work, very often being so effective and efficient that they make themselves indispensable. Their humility allows them great compassion in their dealings with others as well as a capacity to undertake many tasks without pretension or preciousness. It is no accident that Virgo is often the sign of the Monk or Nun. Some Virgos may even take pride in being humble – a contradiction that can help to build strength of character and provide them with a clear focus for their creativity.

Virgos can find great healing for themselves away from the city, the office or the demands of family, in quiet contemplation, perhaps walking countryside trails or pottering around a garden tending vegetables and fruit. Some may even be drawn to work with the earth by volunteering for environmental projects during their leisure time. For the purposes of finding self-healing and balance, the more hands-on the work the better it will be for the Virgoan soul.

VIRGOAN ZONES OF THE BODY

Virgo rules the abdominal region, more specifically the intestines and the spleen. Virgo may often benefit from a balanced earthy diet that includes plenty of root vegetables such as carrots, beetroot, parsnips, turnips and potatoes. Other fresh fruit and vegetables could be of benefit too, as well as a certain amount of grains, pulses and cereals. Of course there is no such thing as the ideal diet for everybody.

Finding a good, healthy diet comes with trial and error and some adjustment as needs change over a period of time.

Certainly the high roughage and water content that comes with the consumption of fresh fruit and vegetables will help Virgo to keep the intestines working properly and clear of toxic wastes. Virgos may enjoy experimenting with the organically produced foods that are becoming more popular now as the effects of chemical pesticides and fertilisers are coming under greater scrutiny.

Some Virgos may even enjoy organic gardening themselves, working closely with the earth to produce foodstuffs that will keep them healthy and balanced. Others may take a delight in preparing and cooking wholesome dishes that combine rustic farmhouse cuisine with the sensuality of Virgo subtlety. Virgo sensuality and health both come with keeping things simple. Not every Virgo is a cook or gardener, but they will all benefit from wholesome, simple foods.

Being the most analytical earth sign and paying great attention to detail, Virgo may occasionally have a tendency to worry, perhaps going to bed while still thinking through the unfinished business of the day. Worry or mental stress can sometimes be held in the abdominal area as an unsettled feeling of discomfort. Virgo will always benefit from talking out or finding some other way of releasing these concerns and tensions before they go to sleep at night.

Some people find great relief in using the simplicity of worry dolls to put aside the heavy thoughts that could build into physical stress. These are sets of tiny dolls in a box that you tell your troubles to before you go to sleep. Each doll is given one worry to take care of while you are sleeping. In turn you 'tell' the dolls of your concerns before placing them in the box and putting on the lid. Usually a set contains six dolls, as having more than six worries at a time is considered frivolous.

There may certainly be psychological and physiological benefits in putting your worries aside in this way; an alternative is to write them down and immediately tear up the paper. It is the process of putting these anxious thoughts outside of yourself that generally makes the difference, clearing the mind and helping the body to discharge the stresses of the day.

Abdominal tensions can also be prevented and released through physical exercise. Simple abdominal stretching can be performed by gently arching the back, and abdominal contractions can be performed by gently tightening and relaxing the muscles around the stomach area. Exercise like this can help to calm, balance and relax as well as aiding digestion. The combination of a full exercise programme, correct diet and a regular outlet for mental tensions can help prevent ulcers, nervous stomachs and many other conditions.

For Virgo, taking care of the spleen is helpful to maintaining health in other parts of the body. The spleen can sometimes be affected by travel. Acupuncturists and Chinese medicine practitioners are often concerned with the effects of the environment on bodily organs; the spleen and other organs can be required to make dramatic adjustments when any of us, Virgo or not, lift up our roots to go on holiday, work abroad or move house. Taking a day after any journey to rest, recuperate and get your bearings will help the body to adjust. Periods spent in transit need to be punctuated with periods of stillness, preferably taken in environments that feel safe, comfortable and secluded.

The central nervous system is also ruled by Virgo. This contains the sensory information and biochemical impulses that are transmitted to and from the brain around the nerves of the body. Again, Virgos benefit from learning to discharge stress, keeping themselves in contact with natural things and close to the earth. Keeping a pet, particularly a cat or a small mammal like a rodent, can be very healing for Virgo, although other animals can be beneficial too. Stroking and talking to an animal can lower the blood pressure, balance the nervous system and regulate the body's natural rhythms.

EXERCISE AND THERAPIES

Virgos need exercise that balances fine-tuning with flexibility. Rigid exercise like body-building, circuit training and some forms of athletics may be appropriate in small, regulated doses, but this needs to be tempered with fluid, receptive forms of movement. Some Virgos love the discipline of dance, perhaps being especially drawn to the precision of ballet.

The ideal fitness programme for Virgo could include very free forms of dance where spontaneity is rated more highly than rigid attention to detail. Courses in Indian dance or Jazz dance may offer a good combination of fluidity and precise routine. Virgos wishing to express their innate, earthy sensuality, while enjoying the company of other people would probably love circle dancing.

Stretching exercises of all kinds may benefit Virgo. Many Virgos have an innate understanding of yoga, which as well as releasing rigidity from the body is good for the nervous system and brings general physical vitality. Gentle keep-fit classes that incorporate stretching with aerobic dance and general toning would also be good. There are now more classes of this nature catering for the elderly, the disabled, and anyone who is unused to strenuous activity, so it is easier to find one that suits your special needs.

Active Virgos may even consider taking up fencing, a sport that incorporates balletic movement, agility, stretching and razor-sharp Virgoan precision. Tennis, too, is a game that allows them to combine general toning with stretching, the development of precise aim and a good dose of fun. A brisk walk will not only provide Virgo with exercise but will also give them space to clear their heads of worries or an over-involvement with petty details.

On the whole, Virgos are not comfortable with being ill and they often tend to keep going regardless of their physical condition. This can be healthy up to a point; it is useful to have a positive view of one's health and not get over-attached to illness. However, they do need to take time out occasionally so that their bodies can regenerate and their minds achieve a state of calm. The trick is to plan for health while being willing to surrender when there is a genuine need to stop and recuperate, physically or emotionally. Probably the best therapy for Virgo is peace and quiet.

Occasionally the Virgoan skills of analysis and criticism can become misdirected and some Virgos may become overly critical of their bodies or their personality traits. Many Virgos, too, are essentially shy, sensitive people who could benefit from learning to promote and express themselves to others. For Virgo the therapeutic effects of a course in assertiveness or self-esteem can be enormous. Viewing oneself in a less judgemental light and choosing to love and accept one's body, personality or lifestyle as they are can be like a magic charm to improving confidence, peace of mind and general health.

Individual counselling sessions, too, can often be at their most effective for Virgo when they deal with retraining self-image as well as providing a space for the expression and release of worries. In discovering their true value, Virgos can transform their relationships, their work and their physical well-being. An easy starting-point is to keep your mind focused on the things that you do well and the aspects of yourself that you are happy with rather than becoming preoccupied with your perceived shortcomings.

PARTNERSHIPS, BUSINESS AND SERVICE

Virgos have a tendency to make themselves indispensable in work or business settings. They are so good at taking care of a million and one important details that colleagues or partners may otherwise miss, that they become the lynchpin around which many projects are based. Virgo will often know where items of equipment are located, who to contact for specialist advice, how to follow complex procedures, and whose turn it is to buy the biscuits. As such, they make brilliant administrators or secretaries.

Behind the façade of a company or team that appears to run smoothly and effortlessly there will often be a Virgo putting in two hundred per cent to keep the wheels oiled and everything ordered. Virgo can analyse, quantify, catalogue and prioritise the day's tasks while other colleagues are still taking off their coats and putting on the kettle. It is not that most Virgos are particularly speedy; it is just that they have minds that are brilliantly ordered and they get stuck into a task with quiet efficiency.

Virgos do need to learn how to blow their own trumpet and make other people aware of what they do. They are often so busy getting on with the job that they do not always pause for long enough to tell others about the value of their work. In extreme cases bosses, colleagues or clients are not aware of the Virgoan flair for excellence until the Virgo has left the job and things have stopped running smoothly.

Virgo needs the balance of working with people who can provide creative innovations, marketing and PR skills. They also appreciate colleagues who can temper their Virgoan order with a dash of chaos, bringing a little lightness and humour to all of that dedication and commitment. Virgo will also be happy if colleagues have an awareness and an appreciation of their careful contribution without them having to shout about it too loudly.

Virgo can find great pleasure, fulfilment and satisfaction through their work. They enjoy being active, using or stretching their minds and providing a service that will aid other people. They are often quite logical or scientific in their approach to work while having an inner core of sensitivity that helps them respond well to the needs of other people. Virgo is good at seeing what needs to be done and responding efficiently so that everyone can benefit.

Virgo often finds a sense of purpose and a degree of self-healing through serving other people in some way. They feel valuable if they can bring practical solutions, order and even healing into the lives of others. Virgos can sometimes be excellent healers, drawn to work with people as surgeons, dieticians, nurses or psychologists. Within the realms of complementary therapies they can be wonderful medical herbalists or homoeopaths.

At its highest vibration, Virgoan service and dedication lends itself perfectly to the higher ideals of science, medicine, global harmony and environmental or humanitarian causes. When it comes to the crunch and lives are at stake or it is imperative that a task be completed for the good of all, Virgos are excellent at putting their egos to one side and getting on with the job, selflessly and with great compassion. They are ultimately too down to earth to let personality differences get in the way of practical, healing solutions.

Earth Affirmations for Virgo

I value my contribution.

My life is filled with the stillness and contemplation of the earth.

My presence is enriching and grounded.

Serving others brings me financial, emotional and spiritual rewards.

I embody pure health.

I digest my life's experience with ease and trust.

I easily discover practical solutions to staying healthy.

My life is successful in every glorious detail.

I easily assert my needs and I ask for what I desire.

I harvest a wealth of opportunities in my life.

Earth Visualisation: The Orchard

Find a quiet, comfortable place and relax, preferably lying down or sitting with your back properly supported and your body open rather than curled up.

Breathe deeply and, as you do, picture yourself standing in a large orchard filled with fruit trees of many varieties. It is late summer and the fullness of fruit surrounds you wherever you look. This place is calm and peaceful and the sun is shining down from above to warm your body.

Imagine yourself drawn to a fruit tree that is magically filled with the energy of youth, health and vitality. Notice what kind of tree it is and thank it for its gifts as you reach up to pluck a ripe fruit from its boughs. See yourself eating that piece of fruit, carefully saving the seeds in your hand. As you eat, imagine waves of healing energy pulsing through your body to regenerate and rejuvenate every cell. Picture yourself growing younger, more alive and more attuned to the joys of life.

See yourself planting the fruit seeds in a fresh plot of rich, fertile earth and immediately witnessing the growth of a new tree. Instantly this tree becomes mature and full of ripe fruit. Imagine that this second tree is magically imbued with the energy of prosperity and abundance. Once again pluck a fruit and eat from the tree visualising waves of prosperous energy pulsing through your body making you magnetic to money, creative opportunities, positive situations and the fulfilment of your material needs.

Once again thank the tree for its healing gift and be aware of any areas of your health, prosperity or career development that you need to give some attention to right now. When you complete this visualisation, it may help you to write down or record any ideas that you have.

Breaths of Pure Air

The element of air brings the breezes of pure, clear thought to the mind and to the higher mind. Virgo is highly attuned mentally and many Virgos have a keen intellect and an ability to analyse that is razor-sharp. The Virgoan mind is able to make detailed assessments that are entirely logical in nature while having the flexibility of thought that all of the four mutable signs can enjoy.

Virgo often has a desire for information; yearning for more knowledge to analyse and put to practical use. Virgos love to learn new things and find ways to hone or sharpen their skills. The broader the picture that Virgo can have of a subject or of an area of enquiry, the more detailed and precise they can become. Virgoan minds take any new body of information and dissect it in a highly specialised, surgical way. The Virgoan mind is often likened to a scalpel.

As we move farther into the age of information technology, the more prized and valued Virgo's mental skills will become. The world is now too fast-moving for most people to stay in one job for the whole of their lives, yet the nature of many jobs has become more specialised. Virgo has the flexibility to change and adapt to new situations, while being able to pick up the increasingly detailed skills required to function in a world of computers, micro-electronics, micro-surgery and multimedia communications.

Some Virgos enjoy using their minds in games of logic, strategy and detailed memory, perhaps poring over a chessboard or mastering the intricacies of computer games in the way that some air sign people do. With Virgo, there will be an earthy intensity and a joy in the process of working through the game that is unique. When Virgo undertakes any task you can often see the underlying thrill that comes with them sharpening their minds a little more.

Virgos may hone their mental skills by becoming scholars, perhaps even drawn to a seat of learning that will allow them ongoing study or research, safe within cloistered walls. Alternatively they can become critics, expressing the practical appraisal of information or creative works.

Mercury's influence can give Virgo a desire to communicate, and often a special talent for precise written communication. Some of the most intricate, specialised or technical ideas can be brilliantly expressed by Virgo on paper. The Virgo mind can be directed to write anything from a meticulous piece of poetry to a clearly presented technical manual or a knitting pattern. Virgos are drawn to articulate ideas that other people can effectively put into practical use.

Poetic Virgos may use precise and powerful metres or rhythms to put across moods, concepts or images. Some may have a fascination for poetic devices or other highly refined techniques of communication. Most instinctively know how to present information, whether in written, verbal, visual or musical form, in ways that are ordered, clear and readily digested by other people.

Air Affirmations for Virgo

My vision is clear, sharp and focused.

It is easy for me to learn and to use what I learn.

I am precisely guided to health and joy.

I am inspired by each new detail of my life.

I tune into the rhythm and poetry of my mind.

My thoughts are positively focused and my mind is sharp.

Air Visualisation: Bird of the Airwaves

Do your best to have a good supply of fresh air as you meditate. Perhaps you could find a quiet, outdoor space or a peaceful indoor spot near an open window. Make sure that you are going to be warm enough though and that you are not going to be disturbed.

Breathe and relax, filling your lungs with fresh air. Picture yourself as a beautiful songbird, winging your way from tree to tree. You are gently caressed and guided by the currents of air to alight on the most perfect branches where you warble with delighted contentment.

Imagine that the air around you is filled with a subtle network of ideas, invisible to the human eye but as this bird you are able to see it and travel through it. Every time you take flight you are able to pluck from the air the minutest details of new, inspirational thought. It is like a fine web of logical brilliance and intellectual inspiration that you can glean from at will. Perhaps you could see these ideas as shiny little threads of silver and gold.

Now visualise your bird-self building a nest. As it does, imagine every twig, feather or piece of straw being woven in with the beautiful threads of these pure ideas. Imagine the nest being formed in perfect detail, woven with delicacy and precision.

Take a moment to think of any ideas that would be of

use for you in your life right now and see yourself putting them into practice, taking care of all the details carefully and with great satisfaction.

When you complete this visualisation you may choose to write down or record any ideas that you had.

A DIP IN CLEAR WATER

The element of water is a comfortable close companion for Virgo. It is through water that Virgo draws a great deal of sustenance and discovers the deeper meaning of life. Virgo experiences water through its opposite Sun sign, the water sign of Pisces. Where Virgo is precise and practical, Pisces is diffuse and mysterious, bringing to Virgo some additional spirituality and delicious sensuality.

Virgos may be precisely focused and detailed in their waking awareness but when they dream they enter a world of expansiveness, intuition, escapism and fantasy. Dreams can bring them much joy and give them a bigger picture of their lives. For this reason sleep is very important for Virgo as it connects them to their fertile imagination and their creative source.

In the early part of their lives Virgos may nurture a secret fascination for spiritual studies, esoteric philosophies and psychic phenomena, perhaps aware of innate mystical abilities buried deep within their unconscious. It is only later in life that they may feel fully confident in exploring these aspects of themselves openly. However, the sooner they are able to enter into and connect with these areas of themselves, the richer their lives will be.

LOVE AND ROMANCE

In love, Virgo requires warmth, trust, peace, safety and gentle coaxing before they fully open up to the sensitive side of their personality. Virgo tends to shy away from relationships whenever there is a hint of an angry scene or when there is what they might consider to be an excess of soppiness. However, under the practical, committed and sometimes cool exterior of Virgo beats the heart of a sentimental romantic who longs to be appreciated.

Virgos can be conventional in their choice of partner, opting for modesty and refinement rather than full-blooded passion and sensual expression. In contrast, the deeper waters that run through the Virgo psyche do allow them to tap into an extraordinary range of romantic and sexual feelings! The key is to have the right partner and the right mental attitude. Love, after all, involves a certain surrender from the values of the outer personality to the more vulnerable world of the inner self.

As marriage partners, Virgos are generally very loyal once they have committed themselves. They will provide for themselves and their partner in many practical ways that keep the relationship running smoothly. Many domestic, financial or organisational details are taken care of by the Virgoan member of the household. Virgo may well be the person who balances the family budget, remembers to take the sun cream on holiday and makes sure that the plumber comes to fix the shower. This is how they direct a great deal of their love to partners and children alike.

The ideal partner for a Virgo will be someone who is able to recognise and acknowledge this loving attention to detail, appreciating Virgo fully without being sentimental. Virgo needs to have lovers who have great tenderness and a generosity of spirit. They will need to be willing to leave their cherished Virgo alone at times when Virgo craves solitude, contemplation and self-actualisation, intuitively re-engaging when Virgo's desire for acknowledgement and companionship returns.

In addition it helps Virgo to have partners or friends who are a little frivolous and who can fill the Virgoan home with the healing sounds of laughter. Virgos need someone to remind them to loosen up and have a bit more fun sometimes. For many, childhood feelings of hurt or rejection can be healed through sharing love and care with others; nothing opens the heart more than shared laughter.

Many Virgos choose not to marry or settle down with a live-in partner, some preferring an independent lifestyle, living on their own while maintaining one committed, romantic involvement that can be enjoyed part-time. This contact may not even be a sexual one but one that is based on intellectual rapport and companionship. Even married Virgos will need to remember that their relationships with other people may blossom fully when balanced with plenty of time out for themselves.

For Virgo, self-actualisation is of paramount importance; there is a need to explore and integrate different parts of their own personality. The time and energy needed for this makes it essential for them to withdraw their focus of attention from the needs of other people and place it firmly on themselves. There are many Virgos who choose to forgo romantic involvements entirely so that they can undertake a life of intellectual study, vocational development or monastic meditation. Perhaps for Virgo the most important love affair to seek is an ongoing one with themselves.

Water Affirmations for Virgo

I love and accept all of my emotions.

My feelings bring me greater clarity.

I am cleansed and purified by my emotions.

I allow myself to be sensual and intuitive.

I discover my true self through my feelings.

My sleep refreshes me and sharpens my senses.

Water Visualisation: The Pool of Fantasy

Find a quiet, comfortable place to relax and settle into a position with a clear open posture.

Breathe deeply and imagine yourself standing next to a pond of clear, pure water. The surface of the pond is shimmering in the warm haze cast by summer sunshine and the wings of a thousand dragonflies buzz and shimmer all around.

In your mind's eye imagine that the haze of light, water and dragonfly wings creates a myriad of fleeting dream images for you to focus on momentarily before they shift and change. The water is so seductive and the effect so beautiful that you find yourself undressing and stepping naked into the pond.

Imagine ripples of sensual pleasure washing through you as you feel yourself relaxing more and more; imersing yourself in the healing power of your feeli your deepest dreams. Any areas of tension wit body easily release as you surrender yourself to feeling and fantasy. In your mind, picture any illness, disease or disharmony dissolving and clearing away in the pure waters of the pond.

Imagine yourself clearly and safely being able to express all your emotions. Picture yourself fully and freely expressing yourself, drawing energy and vitality from your feelings and using them as fuel for your creativity.

When you feel complete, see yourself emerging from the pond looking brighter, fresher and younger than before. See your skin glowing with health, your eyes clear and alive and the air around you shimmering with a mystical haze.

THE HOME FIRES OF VIRGO

Fire is perhaps the most challenging element for people with their Sun in Virgo. The element of fire brings with it inflamed passions, spontaneity and visions of the future. Virgo, on the other hand, prefers to have a cool exterior and a calculated approach to life, and to be focused on the affairs of the present. There is a good reason for this: Virgos need to learn to have a solid sense of their current position in life, rather than dissipating their energy on contemplating abstract future events.

Fire causes people to be outwardly focused and more concerned with doing than with being. The activities that Virgos choose to participate in are generally concerned with attaining a clearer and clearer sense of themselves and as such their lives quite rightly tend to be more inwardly focused. The fires of Virgo are most likely to be the fires of hearth and home. Fire is the element of adventure; for Virgo the great adventure is one of coming home to themselves. Physically, Virgoan homes may reflect this with great emphasis put on the fireplace, candles or some other area of singular focus within a room. This focal point may contain family photographs, inspirational ornaments or other treasured possessions that remind Virgo of who they are and of their finer ideals or beliefs.

Within a family Virgo can become the hearth and home for other people even if they live a life that is essentially independent of the family circle. For example, the Virgo son or daughter with a solitary lifestyle may, on returning home, become the focus for the whole family getting together to share warmth, companionship and an exchange of information. Virgos who choose to become parents will often provide the hearth and home for their children and other family members to return to.

Contact with overtly fiery, passionate or angry people may well be unsettling for the Virgoan soul and may cause Virgo to withdraw. Virgo can find fiery displays of any kind a bit embarrassing or unnecessary as they prefer to practise modesty and restraint. They are not essentially demonstrative and as such do not always understand the need of other people to display their passions for the world to see.

What Virgoans need to learn from friends or companions who exude an aura of fire is how to let their hair down a little and indulge in some fun and frivolity. Virgo can lighten up when they occasionally allow themselves to be drawn out from their special inner focus. After all, to create order, clarity and a sharp practical intent it can be useful for Virgo to have the contrast of a little creative chaos to assess and enjoy.

VIRGOAN INSPIRATION AND CREATIVITY

The creative spark within Virgo becomes finely tuned and clearly focused for practical application. Creative activities of all kinds can bring healing to Virgo and a fertility that can help them to bloom. Some Virgoans discover that they have an aptitude for creative work that involves fine detail such as needlepoint or the painting of artistic miniatures, perfect in every aspect. Others have a talent for delicate beading or beautifully formed sculpture. Certainly Virgo can be talented draughtsmen or women and as such can be inspired architects or interior designers; some may even have a talent for designing industrial components.

Musical Virgos may be fascinated with both the mathematics of music and the precise communication or delivery of it. Many have a natural feel for precise rhythm and tempo and even those who consider themselves unmusical may find themselves wincing at a badly paced piece of music. Virgo is often drawn to string instruments, perhaps enjoying the discipline of playing the violin or listening to the delicacy of the harp or harpsichord.

Some Virgos may develop a lifelong interest in art or music appreciation or criticism. Virgos are natural critics who can turn this skill positively to the evaluation of creative works. Many art, drama, music or literature critics in newspapers and magazines have a strong Virgoan energy; either their Sun sign is Virgo or there is a strong Virgo placement in some other area of their birth chart.

Virgos are inspired by fine aesthetics. They search for beauty wherever they go and would do well to recognise the beauty in themselves and their own personality. They are also inspired by the power of simplicity; a work of art with simple, clear lines perhaps or the direct expression of logical thought into simple, practical steps. For Virgo, less is more. The element of fire is most often appreciated as fine sparks of inspiration rather than as overwhelming rushes of passion.

Fire Affirmations for Virgo

I glow with an inner light of beauty.

I balance the coolness of logic with the warmth of passion.

I communicate my divine spark of inspiration.

I come home to the magnificence of my being.

My inner light radiates brightness and clarity to the world.

My passions bring me purity of spirit.

Fire Visualisation: Bright Inner Light

Breathe and relax. As you do, hold an image of your body in your mind's eye and see it as being sacred or divine. It is as if you have become a god or goddess, or if you prefer, a shining expression of God.

Imagine that inside yourself there is a single pure flame of radiant brilliance. The light is fine and piercingly clear. Imagine this light shining out from you, radiating warmth and beauty to the world around you.

See the light making you attractive or even magnetic to loving, supportive people. People who are healthy for you to be with and who honour your needs and your individuality.

See the light making you attractive and magnetic to numerous creative or spiritual opportunities that leave you feeling fulfilled. Each new opportunity gives you a greater and greater sense of who you are: your own divine spark.

Imagine the light illuminating the way for you. Making your decision-making process clearer and healthier, brightening your thoughts with positivity and filling your life with healthy choices. Picture the light within you growing brighter and brighter every day.

THE SPIRITUAL PURPOSE OF VIRGO

Virgos learn about the whole picture of their lives by breaking down and analysing everything in fine detail. Virgo turns precise thought and clear action into an art form that they continue to refine with increasing awareness throughout their lives. In doing so they are learning to master life itself.

Every logical thought or practical action brings Virgo closer to recognising another aspect of themselves and fulfilling their highest spiritual purpose. Virgos need to rediscover themselves again and again, each time coming to a greater level of self-love, self-trust and self-acceptance.

The purity of Virgo can be said to represent the pure spirit of us all. For each one of us, whether Virgo or not, there is a part of ourselves that always remains innocent, regardless of how old we are or how sophisticated we become. For Virgoans this innocence allows them to shrug off or distance themselves from the complications of everyday life; detaching from the demands of other people when they need to become immersed in the power of their inner world once more.

The fertility of Virgo is demonstrated by the enrichment that Virgos bring to the world in the creative organisation of practical affairs. The spiritual purpose of Virgo includes the harvesting of the material world or enjoying the fruits of being alive. The earth is full of beauty and sensuality for us all to enjoy. For Virgo it is important to savour the richness of each new moment of life and the natural abundance of the earth.

Virgoan self-healing is a process of gentle unfoldment. Virgos are always discovering something more about themselves to love and to integrate as they bring themselves to wholeness. The word 'healing' comes from the concept of being whole or harmonising every part of the self – mind, body, spirit and emotions. For Virgo, the path to wholeness is inextricably linked to the development of practical skills and earthly wisdom.

THE VIRGOAN GIFT TO THE WORLD

The influence of Virgo brings order where chaos once reigned, creating structures from which many wonderful schemes, projects and creations can develop from seed into the full ripeness of maturity. Virgo people can be said to be the guardians of the earth, tending to the many details that help to make life function. Inevitably, many are involved in environmental schemes of one kind or another, from growing organic vegetables to developing products that are environmentally friendly.

Virgos are also to be found among the administrators of humanitarian projects, charities, healing organisations, relief agencies and medical foundations. The quest for self-actualisation draws many to be involved in some form of health work or healing at some time in their lives. Many younger Virgos, particularly, are finding themselves to be naturally gifted healers.

Some Virgoan people make excellent surgeons, nurses, opticians, homoeopaths, herbalists, dieticians, health educators, hygienists or psychologists – all professions that allow them to use their detailed, ordered logic in compassionate service. Virgos are also found in teaching, scientific research, accounting, administration of all kinds, and the practical aspects of creative work. Some may channel their healing or organisational skills through veterinary science.

It is Virgoan energy that helps us all to develop with a humanitarian conscience as we acquire the skills and adapt to the specialisation of the computer age. It is Virgo that teaches us the fine details of information technology. At the same time, Virgo constantly reminds us of our humanness, our humanity and the gifts of being alive.

CHAPTER SIX

CAPRICORN

23 December - 20 January

CARDINAL EARTH

Capricorn is the mountain climber of life, set on a straight, step-by-step course to the higher realms of material achievement. For the dedicated and committed people of this steadfast Sun sign a golden age of spiritual well-being is attainable through persistent effort or focused conviction.

Capricorns are strong-willed, self-contained and committed individuals who create their good fortune through perseverance. Diligent and proud, they often exert their will quietly but effectively, exerting a steady influence on the world and within their relationships.

Capricorn is symbolised by the mountain goat, strong, adaptable and sure-footed. Capricorns are great survivors and people born under this sign are often capable of creating something positive from the harshest of environments. Their diligence can bring rewards that are extraordinary, unique and sometimes unexpected. The glyph or shorthand notation for Capricorn is not unlike the twisted horn of a wild goat (♑), perhaps reminiscent of the indigenous mountain breeds of the Eastern countries where astrology began.

Capricornian ambition is the kind of force that can move mountains. Capricorns will plan their route to the top but rather than become overly involved in future possibilities, they will achieve where others fail by keeping their attention firmly in the present. Capricorns prefer to work with what is real, tangible and solid, carefully carving out their successes little by little.

Saturn, the ruling planet of Capricorn, expresses creativity through chosen boundaries. Saturn drives Capricorn with discipline and control. Many people with Capricorn as their Sun sign or with Capricorn strongly aspected in their birth chart will display an extraordinary amount of self-discipline, able to keep motivating themselves long after other people have given up and fallen by the wayside.

The restrictive nature of Saturn ensures that the correct degree of attention stays focused on the task in hand. For Capricorns this allows them to initiate, follow through and complete any project with admirable effectiveness. Capricorns develop the secret of attainment through an awareness of what not to do as much as by knowing what to do.

The real strength of the mountain goat is stamina. Capricorns have an innate knowledge of how to pace themselves over a great distance. When focused on an objective they will exert their energy effectively over a sustained period of time rather than rushing at a goal and burning themselves out with their initial enthusiasm.

When climbing the mountain it is important to be aware of the peak towards which you are climbing, but it is even more important to be aware of your feet as you climb. Capricorns take great care of their progress, accounting for every step on their route to the top.

CAPRICORN IN ITS ELEMENT

The element of earth provides a firm foundation for its beloved, dedicated soul Capricorn. Earth is a representation of all that is real, solid and tangible; it rules the exploration of the material world with its concerns for bodily health and financial success. For health and psychological balance Capricorns need the day-to-day rhythms of physical activity. Capricorns can find great peace through routines and order; it is as if they always need to return to the solid structure of their lives to find balance and harmony.

Capricorns are often sustained by routine breaks. The regularity of a repeated timetable is as beneficial as the break itself. Activity, too, can be accomplished more easily when undertaken at the same time every day, every week, month or year. Capricorns instinctively know how to programme their bodies and minds to be effective, using the rhythms of the day for support.

Perhaps the trick to this is to listen to your own internal drives, get to know what your body and mind need to be doing at any given time of the day and build a routine around it. After a while we intuitively know when to step up the mental or physical activity. More important for Capricorn, if they listen to their inner needs, they can know when to step down the activity so that their batteries can be recharged.

Successful meditators will often undertake their meditation practice at the same time and for the same length of time every day or every week. In this way the mind learns quickly how to go into neutral and how to become focused on the outside world once again when it is time for more activity.

When engaged with a positive mindset, many routine tasks can be therapeutic and even meditative for Capricorn.

Everyday activities such as cooking or cleaning can be used as sacred tasks. Focusing on the familiar can leave the mind free to relax and wander. Capricorns can develop themselves spiritually, mentally and emotionally by bringing a loving intention to their physical actions.

Some Capricorns may find themselves becoming so engrossed in their work or practical tasks that they achieve a high level of inner peace and harmony from them. Those, particularly, who work closely with nature, gardening, farming, building or clearing the earth can have the experience of becoming one with the task that they are accomplishing. Office-bound Capricorns, too, may find that their efficiency is very healing and stabilising for them. Some Capricorns may even experience a oneness with God as they work.

Capricorns are always healthiest and happiest when there is some degree of structure in their lives and this can best be created through the use of solid, safe environments. They love to create a warm home and hearth where their physical or emotional supports are constant and unvarying.

Unstable environments or too many external distractions can sometimes cause Capricorns stress or distress. They would always benefit from having their own home space to retreat to that is impervious to the frenetic business of the outside world. The warmth of loving partners, friends and family could contribute to this stable home environment, providing a safe haven of familiarity, constancy and support. However, there will be times when Capricorn needs to cut off completely and be on their own so that they are able to recharge their batteries without having to deal with the demands of other people.

The persistent progress of the Capricorn soul can create its own safe environment, providing the people of this sign with some healthy protection wherever they may find themselves. Capricorn or not, when we bring our attention back, again and again, to the task in hand and focus on our next immediate step, we can escape the numerous distractions of the world. Capricorns can have a strong inner sense of their life's journey and can hold their attention firmly on achieving the tasks that they have set themselves. This in itself is very settling and can generate a stability that many enjoy.

Capricorns often radiate an inner peace when they have created appropriate boundaries for themselves within their relationships, their work and their home life. They always benefit from being sure of their role and are happiest when they know what is expected of them. On entering a new job it would serve them to have a clear job description to guide their daily tasks; if one does not already exist it may be helpful for them to sit down with their employer and devise their own specifications. Similarly, in romantic and domestic relationships Capricorn may well be happier and remain healthier if they know where they stand.

The healthiest Capricorns are often those who are willing to learn about their own internal rhythms, listening very closely to the needs of their mind, body and emotions. As they listen they may develop a connection with their innate sense of what is right for them and choose their diets, therapies, careers and relationships accordingly. They benefit from finding their own inner hearth and home, a place of warmth and refuge within that is immune to the external world.

Capricornian Zones of the Body

The special energy of Capricorn provides us all with the structure, foundation and cohesion of the physical body. Capricorn rules the skeleton, the magnificent system of bones that gives the human body its basic solidity. Of all the bones and joints of the body Capricorn particularly rules the knees. Exercises that promote flexibility and bounce in these load-bearing joints will benefit the health or carriage of the whole system. Gentle bouncing on the spot, keeping the knees bent, the feet planted on the floor hip width apart and the upper body straight and relaxed would be good for most Capricorns.

Capricorn also rules the skin, which is the largest organ of the body and through which we experience many of the sensations of the physical world. Our skin provides us with our outer structure. It is both acutely sensitive and highly protective, having an extraordinary capacity to renew and replenish itself as it keeps the body safely contained. The qualities of these two areas of the anatomy say much about the gifts of Capricorn while providing us with effective barometers for the overall health of Capricornian people.

Many Capricorns will have strong bones and joints but any trauma or stress may be deeply held within the skeleton. Aches are often more bony than muscular. Capricorns with deep structural tension would do well to rest and consider their emotional state. Sometimes unexpressed feelings, anxieties or emotional yearnings can be felt in the body as aches and pains. Acknowledging and expressing these feelings can bring physical release.

Massage, although focusing on the muscles rather than the bones, may help to move trapped emotional energy from deep within the body and provide the benefits of a positive, healing contact that Capricorns often need. Capricorns can be so committed to their vocation or in some cases to taking care of other people, that they may need to be encouraged to stop work and allow themselves to receive some loving care. Perhaps this will be all that is necessary for the tensions to discharge. Of course, prolonged skeletal aches and pains would require the appropriate medical or complementary health treatment.

The skin is a very clear indicator of health for us all, whether we are Capricorn or not. Acupuncturists and Chinese medicine practitioners always examine the colour, tone and quality of the skin as an aid to diagnosis. Everything from poor diet to allergic reactions, stress and shock can be seen through the skin. Capricorns who suffer from eruptions, rashes or dry or flaky skin conditions could benefit from keeping a log or diary of these occurrences, using it to become aware of the areas of their lives that require special management to avoid the build-up of tensions.

If, for example, the skin reacts every time there is an increase in workload, then appropriate time management and relaxation techniques could help. By listening to their bodies, Capricorns can take appropriate action to keep themselves healthy. A similar log or diary could be a useful way of checking out and eliminating foodstuffs that are particularly toxic. This can take careful observation over a period of time, eliminating foods one by one until the cause of the allergy or toxicity has been discovered. The increase in comfort and levels of energy can be well worth the experimentation.

When a Capricorn becomes aware of the particular external pressures that create disharmony in the mind or body they can learn, through regular practice, to recognise the early signs of stress. A routine of step-by-step breathing exercises, meditations, visualisations and positive thought techniques linked with the practice of taking regular breaks would diffuse the build-up of worry or mental anxiety that contributes to physical illness.

EXERCISE AND THERAPIES

Trampolining would be a wonderful exercise for more active Capricorns, bringing flexibility and bounce to the knees and other joints of the body while at the same time building strength and stamina on a psychological level. This is just the kind of activity to lighten the life of any Capricorn who becomes too serious or overly focused on work.

Similarly, jogging or light bouncing on a trampette or bounce pad would provide overall fitness while allowing the joints to be exercised without the jarring effect of a hard floor. In addition this kind of exercise is highly aerobic, giving Capricorn a little air to enrich all of the earthy strength. Of course, anyone embarking on vigorous exercise that their body is unused to would be well advised to seek medical advice first, but even the gentlest bouncing could be of benefit.

Capricorns who have tangible, physical problems with the spine, joints and bones would do well to consult an osteopath. Osteopathic and chiropractic techniques manipulate the bones back into position. Perhaps the most wonderful form of these healing disciplines is cranial osteopathy, in which the practitioner is able to make the most profound manipulations using subtle pressures or adjustments to points on the head. In this way the spinal fluid is balanced and the spine and the rest of the body follows suit.

Treatments to beautify or cleanse the skin will be wonderful for Capricorns. Although some may have a tendency to resist pampering of any kind, this is exactly what they need for relaxation and to unearth their sensuality. Capricorns could treat themselves to a body brush from their local health or natural beauty shop and stimulate the skin before bathing. The skin needs to be dry for this and it is best to brush the surface of the body towards the heart, avoiding the face, the genitals and other sensitive areas. Brushing in this way would remove old, dead cells, stimulate the circulation and allow the skin to breathe.

An alternative would be gentle exfoliation of the skin with a loofah while in a warm bath. Capricorns would benefit, too, from taking long, luxurious baths, perhaps filling the bathroom with candlelight, soft, meditative music, pretty flowers and healing crystals while making sure that the bath is filled with the sensual delights of aromatic oils or foaming bubbles. Making any activity sacred or luxurious in this way acts as a positive, practical affirmation of self-worth as well as having the physical benefit of providing quiet time and relaxation.

Capricorns able to take the pampering a little further could visit a beauty therapist or a health spa for other cleansing, toning and beautifying skin treatments. Another way of removing dead skin and stimulating new cell growth is with a salt rub; natural mineral salts are gently massaged into the body before a bath or shower and sometimes before a full massage with oils.

As well as any physiological benefits, Capricorns can expect a psychological boost from skin treatments, particularly if they really do allow themselves to be pampered in the process. Perhaps the best treatment of all for Capricorn is aromatherapy, in which natural essential plant oils are massaged into the body by the practitioner. Unlike other massage therapies, the physical strokes of the massage do not concentrate on a deep muscular or tissue level in most cases but rather are designed to stimulate the skin to absorb the healing oils. Through the skin, trace elements of the oils, specially chosen for properties that match the client's needs, are passed into the bloodstream to be circulated throughout the body producing deep relaxation, stimulation or euphoria.

Sporting Capricorns can tend to work diligently at developing their physical skills and be highly competitive. Mountain climbing, hill walking, and abseiling are all Capricornian activities but all other sports or physical exercise are tackled with a great deal of determination too. On the whole, Capricorns will favour sports that have them individually pitted against an opponent or tackling the challenges of nature single-handed rather than working as part of a team. They need to remind themselves to enjoy the fringe benefits of sport, like taking time to pamper themselves by sitting in the sauna or jacuzzi to relax after a workout. They also need to enjoy the social contact that sports can bring.

PARTNERSHIPS, BUSINESS AND SUCCESS

Capricorns are highly ambitious people, not necessarily for themselves but often for the scheme or project that they are involved with. It could well be a project that they have initiated and they will do the groundwork and follow it through with a strength of will that is admirable. Capricorns do not appear to be daunted by what others might experience as insurmountable challenges; able to win out against the odds by continued and persistent application, Capricorn has the ability to make the most infertile schemes bear fruit.

Capricorn often needs a challenge and delights in continual activity. Within a partnership, team or company Capricorn will be the backbone keeping the whole project going as other members drift in and out. Capricorns provide a great deal of stability for their colleagues, who in turn may bring some lightness or fun to inspire Capricorn and bring some additional creativity to the endeavour.

Capricorns need colleagues able to deal with public relations, communications and the development of new ideas. On the whole, Capricorn is too focused on all that is presently real and tangible to concern themselves with the realms of the possible or be effective with publicity. However, Capricorn would be well advised to learn these skills while also learning to bring a bit more fun to their upward path.

Capricorns have the qualities of the earth itself – endurance, resistance and constancy. They love to climb the mountain of success and the path they tread is straight and directed towards the peak. Capricorns are destined to succeed but the path they choose may be steep and unyielding at times. They would do well to learn that life can be simple and easy; they do not have to struggle to create their successes. A simple change of attitude or belief that can come with the use of positive affirmations, meditations or spiritual practices could make all tasks flow more easily. If you have a struggle mentality then you are more likely to be magnetic to difficulties whereas, if you are willing to put energy and commitment into what you do, while thinking positively about it, then achievement can be created with grace.

The beginning of Capricorn is the midwinter solstice, the

time of Saturnalia. Traditionally this is a time for celebrating the earth, remembering its fertility while it is passing through the barren part of its seasonal cycle. The Capricorn time of year is a time of great feasting, a period of revelling in the gifts of the earth that have been stored and preserved from the summer harvest. It is a time of joviality, merrymaking and frivolity when everyone lets down their hair and explores their earthy sensuality.

For Capricorns to stay healthy they need to remember that there is more to life than work. It is all very well striving for great things in the world but if you cannot allow yourself a few earthly pleasures along the way then you may have a tricky time adjusting to and reaping the benefits of success when you arrive at the top of the mountain.

Earth Affirmations for Capricorn

Strength and stability are mine to enjoy.

I enjoy the fruits of my work.

Each step I take brings me to success.

I allow myself the sensuality of my body.

My life is a feast for me to enjoy.

My bones and joints are always healthy.

My knees are flexible and strong.

I am safe and secure.

My life provides me with firm foundations.

I am structured for health, within and without.

Earth Visualisation: Path to Success

Find a quiet, comfortable place to relax, preferably lying down or sitting with your back properly supported and your body open.

Breathe deeply and as you do, imagine yourself walking up a dry, dusty mountain path. See yourself move forwards at a steady rhythm, pacing yourself as you gently ascend. Feel the strength and stability in your body as you move and imagine yourself with a light bounce in your knees that helps to propel you forwards.

Picture yourself looking down at your feet and see each footfall creating fertility from the dry earth. Every time you visualise yourself placing your foot down imagine lush plants and flowers growing in that spot. As you look behind you see the trail of green and other rich hues that have developed from your progress.

Imagine your journey becoming easier and easier, the little explosions of life beneath your feet giving you a greater spring in your step that moves you onwards effortlessly and with joy. As you advance, see yourself gaining many little rewards along the way: money, fun, laughter, security, stability, peace and love.

When you reach the top of the mountain, see yourself stop to rest and enjoy the view. Notice that your mountain, once dry and barren, has become covered with rich vegetation, much of it in bloom. Sitting at the peak you are bathed with the golden sunshine of success and you are enjoying a golden age of health, prosperity and freedom in your life.

EMERGING FROM THE WATERS

Capricorn has a powerful relationship with the element of water. It is through water that Capricorn can draw much of its sustenance for the climb to success but the drinking of that water of sustenance can be challenging for the Capricorn soul.

Water tells us much about the origins of humankind and particularly about the emergence of Capricorn energy into the world. Capricorn best experiences its relationship to water through its opposite sign, the water sign of Cancer. Cancer can be seen as the foetal waters of Mother Earth from which all life was born. Capricorn can be seen as the progress of evolution that compelled early life forms to climb out of the sea and onto dry land. The Capricorn progress up the mountain can then be viewed as the ongoing evolution of the human race.

In some areas of astrology, Capricorn is depicted as a goat with a fish's tail showing that the past relationship with water has propelled Capricorn into its present exploration of worldliness and ambition. Ancient Babylonians saw Capricorn as a fish-goat. This image was associated with their god Ea, who was the antelope of the subterranean ocean. Legends tell of a hero or heroine who emerged from the waters of Ea and brought the arts of civilisation to shore: agriculture, astronomy, mathematics, architecture and medicine. That hero or heroine could well have been Capricorn.

On a psychological level this emergence from water symbolises a movement from the unconscious mind, with its dreamy formlessness, into tangible external activity and worldliness. Capricorn is fed by this watery inner realm but holds onto structure and continual activity for fear of being pulled back into that irrational inner world. For this reason most Capricorns need to learn to feel safe with their emotions, dreams and imagination.

LOVE AND ROMANCE

Most Capricorns have a wonderful ability to engender love in other people. Something of their commitment, dedication, gentleness and persistent strength brings admiration from partners and friends alike. Many Capricorns will open hearts wherever they go and some may also have an indefinable quality that makes other people want to care for them and protect them. Independent Capricorns may not want this kind of attention but they will certainly benefit from accepting it sometimes.

Romantic involvement can bring inspiration to the world of Capricornian ambitions. Emotions are the water that brings forth new life from the dry earth, awakening the buried seeds of deeper meaning. The route to the top is always helped by a strong sense of purpose and there is nothing quite like a meaningful relationship to make the effort all worthwhile.

It is important for Capricorns to find marriage partners or lovers with whom they can set up a safe home base. Capricorns seeking a partner will usually look for someone who is going to remain a constant, reliable support throughout life; someone who can be a certainty in an uncertain world. In some cases the choice of relationship will be based on practical or material considerations as much as emotional ones. They need to feel that their needs and the needs of their partner will be fully taken care of on all levels.

The healthiest Capricornian relationships are often those where the practical considerations have been clearly agreed and both parties know what is expected of them. Once this has been established the Capricornian soul can feel safe enough to relax and fully explore the sensual or romantic aspects of life with their partner. For those who are willing to do this the rewards are great.

It would be rare for Capricorns to be fully comfortable with a series of affairs or flirtations. This kind of romantic lifestyle would be too emotionally challenging and would unsettle any foundations that Capricorn may wish to make for career or personal development. The occasional exception to this could be the married Capricorn who has made the wrong choice of marriage partner but who is otherwise too conventional or too involved in familial commitments to feel that they can separate. Perhaps having wed the person that their relatives or social group approved of rather than waiting for someone more suited to their needs, they seek some sensitive emotional companionship from outside.

Within committed relationships Capricorns are usually very loyal to their partner or to their partner's family. They often fulfil their side of any emotional or practical contract to the letter. The unspoken agreements that provide the foundations for most loving relationships will be honoured; Capricorn may even sacrifice some personal needs to take care of these domestic or economic expectations.

Those Capricorns who choose a solitary lifestyle often do so because they are too involved in their work or vocation to allow themselves any kind of emotional attachment. This kind of life can also be safe and reliable in its constancy; Capricorns may appreciate the opportunity to stay focused on current tasks without the rhythms and needs of another person deflecting them off-course.

Whether they are in a relationship or not, Capricorns need to remind themselves that they deserve to be loved purely for who they are and not for what they do. All of us, Capricorn included, need to move from wanting to prove that we are worthy of love to loving ourselves fully and accepting the love that other people delight in giving us. Capricorn benefits from remembering that they do not have to earn love; they are lovable because they are alive.

Water Affirmations for Capricorn

My feelings provide a safe foundation.

I am willing to receive love and support.

It is safe for me to be touched.

My relationships nourish my life's purpose.

I balance my inner feelings with my outer desires.

I am always loved and protected.

Water Visualisation: Beyond The Waterfall

Get yourself comfortable and relax. Breathe deeply and allow your body to settle into the support of the chair, bed or surface beneath you. Whether you are sitting up or lying down, keep your body open and comfortable.

Imagine yourself tracking the source of a clear stream up the mountainside. You walk in the opposite direction of the current as it cascades downwards and as you ascend you notice that the stream is an offshoot of a large river of fast-flowing crystal waters. Follow the source of the river upwards until the land levels out a little and imagine that you see a pool that is fed by a sparkling waterfall gushing from the rocks above.

Picture yourself shedding your clothes and wading into the pool. The water is soft and inviting as you approach the waterfall and you allow yourself to be showered by the falling waters. Imagine the water cleansing away all fears, tensions, aches, pains and ailments. The water is cool and invigorating but the effect is warm and soothing.

Visualise yourself going deeper into the waterfall to find that there is a wide open space behind it, a hidden cave in the rock. Here you discover your inner feelings as a magical collection of wet, glistening crystals. Pick them up, touch them and allow the particular feeling of each one to touch you. See yourself discovering the crystals of your intuitions, passions, angers and joys. Each one is safe to touch and acknowledge before returning to its place.

When you complete this visualisation, make a note of any feelings you have that you need to express to someone else or acknowledge for yourself. Find safe ways to express those feelings. For example you might write a letter, send a card, or choose to speak to someone directly at a time when you know that they will be best able to listen. You might say 'I love you' or 'You make me very happy' or perhaps you could tell someone calmly and simply that something frustrates you rather than waiting for that frustration to build up into a state of pent-up anger. Acknowledging and expressing your feelings is a powerful tool for self-healing.

WARMING BY THE FIRE

The element of fire rules the realms of the spirit, creativity and inspiration. Capricorn's relationship to the element of fire can best be seen as a contemplative and cosy warming of the body by a roaring midwinter blaze. Capricorns often love a warm hearth and home to return to through the winters of the soul, as they continue to achieve their ambitions. Fire works best for Capricorns when it can be used as a means of sustenance, physically keeping heart and soul together as they climb the mountain.

For Capricorn, the spiritual challenges of fire and the lights of inspiration come with learning to accept a burst of luxury from time to time. Capricorns can be so committed to the physical tasks of the world that they are reluctant to pause from their labours to enjoy life. They may be so good at choosing self-denial as a way of achieving that they forget to fuel their soul with the pleasures necessary to maintain their health and their quality of living. To travel to the highest pinnacles it helps to be able to refuel your passions and your visions with moments of creative indulgence or frivolity.

CAPRICORNIAN INSPIRATION AND CREATIVITY

The god Pan was represented by the Greeks as a creature that combined the torso, arms and head of a man with the legs, feet and horns of a goat. Pan was the god of wild and untamed nature, spontaneous, sexual, alive and free. Although Pan was a very male image, often depicted with a huge phallus, the untamed forces that he celebrated were both male and female and he brought expression to the feminine sensuality of the earth. Pan celebrated fertility, the inspiration of female sexuality, the dance of all living things and the passionate drives of the natural world.

Pan can be seen as the fiery creativity of the Capricorn nature that seduces Capricorns into playfulness through music, song and sexuality. Pan can provide Capricorns with an irreverent romp, putting a spring in their step as they climb the mountain to its golden peak. This fiery energy can remind the Capricorn soul that even in the winter the earth is fertile, containing the seeds of new life that will sprout in the spring, as well as providing sustenance to evergreen or leafless plants alike. Despite strong tendencies to do otherwise, it is healthy for Capricorns to unearth their sexy, playful nature. There is more to life than work and self-denial.

Some Capricorns express their creativity through the care and decoration of their homes, filling them with soft, pretty pastel colours, floral designs and crafted co-ordination. Perhaps softness and beauty within their home environment can help Capricorns to soften away from the challenges of their work or vocation. By contrast they may dress themselves in practical clothes that are comfortable and non-fussy.

Capricorns may be wonderful gardeners and could express their creativity by building a rock garden complete with alpine plants, herbs and wildflowers. Some Capricorns may enjoy painting pictures of flowers or painting floral designs on the surface of polished stones. Some may also find healing and recreation through carpentry, wood-carving or the polishing of gemstones.

Capricorn creativity can be as rich and varied as any other; it is just that it becomes focused into dealing with the practicalities of life rather than being enjoyed for itself. Normally serious Capricorns would do well to allow themselves some frivolities, singing, playing a musical instrument, painting, dressing in bright colours and merrymaking, purely for the pleasure of life itself and not for some desired end. Becoming playful with life can release deeply held tensions and heal the soul.

Fire Affirmations for Capricorn

It is safe for me to play with life.

My creativity lights the way.

It is safe for me to express my passionate nature.

My imagination fires my ambition.

I now build a warm glow of health, within and without.

I deserve to have luxury in my life.

Fire Visualisation: Pictures in the Flames

Breathe and relax. Picture yourself warming your hands by a bright fireplace, sitting comfortably in a warm armchair and allowing your body to be gently soothed by the heat of the fire.

Look into the hearth at the flames dancing and imagine the rich oranges, reds, yellows and the occasional flashes of blue or purple as the flames crackle and leap. Imagine yourself creating pictures in the flames. See images of your present life: your job, your relationships, your home life, the places you frequent.

Visualise all of these areas of your life becoming warmed by the inspirations of fire, creating energy and vitality in everything that you do and in every part of your being. See the images flicker and change and have the fire show you ways in which you could heal yourself at this time. Do you need to take more time out from work to relax and unwind? What could you do to create a greater sense of play in your life? How could you express more of your passion and enthusiasm for life? What can you best do at this time to bring healing to your mind, body, emotions and spirit?

When you are complete with the visualisation you may choose to write down or record any inspirations that you had before putting them into action.

GUSTS OF MOUNTAIN AIR

The element of air rules the mind. Capricornian minds are often exceptionally sharp and focused on the task in hand. Capricornian ideas tend to be constructive, and they act like building blocks, cemented by physical effort, to create worthwhile, tangible and functional schemes for the greater good of civilisation.

Capricorns are not always free thinkers or original in their thoughts, but their ideas often instigate action. Capricorn people are at their most comfortable and probably at their healthiest when they work with concepts that are reliable or proven. Capricorn tends to think in rather conventional ways, staying with all that is tried and tested rather than exploring the imaginings of new thought.

This is both a great strength and a potential limitation. It is a strength to be able to stay focused on the current reality of a situation and to be able to think clearly about the practicalities of the next step; this is what makes Capricorns such great achievers. However, it is not always healthy or innovative to stay rigidly controlled or to conduct one's life from what is already known rather than finding new solutions.

The healthiest Capricorns will allow themselves some flexibility of mind without getting distracted from their life's journey and the present steps they are taking to reach their desired end. Books or courses in lateral thinking could help Capricorn construct alternative routes or approaches and puzzles or quizzes with multiple choice answers would be a fun, healthy way to strengthen and relax the mind.

The element of air brings with it the winds of change, and this can be unsettling for Capricorns who, while initiating new things, like life to be stable. Perhaps the healthiest way to embrace change – as change inevitably needs to be embraced – is to find certainty within. The Capricornian soul needs to feel safe while learning to harness the new currents of thought that will allow them to bring their innovations to the world.

The speedier thinkers of the world will often burn themselves out while Capricornian thought will adopt a perservering pace that ultimately ensures achievement.

Air Affirmations for Capricorn

My ideas are constructive and fulfilling.

I air my opinions and allow them to take shape.

I always have a firm foundation of positive thoughts.

My mind constructs healthy solutions for every need.

I am clear, precise and focused.

I safely climb to the heights of mental achievement.

Air Visualisation: Gifts from the Air

Find a light, airy, peaceful place to sit or lie down with your body open, receptive and comfortable. Breathe deeply, feeling the air move in and out of your lungs. Concentrate on the feeling of this for a few moments before beginning the visualisation.

Next, visualise yourself sitting on a mountain peak; this could be like sitting on top of the world looking down at the beautiful view below. All is calm and serene, you feel peaceful and rested. Feel the gusts of the mountain breezes as they caress your skin and ruffle your hair. Be comfortable with the rush of air onto your face.

Imagine that the air is filled with creative ideas and in your mind's eye, reach out your hands to collect pockets of it between them. See your hands as cupped and picture yourself drawing the cups of your two hands together to enclose the air. As you do, imagine those airy inspirations becoming real and tangible, taking physical form.

As you draw your hands to you and empty the contents out on the earth at your feet, notice that the air has become piles of money, magnificent jewels, beautiful flowers or anything else that you would like to imagine yourself creating. See the mountain peak becoming covered with wonderful gifts. As you visualise this, imagine that all of these inspirational, prosperous and healthy thoughts are going to drop into your mind over the next few hours or during the next few days.

When you have completed this meditation you may choose to write down or record any ideas that you had.

THE SPIRITUAL PURPOSE OF CAPRICORN

Capricorn represents the evolution of the human spirit through physical incarnation. The spiritual purpose of Capricorn includes a movement from dealing with day-to-day survival to arriving at a golden transcendence of pleasure and practical wisdom. Capricorns are learning to bring about a change of attitude in themselves and others, one that persistently embraces more and more of the beauty and the divinity of life through every simple act or physical task.

The spiritual purpose of Capricorn is concerned with turning the whole process of life into a celebration. Every task in life can become divine, sacred, joyful and fun if we choose to make it so. Even routine chores can have their beauty and splendour; we just need to see the magic that is there.

Capricorn's ruling planet Saturn brings restrictions and creative limitations. Without these creative limitations we would all be unable to achieve anything in the world and learn from our achievements or our creativity. In painting a picture, for example, deciding on our creative limitations such as the size of canvas or paper, the kind of paints or materials to use, the brushes and the range of colours, allows for the creativity to take a tangible form. Within our chosen boundaries magic can take place.

Capricorn people may spend much of their early lives working through their chosen creative limitations. Whether focused on a career or domesticity, Capricorns will self-sacrificingly involve themselves in their chosen tasks or their life's work emerging from their self-sacrifice and dedication in their later years. From midlife onwards the world often appears more golden and Capricorns may feel more able to let their hair down and celebrate.

Years of self-discipline open the way to spiritual understanding and this can bring an air of playfulness to older Capricorns. Once the work is done, Capricorns can divide their time between the deeper mysteries of the universe and frolicking like a young mountain goat – a good balance of activity for the golden years of life.

In Roman mythology Saturn's influence over the world brings us to a golden age of humankind when men and women no longer have to labour. The vines are filled with an abundance of fruit, the rivers flow with sweetness and the sky is blue. Capricorns have the ability through perseverance and commitment to make the earth yield up its richness. Capricorns may experience many challenges in their lives, but for them challenges bring rewards in abundance. There is truly no such thing as failure and Capricorn's committed endeavours inevitably lead to success. Knowledge of this is perhaps the greatest healing of all.

THE CAPRICORNIAN GIFT TO THE WORLD

We need the persistent skills of socially minded Capricorns to provide us with the structures of society and the foundations for the highest ideals of civilisation. Capricorn brings with it the skills of building and administration, giving us all stability, organisation and strength.

Capricorns are drawn to careers in banking, office management, stockbroking, politics and the civil service. They are good in positions of authority and some may serve the community as local government officials or head teachers. Those that choose a more physical lifestyle could turn their hands to engineering, building or the healing skill of osteopathy. Some may choose lifestyles that are close to nature, living with and tending the earth.

Capricorns who enjoy strengthening and harnessing the skills of the mind may make excellent mathematicians, scientists or production analysts. Whatever their chosen career, Capricorn has the dedication to arrive at positive results through prolonged and careful experimentation or testing.

Capricorn reminds us of the gifts of the real world and teaches us all that life is what we make of it. Capricornian achievements are not idle fantasy but glorious realities that open the doors to a better future for mankind.

Healing with Air

A TIMELESS FLIGHT WITH THE AIR SIGNS

Air is the element of the mind. It is logical, light, fast-moving and filled with future possibilities. The people born into the element of air are intellectual, reasonable, communicative and bright.

The three air signs are:

GEMINI – MUTABLE AIR
23 MAY – 22 JUNE

KEY QUALITIES:
PLAYFUL, COMMUNICATIVE, BRIGHT, BUBBLY, JOYFUL, WITTY.

LIBRA – CARDINAL AIR
24 SEPTEMBER – 22 OCTOBER

KEY QUALITIES:
BALANCED, FAIR-MINDED, INTELLECTUAL, ARTISTIC,
HARMONIOUS, ROMANTIC.

AQUARIUS – FIXED AIR
21 JANUARY – 20 FEBRUARY

KEY QUALITIES:
FREE-THINKING, VISIONARY, UNIVERSAL, REVOLUTIONARY,
ECCENTRIC, INNOVATIVE.

CHAPTER SEVEN

GEMINI

23 May - 22 June

MUTABLE AIR

Geminis are the bright butterfly children of the zodiac with an innocent lustfulness to explore the shiny baubles of life. They are expressive, youthful, enthusiastic and energetic. They love to live life to the full so that they can explore new ideas and meet new people. They are sociable, intellectual, bubbly and extrovert.

Picture in your mind a landscape that is teased and freshened by a series of playful breezes, creating new patterns in the grasses, rustling the leaves on the trees and scattering seeds to new locations where they may set and germinate. This is the energy of Gemini, bringing mischievous changes, new ideas and new inspirations to the world.

Geminis are talkative, witty and charming. They are lively, stimulating and full to overflowing with ideas. They are often blessed with an unquenchable desire to see all, do all and tell all. Geminis are often happiest when they are active and when they have a forum of other people with whom to exchange new information, anecdotes and humour.

Gemini is often seeking ways of making their inspirational genius more profitable for them. They are constantly on the lookout for new social, financial and experiential opportunities. Geminis love their ideas to bear fruit in the healthy enjoyment of each waking moment. Life to Gemini is like a magic playground filled with wonderful toys.

Gemini is symbolised by the twins, one heavenly and one human, reflecting the dual nature expressed by most people who are born into this sign. This image also reflects the extraordinary ability of each Gemini soul to be uniquely human and magnificently spiritual at the same time.

If you look at the glyph, or symbol, for Gemini ($\mathbf{II}$), you can see two pillars (the twins) bridged above and below. This represents the challenge faced by Geminis to bridge their inner polarities. For example, finding the bridge between ideas and feelings, logic and intuition, coolness and warmth, freedom and commitment, inspiration and objectivity.

The ruling planet of Gemini is Mercury. In mythology Mercury was the messenger of the gods who zoomed through the element of air to bring heavenly communications and more than a little mischief to the world of mortals. Within each Gemini person the influence of Mercury is constantly present, willingly bringing the gifts of inspiration and realisation to those who are able or willing to hear.

Like Mercury, Gemini has an elegant agility of thought and communication that is a wonder to behold. The Gemini mind travels through the realms of the possible on winged feet to collect and disseminate information, spreading fun and flirtation wherever it goes.

GEMINI IN ITS ELEMENT

The element of air perfectly embodies its communicative child Gemini. Air rules the mind, the intellect and the breaths of higher thought. Pure Gemini energy, when free, healthy and unrestricted, is compelled to express its elemental nature; Geminis love to communicate their fresh inspirations and their unique mental awareness to the world.

Some Gemini people are driven to collect and give out information to as many people as they possibly can, whether through the writing and teaching of new thought or through scattering juicy gossip to eager ears. In most cases the information that they disseminate is optimistic, positively affirming and life-enhancing.

For Gemini, to think is to speak. Rather than analysing to any great depth, Gemini delights in putting ideas straight out for discussion and then, when everyone else is continuing to discuss, moving on to a new idea. Gemini always needs to be discovering brighter, shinier jewels of information, not caring greatly whether the jewels turn out to be genuine diamonds or pretty fakes.

Imagine a child opening a cupboard and pulling out a variety of items in search of a new toy. What's this? What's that? What's this? What does that do? And imagine that child being distracted by the fly that has just buzzed in through the window and being just as fascinated by the fly as by the contents of the cupboard.

Needless to say it is unlikely that the contents of the cupboard will be put back again or that the cupboard doors will be closed. Pure Gemini nature is always onto the next thing, and the next, and the next; someone else will take care of the details. This does not mean that all Geminis negate their responsibilities. Many can become highly efficient and conscientious, particularly as they mature. It is just that life is too full and too interesting to get bogged down in meaningless order and routine.

For Geminis to stay fully healthy and energised it is vital for them to acknowledge their need for freedom. It is essential for them to be free enough to react spontaneously to each new moment; able to drop all restrictions when the adventure of life begins to beckon.

The air of Gemini can be symbolised by the fresh, warm breezes of early summer; currents of positive anticipation that whisper of new life, new growth and new possibilities. A Gemini who becomes blocked, stifled or restricted needs to remember that life is always a joyful adventure. The exciting possibilities of the mind are always calling, bringing thoughts of healing and divine mischief.

The Gemini vision includes a view of the world that is full of interesting people with new ideas to exchange and discuss. The lively Gemini mind delights in social and intellectual interaction of all kinds. Many Geminis have a wonderful sense of humour and some are a never-ending source of amusing anecdotes, embellished stories or jokes. Socially Geminis act like the bubbles in a glass of good champagne; bringing brightness, airy ideas and effervescent energy to everyone that they meet. It is easy to be charmed and seduced by a Gemini.

GEMINI ZONES OF THE BODY

Gemini rules the lungs, the hands, the arms and the shoulders. Areas of the nervous system are also Gemini's domain. Breathing exercises of all kinds will be beneficial for Geminian souls, especially if conducted in a light playful way. Conscious and positive use of the breath can discharge tensions, dissolve anxieties and reawaken the clear perceptions of the mind.

The lungs and the breath would act as a good barometer for

the overall health and well-being of the Gemini soul. The comfort of breathing could help to indicate how free or how stifled each Gemini person has allowed themselves to be within their relationships, career and home environment. Any tightness, weakness or tension of the lungs or chest may demonstrate to Gemini that it is time to make psychological, physical or practical changes in their lives.

A Gemini who has experienced too much restriction or smothering in childhood could be prone to asthma or breathing problems. Geminian nature is usually so free-spirited that overly controlling environments could prove psychologically or physically frustrating. However, because of their need to have some boundaries it is sometimes too easy for Gemini to rely on other people to provide the structures for them. In fact, Gemini's desire to remain the charming child throughout life could attract restrictive people in adulthood too.

Vague nervous complaints or psychosomatic illnesses can be cleared with a change of scene, free expression and a burst of spontaneity. When unwell, a Gemini could ask themselves, 'What do I need to change? What do I want to express?' Liberating the core desire to communicate will always help with the healing process.

Although many Geminis are attracted to the bright lights of the city, holidays in natural settings with lungfuls of clean air are important for revitalisation and balance. Mountain air would be particularly good, especially if you add some snow, skis, bright clothing and new faces. Many active Geminis would love the speed and thrill of skiing, all set in a vast and beautiful open-air playground.

The Gemini need to communicate can be balanced and enhanced by using the hands for added emphasis. By using the hands to move and enliven the air around them, Geminis can add greater power to their expression as well as keeping themselves energised and flowing. They also benefit from the soothing experience of having their hands massaged. When tension is discharged from the joints and muscles of the hands, other areas of the body can relax or discharge tension too.

A full body massage for a Gemini would often be most effective when special attention is given to the shoulders, the upper back, the arms, the hands and the chest. Massage of all kinds can help to release restrictions held in the body. Mental, emotional or environmental stress can often be felt as physical tension. A good massage can sometimes help to create an attitudinal shift that may bring about a more permanent healing of restrictive situations.

EXERCISE AND THERAPIES

Geminis may seek to exercise their lungs and bodies through fun aerobics, acrobatics, trampolining, roller-skating, skipping and juggling. Those who dance may excel at tap-dancing or sparkle down at the disco. Any exercise programme would be better as a group experience rather than an individual pursuit. Classes provide important additional motivation as Geminis are then given opportunities to socialise, communicate and flirt. Geminis will appreciate being led and taught, particularly if an exercise instructor can provide structure and make learning fun at the same time. The trick is to make it so enjoyable that Geminis don't realise the level of structure and discipline involved.

Individual exercise and bodywork routines are also useful,

especially Feldenkrais and Alexander Technique. Over a period of time a practitioner can help to retrain the body to move correctly and to return to a balanced, neutral position when still. Gentle postural therapies are great for realigning the head with the body, the mental with the physical, and the logical with the intuitive, thus bridging that Gemini duality. Gemini may need to remain patient and committed over a period of weeks or months to allow these therapies to work and to receive their full benefit.

Any shoulder tension, although common to us all, is a good indicator for Geminis that they need movement to help them release burdens and restrictions. This could be the physical movement of exercise, moving on to pastures new or moving to new areas of growth and stimulation. In some cases creating physical, mental and emotional activity, all at the same time, can have magical or dramatic healing effects.

Water play of all kinds could help to strengthen the connection between the Gemini mind and the emotions as well as being physically beneficial. Gentle swimming, floating or stretching in water will exercise the lungs and balance the upper body, creating greater confidence in physical and emotional movement.

Water slides are brilliant for more animated Geminis and activities such as water polo, water-skiing or classes in aqua-aerobics would bring additional fun and lightness. For the really sporty Gemini, diving is magnificent. Flying through the air into the depths of water and then returning to the air would act out and symbolise a strengthening of emotional expression.

Geminis who feel themselves becoming caught up in too much nervous energy, becoming too speedy or being unable to ground and manifest their ideas would benefit from walking in the countryside or meditating with their bare feet firmly placed on the soft, warm earth or grasses. Alternatively, collecting a bowl of pebbles or coins to tread on or lay your feet on when you relax or meditate could have a similar effect. The physical sensation of stones, metal or soil next to your skin can disperse that nervous energy and bring you back to all that is real, tangible and practical.

Air Affirmations for Gemini

I enjoy and explore all of my ideas.

I delight in spontaneity.

I am bright, vivacious and lively.

I breathe in the sparkle and the fun of life.

I move through life with fun and ease.

I communicate the brightness of my inspirations.

I play with the pleasure of life.

I am inspired by the wonder of words.

I leap into the game of life.

Life is a wonderful toy for me to play with.

Air Visualisation: Playing with Air

Find a quiet, comfortable place and relax, preferably lying down or sitting with your back properly supported and your body open rather than curled up.

Breathe deeply. As you do, take a few moments to feel the air moving in and out of your lungs, bringing you oxygen, energy and new life.

Imagine that the air filling and releasing from your lungs is like the currents of air or the winds circulating around the natural world. Picture the air moving through the trees or whistling around mountaintops.

Visualise yourself as a bird using the currents of air to support your wings as you glide freely and effortlessly through life. In your mind practise the idea of surrendering to the spontaneity of movement that the air provides. Allow the currents to direct the course of your flight.

Picture yourself alighting on the branch of a tree. As you do, imagine yourself dislodging a seed. See the seed becoming carried by the air. Be the seed for a while and feel yourself being conveyed to your destined place of germination, landing on a patch of fertile earth. As you land, a butterfly takes to the air in all of its transformational brilliance.

Be the delicate prettiness of the butterfly carried to the spot where a child is launching a Chinese kite. Be the child with all of your fun and awareness of the magic of life and at the same time be the kite soaring to the heavens, taking the child's soul with it as it goes.

Be the air itself and visualise the energy of air moving from your lungs to cleanse and heal every cell of your body before whistling off around the chimney tops and beyond.

Play with as many air images as you can and imagine your mind being filled with positive healing thoughts.

See the air clearing away any obstacles that you currently perceive in your life. Picture it blowing away problems, discharging them completely into the atmosphere and freshening the environments in which you live, work and play.

When you complete this visualisation you may choose to write down or record any ideas or inspirations that you had.

EARTHING GEMINI

The element of earth guides the practical, physical and financial aspects of life. Earthly pursuits can appear to be too slow-moving to provide much entertainment for speedy Geminis and certainly it would be a mistake for them to become too earthbound or restricted. However, the realms of earth can support Gemini in creating tangible results from all those bright inspirations.

Geminis often wish to rush ahead of themselves to play with and explore the numerous attractive opportunities that the future may hold. The earth encourages them to slow down and listen to their body so that they can take care of themselves, staying in touch with their inner needs. The practicalities of life challenge Gemini to allow some of their inspirational genius to mature slowly so that when important Gemini ideas emerge into the world they can do so with greater power and impact. This includes taking the practical steps that will turn a dream into a magnificent reality.

Their innocent playfulness and spontaneous sense of fun can see some Geminis taking pleasure in the beauty of the natural world, uncluttered by preconceptions of how life could be. They simply explore any new environment and enjoy taking pleasure in each new discovery. Perhaps it would be useful for Geminis to approach all earthly concerns in the same way, trusting that they can bring their playfulness to the realms of work, finance and organisation.

Pure Gemini energy has a tendency to attract earthier people to help with the areas of life that require order, routine and day-to-day management. Sometimes out of habit and usually with a great deal of charm, a Gemini person can make others around them take responsibility for those aspects of life that they themselves need to learn about and own in order to grow.

PARTNERSHIPS, BUSINESS AND SUCCESS

A Gemini in the workplace can bring fun, lightness and laughter, entertaining colleagues and freeing people from the rigidity of routine thoughts and actions. Their influence can loosen up projects that have become stuck or boring and inject some lateral thinking to get things moving again. A company or professional team will rarely be stuck for ideas when there is a resident Gemini. It is just left for colleagues or partners to discern which ideas will be workable and which will not.

In a business setting Gemini is most likely to be the ideas and promotional person who needs somebody there to administrate, follow through and balance the books. For any of us, whatever our Sun sign, when we get carried away with the very Geminian qualities of inspiration and communication it can sometimes seem to be a chore to bring it all down to earth so that the details can be followed through and projects completed.

Geminis will feel safe and secure when there is someone around to provide boundaries and some attention to detail. The trick is for Geminis to enjoy the mutual benefits of such a partnership while learning how to bring some order to their creative thoughts and communications themselves. A Gemini person who resists this learning process may have a tendency to attract earthier partners, colleagues and friends on whom they feel overly dependent and by whom they feel restricted; this can impede health, growth and development.

The healthiest Geminis will be those who are willing to build some areas of structure within themselves and use that structure to support their inspirational genius. Gemini can use their considerable originality and creativity to help them adapt their career or projects to suit their needs, giving them the bursts of freedom and spontaneity required while managing the details with the minimum effort and fuss. In doing this, Gemini can learn to choose the partners or colleagues who can complement them most constructively.

Geminis can project a persona that is so light-hearted and light-headed, even when they are not feeling it, that they can lift the mood of everyone around them. Such engaging, attractive personalities often make wonderful sales people or public relations officers. Difficult clients or employers are invariably won over by Gemini charm. And a dose of Geminian irreverence may even persuade them to laugh at themselves.

Many Geminis prefer to be an autonomous employee rather than the boss. They love to be part of the team and have contact with colleagues but they still like to be a law unto themselves. Being the boss can sometimes carry too big a burden of responsibility. On the other hand, being just another member of the team can be a little too diminishing. Geminis who do become employers or supervisors may often be great fun to work for. However, their high energy levels and erratic approach to life can leave some members of staff exhausted and lacking clear direction.

It is important to reassure all Geminis that grounding and structure doesn't necessarily have to mean boredom, excessive hard work and being tied down to limited possibilities. In fact, for many Geminis the simple act of slowing down a little to digest ideas, experiences and new insights will greatly assist in the process of manifesting money, tangible results and greater pleasures within all partnerships whether business or romantic.

If a Gemini person can learn to listen to themselves as well as to those around them, then not only will they obtain the ideas and information that will be most valuable, but they will also prevent themselves from becoming too speedy, using too much nervous energy and burning themselves out before reaching the finishing line.

Being bright and inspired, most Geminis will have a big vision of what they are creating in their lives. They can often amaze other people with their creative genius as they enthusiastically expound upon their dreams, schemes and plans for the future. Those that are able to harness their enthusiastic ideas and boundless energy are brilliant indeed, providing the world with innovations and the power of inspirational thought.

Earth Affirmations for Gemini

I am centred, balanced and supported in everything that I do.

I think clearly and act effectively.

My ideas easily take form.

My highest joy now manifests tangibly and productively.

I enjoy the game of making money.

My body is strong, healthy and free.

Earth Visualisation: Digging for Treasure

Be comfortable and relax. Breathe deeply and picture yourself in an idyllic setting of fields and trees. The air is clear and fresh and your mind is powerfully alert.

Imagine yourself with a metal detector, complete with a set of headphones that allows you to hear changes in sound, which locates interesting metallic objects. Picture yourself playing with this metal detector; see yourself walking over the rich, fertile earth, sweeping this gadget over the ground in front of you.

See yourself casting around for treasure hidden beneath the earth. You are filled with expectancy, enjoying the fun and positive anticipation of this search. Very soon you hear a satisfying 'beep' through your headphones and you stop to investigate.

Imagine yourself digging up a small patch of earth, bringing the grains of earth to the air as you search for bright, shiny objects. See yourself discover some beautiful golden coins, perhaps, or other treasures. At the same time imagine that your mind becomes filled with wonderfully creative, prosperous, money-making ideas or positive inspirations for your physical health and well-being. It is as if you are gently unearthing practical wisdom and insight from the depths of your mind.

Lovingly replace the earth. As you do, you may like to see yourself planting a few seeds that will spring to life in this fertile place. Visualise yourself moving on to discover and unearth more wonders in other fertile spots, making a collection of pretty objects that fascinate and delight you.

Finally, imagine yourself sitting with your valuable collection of treasure and visualise it dissolving into the pure golden light of prosperity, health and practical action. See the light spread to fill and surround your body. Hold the thought that all of your ideas manifest tangibly for your health, prosperity and highest joy.

SPLASHING INTO WATER

The element of water provides many growth opportunities for Gemini, creating a fully mature and infinitely powerful range of ideas and expression. Gemini, being the ace communicator of the zodiac, is compelled to communicate every aspect of experience – and that includes the emotions. This can prove to be a challenge, as watery emotions are not normally Gemini's most comfortable playground.

Geminis may analyse or rationalise their feelings rather than allow themselves to experience, fully express and explore them. They can be so keen to stay in the positive, fast-moving realms of the mind that they can skim over the surface of their emotional depths. There can sometimes be an underlying fear of getting bogged down and trapped in areas of irrationality. However, Geminis need to embrace all of themselves in order to maintain their greater health and well-being, and this encompasses the power of their emotions.

LOVE AND ROMANCE

Many Geminis are so bright and attractive that they can easily become the object of desire for other people. The outgoing Gemini personality and the strong urge to communicate inevitably draws attention from others and in some cases will arouse a romantic interest. For some Geminis this can be a surprise as they do not always intend to have this effect and may not even notice that they have created such a profound impression. Most, though, will be completely aware of their impact and they will make the most of each new opportunity to flirt.

Gemini relationships can start with a light-hearted playfulness rather than an intense desire for love and companionship. It is true that Geminis may long for romantic involvements like anyone else, but they are generally so engrossed in the game of life that they can give the impression of being too carefree for it to matter whether they have a partner or not. It is often when they are out in the world playing, socialising and just enjoying being themselves that their interesting romances begin.

Some Geminis have a tendency to be elusive despite their friendly, communicative nature. They can be a bright presence in a social situation that breezes into a room, awakens the interest of other people and breezes out again. Often this elusiveness in itself will invite projections of romantic fantasy from others. Geminis can kindle flames of desire in other people that could burn brightly for years without any romantic developments or any real hope of consummation.

Some long-term relationships may start off as friendships. There may be a stimulating intellectual rapport or a mutual enjoyment of fun and frolics that can draw the friendship together before the inevitable flirtation ensues. In other cases, what starts out as an affair could settle down into a committed, lifelong friendship that provides mutual support and companionship for both parties. Some Geminis develop friendships that can become on and off affairs for many years subject to mutual convenience and the appearance of newer, more compelling romantic interests. It is no surprise that many Geminian friendships can leave all parties confused as to where friendship ends and romantic love begins.

Geminis may enjoy a series of loyal, committed relationships before they finally choose to settle with the one person with whom they feel the most emotionally secure. It is important for Geminis to find partners, lovers and friends with whom they feel safe enough to express their innermost feelings. Slow and gentle expression over a period of time can prevent the build-up or damming up of emotional energy that can send Geminis off-balance both physically and mentally.

Many Geminis will jet out when relationships become too emotional or too involved, preferring to be seen as some charming, elusive butterfly, rather than become too immersed and risk the emotional demands of a committed relationship. In fact, Gemini's dual nature can find itself both attracted to and frightened by warmth and intimacy.

Some Geminis can resist marriage and full-time committed relationships in the early part of their lives, wishing to remain free and perhaps even fearing the idea of commitment. When they do commit themselves, most are very loyal, even if they take time to make the adjustment to more mature and involved levels of communication. They may still enjoy the opportunity to flirt in social situations, but generally they do not intend their flirtations to go beyond the realms of stimulating banter.

The healthiest Geminis are those who are willing to accept and communicate their own feelings rather than make their partner responsible for acting out the irrational and intuitive aspects of the relationship. A more emotional partner can teach Gemini to explore a wider range of emotional expression, creativity, vulnerability and compassion. In return Gemini fills the relationship with brightness, positivity and fun.

Water Affirmations for Gemini

I dive into refreshing sensations of love and joy.

It is safe for me to talk about my emotions.

The more I explore my depths, the more I discover my lightness.

I am open and sensitive to other people's feelings.

I express my emotions with ease and joy.

I wash away the past to have a brighter present and a brighter future.

Water Visualisation: Pearls from the Sea

Imagine yourself to be a South Sea islander anchoring your boat in a jewelled bay of turquoise sea water. See your body as supple, flexible and strong as you dive off the side of your boat and glide through the air into the waters below.

Know your lungs to be strong and full of life-giving oxygen as you hold your breath and swim downwards towards the ocean bed. The strength of your hands and arms pulls you firmly through the depths, your legs pushing from behind to give you rapid propulsion.

Reaching the bottom with its multicoloured landscape of sand, rocks and coral, see yourself gently moving past schools of fish, seduced by the visual splendours of this world. With your inner eye, discover a marbled oyster shell fastened to a rock. See yourself pulling it free and placing it in your waistband before swimming with it back up to the surface.

As you surface, picture yourself relaxing and taking full breaths of the air readily available to nourish you. Clamber aboard your boat and open your oyster shell with a knife, seeing yourself find a perfect pearl within. You hold the pearl in your hands as it shimmers in the sunlight.

Repeat this sequence of images over and over again; each time you do, know that you are strengthening your ability to dive into your emotions and discover the bright gifts available to you through your emotional expression.

Bright Sparks of Fire

For many Geminis the element of fire is a complementary and attractive cousin. Geminis best experience the spiritual and creative realms of this element through their opposite Sun sign, the fire sign of Sagittarius. All signs contain a quality and an innate awareness of their opposite, so it is not surprising that on a deep cellular level Gemini is able to access the dynamic, inspirational and visionary magic of fire. It is through Sagittarius that Gemini can discover an interest in travel, philosophy and the higher realms of spiritual or intellectual study.

Imagine a child looking at a huge bonfire, watching the flames dance and change so rapidly; fascinated by the sparks randomly shooting off in all directions. If the child is Gemini you can be sure that they will be moving around the bonfire, unable to keep still, inspired by the brilliance and the activity. Fire is a motivational gift for Gemini and therefore it is an essential resource for Geminis to discover within themselves, as well as in the world around them.

Fire is the bright morning sunshine that wakes up any Gemini who has temporarily fallen asleep and forgotten their own spontaneous nature. Fire is the strongest element in all positive thought and affirmation. Any Gemini who has become stuck or feels unmotivated could spend some time exchanging any limited, restrictive thinking for new positive thoughts. In many cases this will easily create the movement that is desired. Any of the affirmations in this book, particularly the affirmations within the Gemini section, will prove a useful launch pad to greater realms of positive thought and action.

Gemini, as the child of the zodiac, delights in anything

bright and shiny, so friends, partners, lovers and colleagues with more than a touch of fire will be attractive to the Gemini soul. Visions of the future are always available to Gemini through its relationship to fire, and this too is attractive for the child who is always fascinated by the new. The element of fire helps keep Gemini supplied with the new inspirations that they delight in communicating to the world.

GEMINI INSPIRATION AND CREATIVITY

Gemini creativity contains more than a touch of fire. Whether writing, drawing, performing or devising a computer programme, Gemini's creative world of ideas will frequently find its motivation in fire and light. It is fire energy that will often provide the activating force to awaken dormant creative potential. Geminis who feel a little stuck may benefit from sitting by a large window. A holiday in the sunshine can also reawaken the creative urge.

Many Geminis are inspired by the beauty of light. Meditations using visual images of light are wonderfully transformational for us all, and for some Geminis, even the thought of light can awaken latent passions and increase energy levels. The brightness of the sunshine or the bright lights of a night on the town can illuminate, entertain and create positive action, reminding Gemini that they can have as much fun and entertainment in their lives as they want.

Geminis are often fired up to create vehicles or forums for the expression of their inspirational ideas, although they may well be more passionately motivated by the opportunity to communicate than by any particular creative medium in itself. Creativity is often seen as a means to an end, although one that can bring pleasure and enjoyment. Many Geminis love the creative play that video cameras, synthesisers, still photography and other modern gadgets or sophisticated toys can bring.

Geminis love to express their inspiration and originality through their appearance. Men and women alike may enjoy creating a look that is fun; they may choose colours, patterns or shapes that are bright, bold and inventive, perhaps set off by an interesting hair tint or an accessory that reflects the Gemini sense of humour. Some Geminis may favour large earrings, amusing badges or brooches and trendy designer fashions. Many Geminis like fabrics or jewellery that are pretty and catch the light; some may turn up for work as if they are dressed for a party. Whatever they are wearing, Geminis often like to use their appearance to make a statement.

Fire Affirmations for Gemini

I have the energy to create, communicate and play.

I spread my brilliance to others.

I am the bridge to new creations.

I am always motivated and inspired.

Light exists for me to play with.

I fire myself up to create and explore.

Fire Visualisation: Angel of Light

Close your eyes and visualise an angel or a magical being of light standing a few metres in front of you, glowing with brilliance, warmth and gentleness. You feel soothed and protected by this special presence as it shines with the golden orange lights of creative power, radiating an abundance of love and acceptance in your direction.

Breathe very deeply. As you do, imagine a particularly brilliant spark of light shooting out from the heart of your angel to land at the centre of your chest. As you breathe, picture that spark being drawn in to your body, magnetised by the air that is entering your lungs. Visualise this spark expanding to become a warm, gentle golden sunshine that glows throughout your chest and shines light throughout the whole of your being.

Have this sunshine send light into your brain to transform your thoughts and inspire you with new ideas. Have it send light through your shoulders, down your arms and into your hands to enliven your expression or communication. Imagine the light filling every part of you and shining its brilliance into the world around you.

Thank your angel for its gift of enlightenment and return to this image whenever you feel the need for a little extra motivation, brightness or healing.

THE SPIRITUAL PURPOSE OF GEMINI

The concept of duality is fundamental to the spiritual purpose of Gemini. Most people of this sign will be drawn to areas of life that provide them with opportunities to express their dual nature and help them to balance their powerful internal forces. The twins of Gemini can be seen to represent the spiritual and the human aspects of the soul. The purpose of Gemini is to fully express both twins or aspects of the self while discovering a bridge between the two, a perfect union that allows the whole being to be greater than the sum of its two parts.

Gemini people can sometimes switch moods, ideas or an approach to life within an instant. During a discussion Geminis can present a strong case for one point of view before seamlessly turning the tables to explore its opposite. This can be seen as the other twin of the Gemini soul coming forward to create a balance in energy or atmosphere. In many cases a Gemini person can appear to be unaware that they are contradicting themselves and this is perhaps because they are learning to tap into their greater awareness and know that nothing is completely black or white. Expressing all aspects of an argument can bring the realisation that there is no such thing as absolute truth.

The spiritual twin of Gemini exists in the realms of higher compassion or reason. This is the part of the personality better able to see the bigger picture of life and the subtle nuances of the Geminian spiritual purpose. This higher self can make sense of the life path, holding and co-ordinating the threads of new thought as they stretch into the future. The spiritual twin acts like an older brother or sister guiding its human half to higher awareness. Being the guardian of the soul's journey it has the power to give meaning to its human self and inspire the world with its brilliance and higher knowledge.

The human twin of the Gemini soul, although not earthly

by nature, deals with the day-to-day rhythms of being in the world and the adventure of expressing itself through all that is physical or in form. Its life journey is as a messenger on the earth, mirroring the heavenly movements of its planetary ruler Mercury. The human gift to its spiritual twin is to provide a vehicle through which all of those ideas and inspirations can take form. It is the power of actualisation in spreading all that is new and fun to eager ears.

THE GEMINI GIFT TO THE WORLD

Just as we all need the circulation of air throughout a room to provide us with life-giving oxygen, we need Gemini people and Geminian energy to circulate ideas and information throughout the world. It is as if Geminian energy acts as the impulses of the group mind stimulating us all with new thought.

It is no surprise, then, that many Gemini people find employment in the media or communications industries. Geminis are drawn to writing, performing, teaching, networking, marketing and all career positions that allow for contact with others so that Gemini can pass on and receive new concepts, new techniques and up to date gossip.

It is Geminian energy that helps the world to keep moving forwards, broadcasting the changes and new discoveries that inspire more change and discovery elsewhere. Gemini also reminds us of the gift of remaining childlike, forever curious, constantly open to life's adventure and demonstrating that life is for living and enjoying.

CHAPTER EIGHT

LIBRA

24 September - 22 October

CARDINAL AIR

Libra is the beautiful rainbow of harmony and balance that inspires the world with its aesthetic grace. Libra is the sign of the zodiac that brings a measure of peace and rights all that is out of kilter or unjustly biased. The special energy of this sign constantly instigates and maintains a delicate equilibrium in all that it touches, creating love, tranquillity and healing wherever it goes.

Libran people are diplomatic, charming and romantic. They have a clear and perceptive intellect that is attuned to making fair judgements, peaceful compromises and logical choices. They are often wise, insightful and persuasive, and have a calming influence on everyone with whom they come into contact. Librans have an extraordinary capacity to create healing solutions when others cannot.

Libra is the sign of high aesthetics and fine art. Libran souls often carry a concept of divine perfection within the higher realms of their sensual minds. This awareness of the perfect order compels them to seek beauty, refinement and artistic precision within the world. They often spread good taste, balance and intellectual ecstasy wherever they go.

Many Libran people are fascinated by the idea of happiness. They love to manifest happy, romantic, social and familial relationships where the needs of all parties are given equal importance. They like to ensure that everyone around them is being catered for to the best of their ability. Demonstrations or rituals of happiness and love such as weddings, family celebrations and refined social gatherings are Libra's domain, all executed with good taste and restraint.

The symbol for Libra is the scales which represent justice, harmony and divine balance. Librans of all ages display an extraordinary ability to see all sides of a story. They are often able to analyse the legalities of any situation, weighing them up with a naturally developed sense of higher moral law. They love finding clever compromises that will instigate a new equilibrium and bring a measure of happiness to all concerned.

The glyph, or shorthand notation, for Libra is of two horizontal lines, one above the other (♎). The upper line has an arch or a pivot at its centre. This symbolises the scales of Libra or the beam of balance. Some may see it as a yoke, ready to carry objects, thoughts or beliefs of equal weight and balanced dimensions.

The ruling planet of Libra is Venus. In mythology Venus was the goddess of love, inspiring the realms of the gods and the world of mortals alike with her beauty and charms. Venus can send Librans on a lifelong quest for ideal love, giving them a romantic vision of the world that colours their every mood and action.

Venus endows Libra with high romantic ideals. Libra is the sign of marriage, and many Librans seek to create the perfect union with their chosen partner. They may also seek to create highly romantic, platonic love where everything can remain perfect because it is never fully consummated. Libra is a sign of mental awareness and Librans often fall for the fascinating mind of another person.

LIBRA IN ITS ELEMENT

The element of air carries the higher concepts of form, vision, love and beauty to the Libran mind. Air is the element of mental agility and higher thought; Librans love to engage in discussions of reason, logic and creative philosophy. Most Librans are bright, intelligent people who love to exercise and demonstrate their clear mental faculties.

The air of Libra can be like a breeze gently moving through a garden of roses. Each flower is softly caressed with a breath of air that is as sensual as a lover's sigh, lovingly gathering the heady scent of roses to bring to all who will imbibe. The influence of Libra can open the minds and hearts of all who come into contact with the sensuous people of this sign.

The minds of Librans themselves are often open to seeing the artistic beauty around them whether in the natural world or in the visually stimulating creations of human kind. Librans enjoy discussing literature, poetry, art history, cinema, theatre and fashion. They like to bring themselves and others to a finer and finer awareness of form, shape, lighting, mood and symbolism.

Most Librans are positively focused and optimistic. If their current environment does not live up to their aesthetic ideal then they are often willing to make the creative effort to change it. They are good at holding and implementing a vision of the future in which everything has been re-formed in balance and perfection. Librans can be wonderful at motivating other people to improve their lives and to make social or environmental improvements.

Librans are particularly good at subtle persuasion and diplomacy. It is not the Libran style to get things moving through aggression, passionate outbursts or an obvious force of will. They prefer gentle reasoning, peaceful negotiation and seductive ideas that build into an irresistible force. Some Librans even wield power through passivity; seeming to do or say very little, they can encourage other people into action as a natural balance for their own restraint.

Although Libra is a male sign of the zodiac it also displays a strong sense of feminine, receptive power. By being open and willing to receive a feeling, an action or a positive outcome, many Librans are able to manifest what they desire. They do not always have to pursue what they want; sometimes they do, and sometimes it just seems to fall into their laps. Librans are often looking for the balance of masculine and feminine qualities within themselves and some can be a little androgenous or at the very least capable of empathising with members of the opposite sex.

Some of the healthiest people emotionally, mentally or spiritually are those who have found a balance of male and female qualities in themselves and their lives. In modern culture rigid gender roles are no longer appropriate; there is nothing more wonderful than watching a strong career woman excelling in her chosen field or observing a man nurturing and caring for his children. Perhaps the healthiest state to attain is one of flexibility, in which roles can be expressed and discarded as social, economic and family needs change. Libra is always looking to create new roles for themselves that will balance their personality and bring harmony to their relationships.

Librans are often able to understand and appreciate many points of view. They can usually see all sides of an argument and appreciate the needs of all parties in a dispute or disagreement. This ability to reason and understand can help Libra to be an extraordinary peacemaker, finding compromises or solutions when others cannot. However, Librans do need to learn to assert their own needs. They can sometimes be so reasonable that they negate their own desires and they can talk themselves out of claiming the rights, recognition or rewards that are justly theirs. A true balance comes with regarding your own happiness as important so that you do not become swamped by the needs or demands of others.

Many Libran souls enjoy poetic ideas or visions that can transport them away from the everyday world of work to a fragrant world of higher imagery and justice. Librans delight in the clever use of language and the power of words; their mood can be lifted by a beautifully delivered passage in a book or by an eloquently presented debate or anecdote. Some people more readily think in words or concepts while others think in pictures or symbolism; Libra has the potential to do both. Many Libran minds can skip nimbly from words to images and back again, embellishing what they read or hear with their own inner poetry.

The positivity and cardinal strength that many Librans possess can help them to put their high ideals into practice. They are often able to instigate positive changes in their corner of the world that can move the physical reality a little closer to their peaceful, harmonious vision; bringing healing, equal opportunities and a little piece of Utopia for all to enjoy.

LIBRAN ZONES OF THE BODY

The energy of Libra rules the kidneys and the lumbar region of the spine. The kidneys are sometimes said to be the batteries of the body; their ability to function well helps to keep the whole system charged up and lively. Numerous health problems affecting other parts of the body can sometimes be felt as tiredness because the kidneys have become depleted or sluggish. For Librans, particularly, the health and comfort of the kidney area can be a good barometer for overall balance and well-being.

Librans would benefit from drinking lots of pure, clear water to help cleanse and release toxins from the kidneys. Periods of abstinence from alcohol, rich foods, caffeine and nicotine would also help. The kidneys always benefit from having a rest so that they can clear the residue of the rich diet that many of us consume.

The ideal diet for many Librans would be one that includes large quantities of fresh fruit and vegetables. When eaten raw, these foods have a high water content that can help to flush out the system. They also contain easily digested natural sugars that feed the body and the brain without disturbing the balance of the organs or the tissues in the way that refined sugars do. Of course, there is no such thing as an ideal diet for every single person. We all have different physiological needs that are based on our heredity, our environment and our individual lifestyle.

For Libra, the popular wisdom of eating a balanced diet is probably particularly important. This doesn't just mean finding a good balance of proteins, carbohydrates, vitamins, minerals and roughage; it also means creating meals that have a balance of colour, texture and aesthetic beauty. Librans love good food and they tend to eat with their eyes. Food that is beautifully displayed can lift the spirits, enhance the joy of eating and even aid digestion.

A good general exercise programme can help the kidneys

to function at full efficiency. Regular brisk walking can squeeze the fluids and toxins through the kidneys, aiding all aspects of physical or mental digestion and elimination. Some forms of strenuous exercise, such as body-building, when executed with too much force or stress on a regular basis, can be draining for the kidneys. This kind of exercise can be wonderful when the body is given time to rest and when it is balanced with more feminine, receptive kinds of movements such as dance or Tai Chi.

Like most people, Librans will benefit from massage of all kinds, particularly back massage that concentrates on the muscles surrounding the lumbar region of the spine. All exercises that help to maintain the strength and flexibility of the back will be wonderful for Libra, helping them to maintain mental strength and flexibility too. In holistic medicine, the mind and the body cannot be seen as separate entities; any imbalance of thought will often be reflected in the body and the same principle operates in reverse. When there is a health problem a Libran would benefit from asking: 'What areas of my life, thoughts, beliefs or emotions need to be balanced at this time?'

EXERCISE AND THERAPIES

Librans benefit from the rhythm and regularity of exercise; little and often is better than prolonged periods of physical activity and extended periods of inactivity. When the body is conditioned to expect exercise on a regular basis it can maintain itself in balance and stability. Sudden jolts of exercise after long stretches of passivity can be a shock to the system.

All exercises and physical disciplines that develop balance

and poise would be beneficial for Libra. Trampolining can be a wonderfully balancing aerobic exercise for more active Librans. Anyone who does not have access to a full-sized trampoline could also have fun bouncing up and down or jogging on a bounce pad. Yoga exercises can provide balance as can all forms of gymnastics from floor exercises, stretching or tumbling to vaulting or working with beams and bars.

Librans who are more intrepid may enjoy open-air activities like hang-gliding, parachuting or abseiling. Most, though, will benefit from exercise that is conducted in the open air rather than indoors, even if their choice of activity is a little less adventurous. For fun, Librans may enjoy maintaining their balance while ice-skating, skateboarding or roller-skating. Some Librans have a natural talent for circus skills that require a sense of equilibrium such as juggling and unicycling.

Perhaps more than any other sign of the zodiac, Libra is associated with ballet; many Librans enjoy taking dance classes, and many more enjoy going to the ballet and losing themselves in the romance of balletic performance. Ballet can be an excellent form of exercise for Librans as it is concerned with balance and precision; it can help to build up strength, flexibility and stamina while enhancing poise. Ice dance, too, may hold a fascination for some Librans, combining balletic movement with gliding motion and speed.

Librans would be well served by creating and maintaining a postural balance, utilising anything from deportment classes to the training in correct movement offered by Feldenkrais practitioners. It benefits Librans to maintain the strength and flexibility of the spine. Cranial osteopathy can help them to keep their back properly aligned. By subtle manipulations of the head, cranial osteopaths can adjust the spinal fluid and rebalance the vertebrae.

Like all air signs Librans can be drawn to counselling and psychotherapy as a way of analysing and making sense of their life experiences or life choices. They prefer a therapist with whom they can reason out their motives and their path of development. This can be a wonderful support for short periods of time but it does not serve most Librans to over-analyse themselves for too long or spend too much time weighing up the pros and cons of their life situation when what they most need is direct, practical action. The best therapy for Libra would also allow them to move beyond their intellect into their emotions, their body and their spiritual awareness. A combination of counselling and bodywork could be the answer, or a counsellor who is able to give spiritual or psychic guidance.

Air Affirmations for Libra

I am balanced and harmonious, within and without.

My mind is filled with loving, peaceful, healthy thoughts.

I am open to receive the breaths of higher thought and healing.

The currents of love, harmony and beauty flow into my mind and through my body.

My environment is always tranquil and serene.

The organs and joints of my body are in perfect balance.

My spine is strong, supple and perfectly aligned.

I am treated with fairness, kindness and love wherever I go.

Every part of me is attuned to vitality and joy.

I breathe in the sweetness and the sensual pleasure of life.

Air Visualisation: Music and Fragrance

Find a quiet, comfortable place and relax, preferably lying down or sitting with your back properly supported and your body open rather than curled up.

Breathe deeply and, as you do, imagine yourself in a beautiful garden filled with roses, gardenias and other fragrant flowers and herbs. The sun is shining and the air is clear, fresh and a little breezy. Picture some beautifully crafted wind chimes hanging from the branches of a tree that is located at the centre of this magical place.

Find yourself a comfortable spot beneath the tree and picture yourself sitting or lying there and breathing in the special fragrances of this place. Imagine the air currents bringing you sweeter and sweeter scents; breathe deeply and visualise your lungs filling with the healing power of these exquisite smells.

Imagine that the healing power of fragrance spreads throughout your body, into your kidneys, into your back and into every other part of you, bringing balance, peace, alignment and health. The scent dispels any negativity, tension or disharmony from your body replacing it with vitality and well-being.

Next, visualise the air currents playing with the wind chimes; surrounding you and filling you with exquisitely beautiful sounds. The notes are bright and perfectly tuned, each one filling your mind with positivity, balance, harmony and joy. As you listen to this music of the air, imagine it filling you with wonderful new ideas and inspirations. Perhaps you could picture your mind receiving seeds of new, healing thought, each one grow-

> ing within you over the hours and days that follow.
> When you complete this visualisation you may choose to write down or record any ideas or inspirations that you had.

THE POETIC WATERS OF LIBRA

The element of water challenges Librans to wake up to their poetic or mystical vision and move from their abstract concepts of love into the full emotional reality of loving relationships. Water is the element of deep feelings, shifting moods, intuition and psychic awareness. The currents of water take Librans from their familiar territory of logic and reason into an uncertain world of irrational drives.

Many Librans prefer the idea of emotional intimacy to the feeling of vulnerability that close relationships can bring. Some may even need to find a healthy balance between their romantic ideals and their inner emotional nature that could surface during times of intense physical, sexual or spiritual contact. For those Librans who are able to create the right marriage between head and heart the gifts of joy flow with abundance.

LOVE AND ROMANCE

Librans bring the gift of love to all their relationships. They are so filled with romantic thoughts and loving ideals that they easily awaken the minds of others to the beauty of the world. Some Librans spend their lives seeking ideal romance and in doing so they invariably attract potential suitors who are drawn to their beauty or to their intellectual brilliance.

Many Librans are in love with love. They often engage in the romantic rituals of courtship, wishing to exchange flowers, cards or beautiful gifts. Some Librans send gifts of their favourite literature, poetry or fine art hoping that the object of their desire will be wooed and inspired by the same concepts of beauty that they themselves enjoy. Perfectly stage-managed settings for romance, including exquisite meals, seductive lighting, sensual perfume or enchanting music are all favoured by the Libran who wishes to attract a new mate or bring some breaths of fresh air to a long-term relationship.

Librans can find healing and inspiration by learning to love and care for themselves in the same way that they would care for the object of their desire. Whether they are in a relationship or not, Librans could choose to spend solitary time creating rituals that would make them feel special and cherished. If you can treat yourself to a romantic meal for one and learn to take pleasure in your own company, as you nurture yourself, then other people will begin to notice and respond to the contentment that you exude. The more that you learn to love yourself, the more others will love you too.

Libra can sometimes move from one relationship to another, filling their lives with a series of monogamous affairs. Most Librans prefer to focus on one person at a time, and on the whole they do not enjoy being unfaithful or disloyal. Those with a tendency to move on often do so because they are searching for perfection. When their relationship does not match their ideal then they go off in search of one that does.

Libra is often the person who begins a relationship, exerting subtle forms of persuasion that become more and more compelling as the courtship develops. The object of Libra's desire may find it increasingly difficult to refuse their romantic advances and highly reasonable approach. Libra can be so patient, bright and charming that it would seem unreasonable to refuse them. However, Libra's reluctance to offend, distress or force their chosen partner in any way can mean that the decisive, active move may need to come from the other person. Librans seldom make the marriage proposal or lead their partner to the bedroom unless they are pretty sure that they are on safe ground.

Married Librans are often consistently sweet and caring to their partners. In a long-term relationship, Libra is generally very committed to keeping the romance alive and they will do what they can to maintain or recreate the spark of ideal love or perfection for which they yearn. If there are moments of discord then Libra will do their best to restore harmony. However, the Libran discomfort with powerful feelings could see some Librans backing off or becoming cool and logical at times when their partner most needs them to engage in a passionate exchange. Librans could do well to remember that the occasional argument or passionate demonstration of love can clear the air and bring everyone closer to true romance.

The ideal partner for a Libran will be someone with whom they can maintain a good friendship and intellectual rapport when the initial mystery and romantic illusions have dissolved. Libra also needs someone who can balance their cool reasoning with some fiery passion and a touch of watery sensuality that can put them in touch with their deeper feelings. True, sustaining love comes when Libra can be seduced out of their heads and into their hearts; the concept of love becomes richer when it is touched by real emotion.

Water Affirmations for Libra

I bathe in the romance and sensuality of my emotions.

It is safe for me to be intimate and emotionally open.

I balance the beauty of my mind with the sensuality of my heart.

I am intuitive, poetic, sensual and serene.

I heal my emotions with ease, tranquillity and peace.

I awaken to greater depths of love and sensuality.

Water Visualisation: Pool of Sensuality

Find a quiet, comfortable spot and relax. Breathe deeply. As you do, imagine that you are in a forest clearing enriched with a multitude of wild flowers. The air is sensual and warm, filled with the scent of rich earth, blossoms, ferns and trees.

At the centre of this clearing, surrounded by lush vegetation, is a beautiful pool of crystal water. The sun is shining, its radiations warming the water and bouncing pretty lights upon the surface. It looks so pleasant and inviting that you imagine yourself slipping off your clothes and stepping into the pool.

As you step in feel your body relaxing deeply; the water is soft against your skin, awakening you to the sensual power of your body and your emotions. All physical or emotional tensions wash away from you; any illness, disharmony and distress dissolve harmlessly away.

As you bathe, you feel your skin becoming softer and

younger. Picture yourself moving through a beautiful range of emotions from a sweet sadness to joy, bliss and ecstasy. See yourself becoming more beautiful, more handsome, healthier and more alive. You are filled with a fluidity of feeling and a limitless supply of sensual power.

Knowing that you can return to the pool whenever you choose, see yourself now stepping out of the water and back on to dry land. You look like a god or goddess as you emerge. Imagine that your clothes have been replaced by new ones, more beautiful, more sensual and more comfortable than before and see yourself dressing with pleasure. Every part of you is feeling balanced and serene.

THE MOTIVATIONAL FIRES OF LIBRA

The element of fire is a wonderful companion for Libra; it is inspirational and warming. Fire brings joy, motivation and the sparks of spirituality to the cool, reason of the Libran soul. It is through fire that Librans can discover greater assertiveness, strength and passion to help them to instigate their creative or artistic endeavours. It can also bring to them a sense of adventure and a feeling that their life is a romantic, heroic journey.

Librans perhaps best experience fire through their opposite Sun sign, the fire sign of Aries. The Arien influence can endow Libra with greater physical strength, a force of will and a youthful vitality to enliven their serene calmness. Aries can balance the passive persuasion of Libra with the power to instigate through direct, bold action, challenging Libra to make a firm stand and campaign for their rights.

When persuasion or diplomacy breaks down and peaceful negotiation is having no impact, some Librans may be prepared to fight for justice in the world. Librans can become so incensed by injustice that they get angry enough to campaign for human rights. Then they will passionately defend justice, equality and the needs of those less fortunate than themselves. Sometimes the most powerful healing of the Libran soul can come with a willingness to act.

Libran thought is usually fired with cheerfulness and optimism; Librans can often move mountains with their positive self-belief. The Libran mind is so powerful that a simple change of attitude from cynicism to openness or from extreme caution to positive anticipation can instantly bring a burst of new energy and in some cases a sense of healing liberation. The beliefs and attitudes that we choose to hold dramatically affect the experience that we have of our lives. For Libran health and well-being, choosing to use those vast mental powers positively is essential.

LIBRAN INSPIRATION AND CREATIVITY

Librans can express the healing power of their creativity through their appearance and presentation. Many Librans love beautiful clothes and they often dress meticulously, displaying exquisite taste and a flair for design. They are also known to take great care of their hair. Libran hair is often silky and shiny, expressing an air of sensuality. Their overall appearance is likely to show colour sense and elegance.

Librans may express their creativity through the crafting of fine art. Librans who turn their hand to painting often do so with a delicacy and refinement that is inspirational for other people. They also display fine aesthetic judgement in the framing, hanging and lighting of artwork; pictures are often chosen to complement or balance their setting in the home. Librans who do not paint or draw may turn their attentions to art appreciation to exercise the creativity of their intellect and their eye for beauty.

Libra can often be a naturally gifted poet, finding an outlet for self-healing through the clever use of words and images. Librans express the fire of the soul and the clear aesthetic visions of the mind through all kinds of writing. Libran letters, reports and essays are often evocative, poetic and stimulating.

Dressmaking, tailoring and fashion design can be excellent creative outlets for Librans. Some may love to work with fine fabrics, luxurious textiles and sensuous colour. Librans may favour silks, satins or finely woven cottons. They may also have a flair for millinery or the design, choice and creation of other fashion accessories.

When Librans are not surrounded with beauty then they will either acquire beautiful things or create them. Librans bring great healing to themselves by healing and transforming their environment. Libran homes can often be a sensual delight; even those that are simple can be beautifully presented and luxurious. Libra may also design and create elegant gardens; roses may be favoured as may other fragrant flowers and herbs. They often love the grand gardens of stately homes and may wish to emulate them by creating their own plot of serenity.

Fire Affirmations for Libra

I balance my diplomacy with direct action.

My life is filled with romance and adventure.

I exude positivity, optimism and health.

I discover light and beauty within my environment.

I am enlightened and enlivened with creativity and love.

I create brightness, beauty and harmony wherever I go.

Fire Visualisation: The Morning Star

Breathe and relax, and imagine yourself looking at the early morning sky just as the dawn is about to break and only a few stars remain visible. The air is quiet and peaceful and there is a fresh, invigorating feeling all around you.

As you look up, imagine a single brilliant star appearing; a star of the morning with a light that is penetrating yet soft. It looks so beautiful that you become transfixed by its pulsing, twinkling radiations.

Visualise this star sending down a single beam of brilliance filled with spiritual healing energy. This shaft of light is directed specifically at you to touch and surround you with a loving embrace. Imagine your whole body illuminated in a pool of harmonising starlight and picture the cells of your body able to drink in and assimilate these fine radiations.

The morning star sends subtle information to your

body, mind and emotions; rebalancing you throughout and attuning you to health, beauty, positivity, joy and enthusiasm. Imagine the light strengthening your will-power, firing your passions and improving your ability to assert yourself.

See the morning star gently receding from view as the sun comes out, leaving you with a sense of well-being and new inspiration. Return to this image whenever you feel the need for the special healing vibrations of this light.

THE EARTHLY DELIGHTS OF LIBRA

The element of earth rules the material world with its concerns of physical well-being, earthly pleasures and financial success. Libra perhaps best experiences the element of earth through its planetary connection to the earth sign of Taurus. Libra and Taurus are both ruled by the planet Venus and both signs have a love of luxury, sensuality and the good things in life.

Librans are often generous with money, while wishing to exercise a degree of financial caution. They like to keep their financial affairs in balance and they are often quite sensible about how they use their resources. However, a desire for luxury may see Librans spending their earnings on comfortable furnishings, beautiful paintings, fine wine, good food and holidays in carefully chosen locations.

Some Librans can be so involved in their world of poetic beauty and higher aesthetics that they find all discussion of money rather coarse, or at least challenging. They could even be quite secretive or elusive about their financial transactions, wishing to keep them separate from the rest of their lives. Most Librans, however, realise that money is a necessary part of maintaining their chosen lifestyle and providing for themselves or the people that they love.

The earth challenges Libra to step out from their world of abstract thought and into the realms of all that is tangible, present and real. Librans need to marry up their aesthetic vision of life with the day-to-day realities that they experience around them. Fortunately, Libran mental skills, good judgement and creative awareness are usually in demand, and so they are greatly encouraged to develop the practical side of their nature, bridging the gap between their higher awareness and the physical world.

PARTNERSHIPS, BUSINESS AND SUCCESS

Librans generally work best with other people, usually as the creative or ideas person working with partners who deal with more practical aspects of the business. Even self-employed or freelance Librans working on their own tend to create a feeling of partnership around them as they work with clients, business contacts and other freelancers. Librans can be excellent at creating their own jobs, seeing where there is a need and developing an exciting new post. They can come up with the ideas to develop new markets or create new services.

In some companies Libra will be the lawyer, handling contracts or legal transactions and assessing rights or liabilities. Libra's balanced judgement will often be highly sought after by business partners, colleagues and junior employees alike. They may find themselves weighing up the pros and cons of new company policies or settling disputes between team members.

To maintain health, balance and their innate capacity for fine ideas, Librans need to work in surroundings that are peaceful and aesthetically pleasing. Loud jarring noises, overly aggressive colleagues, airless offices or oppressively dark places can adversely affect the health of many people. Librans particularly would benefit from locations that give them air to breathe, tranquillity, and space to think. Some may consider bringing about improvements in their work environment – or, alternatively – finding a job elsewhere.

Librans with their own business, and those in charge of departments in large companies, make very fair bosses. They are often able to anticipate the needs of their staff and they are willing to see everyone's point of view, giving people a fair opportunity to develop within the organisation. In some cases, though, Libran bosses and heads of department need to learn to be firmer or more assertive with team members. Sometimes they will be required to put the needs of the company or their own needs first and this may conflict with their desire to keep everybody happy at all costs. In most situations people prefer to have clear direction and clear boundaries, and may be happier if their boss does not sit on the fence when there are firm decisions to be made.

Librans benefit from having clear goals for their work projects and their career development. They often like to have some focus to measure their progress by, whether it is a company directive or a personal goal that they have set for themselves. Some Librans are excellent at drafting business plans or creating a plan of personal development for the months and years to come. Sometimes just writing down and declaring your desires is enough to get things moving and encourage you to instigate some positive changes in your life.

The ideal colleague for a Libran will be someone who can complement their brilliant reasoning powers with some passionate, fiery action, creating the perfect balance for instigating new ventures. Libra may also benefit from working alongside an emotionally based person who can bring some sensitive creativity to Libra's brilliant, inspirational ideas. Libra's capacity to create a healing equilibrium within their work environment will often see them finding colleagues who complement them perfectly, providing skills that they themselves do not possess or need to learn more about.

Success for Libra is often equated with creating perfection. Librans can love the satisfaction of a job well done, with everything in its place and the way clear for something new to happen. They are often committed to persisting with a project until every detail has been taken care of and all has been finely tuned to their high standards.

Perhaps true success for Libra comes with creating a sense of inner peace while enjoying the abundance of sensual pleasures that life has to offer. It helps to develop a trust that there is a natural order to things and that everything has its own innate perfection; even when it is constantly growing or changing. A beautiful flower is never quite the same from day to day but it is always perfect and special. Even when it sheds its seeds and dies, it is still perfect, making space for new flowers to grow in the future; just as beautiful in their own unique way.

Earth Affirmations for Libra

I am in tune with the rhythms and order of nature.

I have the time and resources to do everything that I enjoy.

I attract the luxuries and the pleasures that I desire.

My brilliant ideas easily manifest the prosperity that I need.

I create the lifestyle that supports me in health and joy.

I always work with people who are loving and harmonious.

Earth Visualisation: Feast of Fine Healing

Breathe and relax, imagining yourself sitting in a beautiful meadow filled with wild flowers and bordered by beautiful trees. In front of you is a crisp, clean tablecloth that you have spread out onto the ground. Picture a beautiful feast materialising on that cloth and visualise some people whom you love or some new friends appearing, too, to share this sumptuous feast with you as you begin to picnic in the open air.

Imagine that the food is healthy and delicious, imbued with the fertile riches of the earth. As you eat, you notice that the air is filled with peace, calm and the musical sounds of laughter and joy. With every mouthful you take you feel your body being balanced and transformed by the special healing energy of this good food. You eat only what your body needs before sitting back to enjoy the beauty of this environment and the companionship of your good friends.

As your body digests the food and fine friendship, imagine yourself growing physically stronger and becoming magnetic to prosperity and joy in every area of your life. Think of some of the material or financial things that you would like to manifest and see yourself creating them easily and in balance with the needs of the earth.

In your mind thank the earth for its fertile gifts and your friends for sharing the good things in life with you. When you complete this visualisation you may choose to write down or record any prosperous ideas that you may have before putting them into action.

THE SPIRITUAL PURPOSE OF LIBRA

The spiritual purpose of Libra is concerned with the harmonising of natural laws and the instigation of new, positive avenues of thought. In ancient Egypt the goddess of equilibrium and justice was called Maat. She was the spirit of truth that moved within and around all things. The Libran mind has the ability to tap into the spirit of truth and create fairness, positivity and order within the world.

In instigating balance and harmony, Librans are learning to strengthen or fine-tune those qualities within themselves; coming to a point of completeness and moderation where they can tread the middle way in all things. In practical terms this can mean Libra exorcising all extremes of behaviour, any thinking that is negatively focused or out of balance and excesses of consumption.

Librans are also learning to fine-tune the way in which they value themselves. Some Librans overly judge themselves by their appearance, feeling good about themselves only when they think that they are looking good. The image that we have of ourselves from moment to moment can be so illusory and subjective that it is never a sound measure of our worth.

Many Librans are physically beautiful and have wonderfully engaging smiles and personalities. The care and good taste that many apply to their dress and presentation can certainly uplift them and make them aesthetically pleasing to other people. However, the more that Librans can feel good about themselves regardless of how they look, the happier their lives will become. What is more, when they stop worrying about how other people see them, their inner beauty can begin to shine more brightly.

Librans can esteem and value themselves by learning to take care of their own needs and by asserting themselves. They would benefit from being as kind and patient with themselves as they often are with other people. With their desire to keep other people happy, Librans need to remember that their own happiness is important too. A true balance comes with loving yourself enough to say 'no' to the requests and demands of others from time to time. What is more, learning to love yourself can connect the awareness of the mind to an ever-expanding heart that grows in love and compassion for the world.

THE LIBRAN GIFT TO THE WORLD

Libra blesses the world with an interchange of ideas, pleasant social contact, beauty and aesthetic brilliance. We need Librans to provide us with wisdom, a refined sense of awareness and clear objectivity. Librans instigate the many changes that make the world a fairer, more peaceful and a more harmonious place.

Librans may find employment as lawyers, solicitors, judges or diplomats. They may also concern themselves with the rights of other people by becoming staff welfare officers, personnel officers or counsellors. The Libran skill for evaluation and assessment could see some working as valuers or auctioneers.

Creative and aesthetically attuned Libra could be an artist, writer, fashion buyer, dressmaker, textile designer or hairdresser. Some Librans may work in art galleries or stately homes while others put their good looks and personality to work as a host or hostess, a model or a receptionist. Libra may also be a ballet dancer, choreographer or theatrical set designer.

The gift of Libra is one of alignment to the higher realms of thought and inspiration. Libra reminds us of innate balance within all things and the healing gift of balance within our lives. Libra also helps us to remember the wealth of beauty and abundance in the world to be shared and enjoyed by everyone; with the energy of Libra present we can establish peaceful co-existence, harmony and love.

CHAPTER NINE

AQUARIUS

21 January - 20 February

FIXED AIR

Aquarius is an electrical bolt of new thought, scientific exploration and dramatic change. Aquarian people are unconventional, erratic geniuses with minds that move like lightning into sparks of visionary ecstasy. They are highly intelligent, inventive and logical; able to shift gear from one mode of thought to another with rapidity and agility.

Aquarius is a highly idealistic sign and Aquarians can have utopian visions that are ahead of their time. Aquarius speaks of brotherhood, sisterhood, equality and humanitarian convictions. Aquarians seek out and promote truth, fight injustice and concern themselves with the future welfare of society.

The symbol for Aquarius is the water-carrier. This is usually a woman, perhaps a priestess, with a jar or pitcher of water that she pours ahead of herself into the future, tapping into the realms of new thought and vision. When this inspired thinking is channelled or released into the world it has a forward momentum that brings the inevitability of change.

Although the image generally depicted is female, Aquarius is a male sign but one that brings with it a freedom from rigid gender roles. Aquarius is too unconventional to be traditionally male or traditionally female. Some Aquarians may even demonstrate this by having a powerfully androgenous look or by being the epitome of the new man or new woman seeking sexual equality in the workplace and at home.

The glyph, or shorthand notation, for Aquarius is made up of two rippling lines, one above the other, that are reminiscent of waves (♒). These lines can be most appropriately interpreted as electrical waves of pulsing energy rather than the waves of water. They are powerful impulses of the mind and not the ripples of emotion.

Aquarians are highly individualistic, often reacting against traditions or authority. They can be fiercely independent to the point of being detached and aloof at times, although they are basically friendly people with a high regard for others. Their originality is often expressed through eccentric mannerisms, attitudes and clothing or the championing of new causes.

The two ruling planets of Aquarius are Saturn and Uranus. These are planets with very different properties that can appear to be contradictory at times and complementary at others, perhaps helping to explain the unpredictable nature of many Aquarians. Saturn is the planet of structure, creative limitations, boundaries and foundations. It is through Saturn that Aquarius defines its fixidity, bringing a sense of stability that aids the construction of logical thought.

Uranus, on the other hand, is quite different: it is the planet of change, disruption, invention and liberation. It is Uranus that brings the Aquarian compulsion for freedom; Uranus is shocking, rebellious, pioneering and creative. Together, Saturn and Uranus bring about the formation, dismantling and rearranging of personal structures.

With Aquarians no foundation is safe: there will always be new approaches to take that will render tried and tested systems or patterns of behaviour obsolete. Aquarians approach life as if it were a series of scientific or electrical experiments. Some will constantly change their approach to relationships, career and health, curious to see what differences they can make. Others, however, may fix themselves upon one approach to numerous relationships and shifting circumstances; experimenting with life by holding firm to their beliefs while attracting change from the outside.

AQUARIUS IN ITS ELEMENT

The air of Aquarius is the air that carries radio waves, electrical impulses, radiation and futuristic thought. The Aquarian mind can be like a radio, tuning in to positive possibilities that are beyond the boundaries of normal human awareness. Aquarian people can sometimes appear to respond to subtle impulses from outside of themselves, calling them to explore the new and expand the science of living.

Many Aquarians are intellectually brilliant and highly ingenious. It can seem as if original thoughts are able to place themselves in the Aquarian mind to be discovered and played with. The speed and frequency of these thoughts can be dizzying and quite spectacular. Aquarians may delight in discussion or debate, enjoying the opportunity to experiment with their limitless supply of ideas.

Aquarian people may start a discussion, emphatically exploring one idea and then shift gear rapidly when a new idea drops into place. Continual change is a fundamental part of Aquarian energy, and people of this sign can change their minds frequently. They are able to view the truth of a situation from all sides, experimenting with the quality and substance of each new thought.

Some Aquarians can appear to change their minds about fundamental life choices from day to day. On Monday they are in love, on Tuesday they are contemplating a spiritual retreat, on Wednesday they are planning a new career, and on Thursday they are in love again. The healthiest Aquarians are those who remember to take a long weekend off occasionally to give their minds a rest.

In contradiction many Aquarians may have an underlying fixidity of purpose that comes from the controlled nature of Saturn, one of the ruling planets of Aquarius. This gives them some stability within their ever-shifting world of mental electricity and helps them to keep their mind running on its own course. To develop special new ways of thinking it is essential not to be overly influenced by other people's rhythms and patterns.

It is perhaps the contradictory nature of Aquarius, coming from the dramatically different characteristics of its two ruling planets, that makes many Aquarians tricky to spot. The influence of Saturn can make some Aquarians appear to be highly conventional while the influence of Uranus can make others appear to rebel against and shun convention of all kinds. Whatever the external appearance you can guarantee that it will be contrasted or balanced by the opposing inner beliefs and attitudes.

Aquarian airwaves bring broadcasts of new technologies, philosophies and ideals. It is Aquarius that rules much New Age thinking, self-exploration and the expansion of the higher mind. For Aquarians it is healthy to practise mind-clearing techniques from time to time, perhaps writing lists, talking with a friend to externalise thoughts and beliefs, or meditating to still the mind. Clearing mental noise can create space for greater inspiration, balanced insights and a sense of peace.

Aquarians can be quite psychically attuned but unlike the water signs Pisces, Scorpio and Cancer, Aquarians tend to receive information through the intellect rather than through the intuition. Their minds have the ability to unscramble thought waves from other people and convert them into mental images or concepts rather than gut feelings or sensual awareness. Having powerful minds that are able to receive and transmit vast amounts of information it is essential for Aquarians to learn to think in positive, healing ways. Fortunately many are born with a gift for positive thought.

AQUARIAN ZONES OF THE BODY

Aquarius rules the region of the body from below the knee to the ankle. This includes the shins, the calves and the circulatory system within the lower legs. All forms of exercise to strengthen the leg muscles will be beneficial to the whole system; this could include walking, running, circuit-training, weight-training and dance.

Increasing and maintaining flexibility of the ankle by regular stretching or flexing of the feet will benefit Aquarians in many ways. This can be done by pointing the toes alternately away from and back to the leg a few times before circling the foot clockwise, then anticlockwise, from the ankle joint. As well as increased flexibility, greater strength and improved circulation, Aquarians may also find that this exercise gives them a psychological boost.

Health and suppleness of the ankles can sometimes be a reflection of the joyfulness and flexibility of the mind. The whole area of the lower leg can represent the stability and support of the human body and the psychological or emotional ability of a person to advance in life, responding to the many changes or challenges that life can bring.

Aquarius walks a balancing line between structure and revolutionary change; conventional patterns of thought or action and a radical breakdown of these patterns so that they may be replaced with something new. The strength, fluidity and circulation of the legs and ankles for an Aquarian person can sometimes indicate how effectively they are finding this balance.

In some ways Aquarius can also be said to rule the subtle electrical impulses that connect the human brain and nervous system. This would include the electrochemical impulses that instruct the arms and legs to move, the muscles to work and the body to assimilate and digest. General exercise and fitness will help to maintain the effectiveness of these impulses but sports or games, like squash or tennis will be of particular benefit by speeding up mental and physical reactions. As well as the circulation of the lower legs the Aquarian influence can be seen in the circulation as a whole. It is essential for Aquarians to get prolonged bursts of clean, fresh air. An active outdoor lifestyle will help Aquarius to oxygenate the blood and to stimulate the brain.

Regular breathing exercises would also help. Simply filling the lungs to a count of eight, holding the breath for a count of four, and exhaling for a count of eight will keep the oxygen circulating and the mind focused. With practice, the length of the out-breath can be extended by a few counts. This is wonderfully relaxing and will help to balance the whole of the Aquarian mental and emotional state.

Aquarians generally fare better with jobs and lives that allow them to be outdoors, on their feet and able to circulate. For office workers or homebound Aquarian people it helps to work next to open windows, take advantage of breaks to go outside for a walk and stand up to perform as many daily tasks as possible.

EXERCISE AND THERAPIES

Many Aquarians tend to have a go at most exercise routines, therapies and diets. Aquarians can latch onto something as being a good idea and leap into it with great enthusiasm and force of will. Some Aquarians will have dabbled with so many new routines, regimes and fads that they can become quite an expert source of information for other people.

This tendency to skip from one thing to another can be quite healthy for Aquarians. They often need the stimulation of regular change to keep their minds interested and involved as they focus on physical fitness or emotional healing. However, Aquarians do need to slow themselves down enough so that they can allow the latest programme or treatment to have a lasting impact. Their speed to try new things can sometimes inhibit them from being deeply touched by what they are doing. For many forms of healing to work they need time to go beyond the intellect to the emotions, the body and the spirit.

Quiet meditation is always wonderful for Aquarians as a way of stilling and sharpening the mind. If done regularly and for long enough it can help them to contact their inspired inner selves and integrate different aspects of their personality. Meditation can be as simple as sitting comfortably and quietly breathing in and out deeply while gently noticing the thoughts that pass through the mind. For Aquarians it may also help to give the mind a focus to aid stillness. A mantra is a word, sound, phrase or affirmation that can be repeated as a chant over and over again, inside the head. Aquarians could choose any word with a pleasing sound and a positive meaning, to use in this way.

An alternative tool for meditation could be a mandala or visual focus. This can be something to gaze at physically such as a candle, a flower or a beautiful wall-hanging, or it can be a visual image that is held in the mind while the eyes are closed. Some people like to start the meditation with their eyes open and then close them when they become tired, internalising the image of the object that they were focusing on. Meditation can lower the heart rate, regulate blood pressure and relieve mental, emotional or physical stress.

An ideal meditation for Aquarius is one that is combined with a physical activity of some kind. A half hour of yoga or Tai chi exercise before a still, silent meditation will help Aquarians stay physically or emotionally integrated and not overly focused on the mind. Alternatively the combination of a still meditation with a walking meditation may be good.

Walking meditation can be performed indoors or outdoors. The meditation comes from placing the attention on the act of walking rather than on the environment through which you walk. Walking very slowly in a circle or a rectangle while staying conscious of each footfall, watching and feeling every step that you take is a wonderful way of stilling the mind while training yourself to have a heightened awareness during all daily activities. For Aquarians the combination of still meditation and meditative physical activity will bring stability to that highly changeable nature and healing to any areas of emotional distress.

Contrary to some texts on meditation, there is no absolute right or wrong way to meditate. It is enough to keep yourself calm and still for ten minutes a day to achieve some degree of meditative balance. Aquarian minds are so active that any practice that will encourage the mind to rest will be of benefit. Meditations that employ visualisation or positive thought techniques will also be helpful.

Aquarius rules much of the new, electronic technology of mainstream modern medicine as well as the gadgetry of complementary techniques. The Aquarian influence can be found in the electronic diagnostic machines that some practitioners are using to detect allergies, dietary imbalance and the effects of environmental toxicity. One form of this is called Vega testing. Here, a machine is used to measure the subtle changes in the body's electricity caused by the presence or lack of various substances.

Certainly, Aquarians are attracted to gadgets of all kinds as a way of finding healing or a positive stimulus for their lives. However, many of them will benefit most from simple, natural therapies and exercise. Regular walking will be physically and psychologically uplifting for most Aquarians, as will cycling.

Aquarians often love electronic gym equipment like jogging machines or exercise bikes that tell you how fast you are going and how many calories you are burning off. These machines, if used wisely, will be of great benefit. However, doing the real thing in the open air will benefit Aquarians even more and ultimately bring them more pleasure.

Aquarians may also respond well to the ancient Chinese medicine of acupuncture. Acupuncturists insert needles into points on the body that can adjust the circulation of energy that moves through subtle circuits called meridians. For Aquarians this can be a bit like rewiring the body's electricity. As such, they tend to react favourably and in some cases quite rapidly.

Air Affirmations for Aquarius

My life is filled with healing changes.

I bring exciting new ideas to the world.

My circulation is healthy and charged with energy.

My thoughts are filled with flexibility and strength.

I tune in to new and wonderful thoughts.

My natural electricity is vital and alive.

My mind is meditative and peaceful.

I explore the electricity of my higher mind.

I am wired, tuned and programmed for health.

I enjoy and appreciate my originality.

Air Visualisation: Tuning The Airwaves

Find a quiet, comfortable place and relax, preferably lying down with your back properly supported and your body open.

Breathe deeply. As you do, be aware of the air filling your lungs as you breathe in and being released from your lungs as you breathe out. Take a few moments to appreciate the circulation of air in and out of your body.

Think of the air circulating around you too, outside of your body, and imagine all of the subtle messages, new thoughts, original ideas, electrical impulses and radio waves that are travelling through the air, unseen by the human eye.

Picture yourself as magnetic to the most positive, healing messages and impulses moving through the air waves. When you breathe in, visualise yourself drawing in air that contains positive, healthy thoughts; if you could see them they would look like flashes of sparkling, electrical light.

As well as filling your lungs, imagine these flashes of light whizzing around your body and into your mind, where they become the healthy inspirations of originality, liberation and peace.

Next, imagine yourself breathing in electrical impulses that are specially attuned to the healing, revitalisation and rejuvenation of your body. From your lungs these safe but powerful bursts of subtle electricity move to your heart and from your heart they travel around your circulatory system.

Your circulation carries this special healing to wherever it is needed in your body. Picture vulnerable, weak or imbalanced areas filling with electrical light that charges them up with health. Any excess electricity discharges itself safely into the atmosphere.

Particularly fill and surround your lower legs and ankles with a bright, electrical light that will strengthen and protect them. When you complete this visualisation you may wish to write down or record any new healing thoughts or inspirations that you had.

THE LIGHTNING FIRES OF AQUARIUS

The element of fire is a comfortable and inspiring force for Aquarians to draw from for sustenance, motivation, optimism and expansion. Aquarians best experience the realms of fire through their opposite Sun sign, the fire sign of Leo. Through Leo, Aquarians can be motivated to step into the spotlight once in a while and be the hub of social situations, creative endeavours and arenas of new thought. Despite their independent streak, Aquarians can often find themselves becoming the central focus of inspiration for others.

Sunlight will be powerfully motivational and healing for Aquarius. Nothing can quite shift the mood and magic of life more than waking up to bright sunshine streaming in through the window; awakening joys and energies that have become buried or forgotten. For Aquarians, bright, sunny mornings will often inspire them to throw on some clothes and dash straight out into the open air.

The sun can be used as a wonderful healing tool. After covering up and protecting the skin, a little time in the sun can warm away stress, lift depressions and stimulate new cellular growth. For Aquarians, all forms of exercise that can be taken in the sunshine and open air will be of benefit physically and psychologically. During times of stillness it would be good to use the warmth of the sun to relax and expand the chest area.

The element of fire also comes to Aquarians through the ruling planet of Uranus. This is the fire of natural electricity and lightning flashes of creativity. The period after an electrical storm can be one of intense creativity for many Aquarians. At these times the earth is renewed with rain water and the air recharged with negative electrical ions. This can provide energy for Aquarians who know how to channel and use it. They can feel refreshed and reborn, experiencing great clarity, and raring to go.

INSPIRATION AND CREATIVITY

Aquarian people have highly inventive minds that are filled with creative thoughts and innovative ideas. Aquarians are often able to devise new approaches to traditional creative arts and bring lateral thought to the re-creation of functional objects and the execution of original designs. They are fired by a passion to express their innate genius for creativity in as many different ways as possible.

Aquarians bring heightened creativity and the bright lights of inspiration to new technology of all kinds. Many inspired computer systems or computer programs are devised by people with their Sun in Aquarius or with Aquarius strongly featured in their birth chart. Even Aquarians who are not particularly computer-literate will often be fascinated by the things that computers can do. Aquarian artists may enjoy the fun of painting by computer or playing with three-dimensional images on a computer screen.

Aquarians may be drawn to create or collect pieces of artwork or sculpture that incorporate the use of light or electricity in some way. Lasers, holographic images, trick photography and clever uses of circuitry will all delight and amuse. Aquarian painting or writing may also be quite electric in nature, involving luminous colours, flashes of light, startling words or concepts and rapid changes of mood or direction.

Aquarians are often willing to experiment with any number of creative forms. They often show an innate ability to do many things well on the first attempt but some do not always persist for long enough to become expert. Some Aquarians can lose interest in a project very quickly, particularly if they grasp the basic skills quite readily. Perhaps they are always keen to be sampling something new.

When creating anything from a poem to a pasta dish, Aquarians can find great healing, satisfaction, fun and balance in the creative process. The trick is to keep going with a project regardless of the distractions.

The Aquarian mind can also swing dramatically between overly judging the object of creation and not being discerning enough. The former can kill the seeds of creativity before they begin to grow, not leaving them the space to find their own organic way and the latter does not allow for creative maturity. The way to a healthy balance is to create, write, paint or draw first without judging and then when the initial outpourings are complete, the genius Aquarian mind can gently assess the changes or improvements that need to be made. The process of seeing the project through will bring about a sense of peace and well-being.

Fire Affirmations for Aquarius

I have a constant circulation of bright, creative ideas.

I see a healthy future with my clear vision and bright thoughts.

I re-invent myself in brightness and beauty.

I am fired by my laser clarity and creative brilliance.

I persist in my creative passions.

I am free to follow my guiding light and higher purpose.

Fire Visualisation: Charging up the Aura

Breathe and relax. As you do, imagine yourself surrounded by a field or aura of subtle electricity. This may look like a mass of laser lights or a fine web of electrical blue or white threads.

Notice any area where this aura of energy is weakened or depleted, perhaps because of illness, imbalance or fatigue. You have the ability to strengthen this energetic field and replenish these weakened areas. See yourself drawing in natural electrical light from the air around you that instantly repairs these areas, enhancing your power and vitality.

Imagine yourself being able to contract and stretch this aura at will. With a single thought see yourself draw in this subtle electrical field to within a couple of inches from the outline of your physical body and then spread it out a few feet in all directions. In your thoughts, picture yourself practising this a few times until it is both strong and elastic. In the process of doing this, see that your electrical lights are growing brighter than ever.

Once again see your aura contract and, as it does, imagine it becoming imbued with your inspirational, creative thoughts. When the field of light expands out again, imagine it creating many beautiful, innovative and healing things around you for you to enjoy. Your creative abilities also expand as you see your auric light conjuring up beautiful crystalline shapes, perhaps, or sculptures of shining metal and light, potent words or anything else that would heal and inspire you at this time.

> When you complete, imagine your aura of electrical
> lights coming to rest in a healthy, regenerated state just
> a few inches around every part of your physical body.

EARTHING AQUARIUS

Aquarians have an abundance of mental energy and quick-
witted genius that they need to learn to harness and use in
practical, down-to-earth ways. The element of earth
challenges Aquarius to bring all of that vision, abstract logic,
conceptual awareness and idealism into a tangible form that
can have a practical, social impact. This is both exciting and
testing for Aquarians who can be so far ahead of themselves
with their thoughts that they are compelled to bring their
attention back to the present from time to time in order to
achieve this.

Aquarius best experiences the element of earth through its
ruling planet Saturn. Saturn provides Aquarians with stability,
boundaries, structures and a sense of creative limitation or
mental rigidity that allows them to retreat from the frontiers
of the abstract for long enough to get things done. The
Saturnine influence can even make Aquarians surprisingly
conventional around some aspects of career, home and family,
despite their essentially revolutionary nature.

Teamed with Aquarius' other ruling planet, Uranus, Saturn
brings form out of chaos, structure from continual electrical
change, and a safe resting place from the instability of new
thought. Once Saturn has built up the structures though,
Uranus comes zinging back in to break them up again so that
newer and better ones can be created. Nothing is held onto

indefinitely in the lives of most Aquarian people. The combination of Saturn and Uranus brings with it a powerful force of will that can sometimes seem invincible. This allows Aquarians the courage to defend new concepts that go against the norm, challenge authority and create new paths of evolution.

Aquarians can often appear to be working with a creative tension. If they become too focused on getting things done in a structured way, step by step, then they risk losing their spontaneity, getting bored and abandoning valuable projects in their entirety. If they surrender totally to their revolutionary nature then they can become unstable and risk losing their ability to have their genius come to maturity or manifestation. A healthy balance needs to be sought that keeps the mind interested and inspired while projects are allowed to come to fruition.

Aquarians love to have principles or ethical guidelines for their lives and work. If principles are drawn from their highest ideals and greater vision then they can give Aquarians the sense of responsibility that they need to be able to maintain that balance. The happiest, healthiest Aquarians are often the ones that have a greater goal or a group cause to work for. The group cause can be the well-being of the family, the collective goals of a community or professional team or even the greater good of society as a whole. Aquarians are inspired to make the world a better place.

PARTNERSHIPS, BUSINESS AND SUCCESS

Aquarians can be fiercely independent and want to work as a law unto themselves while at the same time loving to be part of a team with a common interest, striving together to achieve great things. They can expect a great deal from colleagues, employers and junior staff alike, fluctuating between being challenging or confrontational, and being highly compassionate towards the needs and shortcomings of others.

Aquarians often love to work with fiery, passionate people who bring warmth and motivation to their cool logic and high ideals. They may also need to have some solid, earthy people around them who can balance the revolutionary zeal of Aquarius with a practical, straightforward approach that ties up loose ends and ensures that ideas are workable.

Within any team Aquarius will be the innovator, the inventor, the technologist and the activist. Aquarian people are the ones who will often be developing new systems and fresh approaches for colleagues to follow through or put into action. They will find or invent the means for projects to be achieved when normal avenues or standard approaches fail.

Aquarians may sometimes find themselves as the negotiator or spokesperson for the team. They will be moved to campaign for human rights, better facilities and the funding needed to instigate worthwhile tasks. Willing to defend others who are unable or unskilled at defending themselves, Aquarians often make good union representatives, project managers and team leaders. However, they often prefer to have someone else in overall authority, above them, to negotiate with or even kick against from time to time.

Healthy professional relationships can be maintained by an appropriate sense of personal responsibility. Aquarians can be so universally fair-minded that they can sometimes make themselves overly responsible for the needs or failings of other people. Aquarians need to remember to take care of their own personal or professional development, tending to everything within their control that will make their work as fulfilling as possible while allowing others to do the same. Clear boundaries in working relationships will keep Aquarians happy and balanced.

Aquarians are often very capable at making material provision for themselves or for the people they love. Many Aquarians will have a basic feeling that they can always create money when they need it. However, it is rare for them to judge success by material gain and increases in prosperity. Money is often viewed quite dispassionately; it is frequently seen as a necessary tool that can buy experiences and provide some level of control over unforeseen circumstances.

Success for Aquarians tends to be more associated with everyone being taken care of, fed, nurtured and respected rather than with self-advancement. Aquarians will also equate success with personal recognition and being valued for the contribution that they make to a project, an environment or a social situation. In addition, success is inextricably linked to personal freedom and independence.

Earth Affirmations for Aquarius

I am free to move from success to success.

When I am successful, everybody wins.

I step forward into a financially successful future.

I work towards my greater good.

I develop a healthy, happy connection to the earth.

I tap into a healthy circulation of prosperity and abundance.

Earth Visualisation: Lightning Tree

Breathe and relax. Imagine yourself walking through a forest of tall, fragrant pine trees. It is the morning after a storm and everything is charged up with natural electricity. Feel yourself relax as you are energised by negative electrical ions, feeling a gentle breeze on your face and soft earth beneath your feet.

In your mind, as you picture yourself walking, picture, too, your own natural electricity buzzing around your mind, filled with power, positive intentions, creative concepts and healing thoughts. Your mind has a limitless supply of energy and inspiration.

Find a tree that is particularly beautiful or majestic and in your thoughts ask it to help you earth and utilise all of this energy. Visualise yourself placing your hands on the trunk and, as you breathe, see all that electrical energy moving from your mind, down your spinal column, down your legs, through your feet and into the earth. The tree is stabilising you and helping you to connect to the ground beneath you.

As you discharge this energy, imagine an equal and opposite charge of earth energy moving up through your feet and circulating around every part of your body, filling you with the balance and structure you need to complete tasks and help your ideas to bear fruit.

In your mind's eye, look around you and see that the forest is filled with wonderful, tangible things that your thoughts have created. See images of the material things that you wish to create: money, a new home perhaps, a healthy body, a better working environment for you and your colleagues; whatever it is you currently desire. Thank the tree for its help and remove your hands from the trunk so that you can move around and physically touch the material objects or situations that you have created.

When you complete this visualisation, write down or record any practical steps you can think of that will help you to create these things in your life on the physical plane.

CARRYING THE ELEMENT OF WATER

The element of water can be both a challenging and a fulfilling companion for the Aquarian soul. Water is the realm of the emotions, an uncertain area of experience for rational, detached Aquarius and yet there is a special relationship that allows Aquarians to discover many gifts within this world of feelings.

The Aquarian image of the water-carrier can represent many things. It can be seen as Aquarius' tendency to harness emotional energy and carry it to higher realms of expression. This may be demonstrated by the many Aquarian people who become angels of mercy in times of crisis or human need. Many are able to transform life situations with a detached compassion that allows them to take the necessary practical or logical steps. They are able to take appropriate loving action because they are not too emotionally involved.

The image of the water-carrier can also represent the Aquarian tendency to direct their emotional energy into higher visions of the future; psychic or prophetic abilities and the expansion of higher awareness. Many Aquarians are highly intuitive but this is a more conceptual intuition than the gut feelings of water signs. The waters of emotion are carried upwards as fuel for a visionary mind and are often expressed through the concepts of universal love or brotherhood.

Another interpretation of this image is of the Aquarian soul who is unable to deal with the irrational power of their emotions, perhaps containing them or detaching them from the rest of life. This is the Aquarian who conceptualises or over-analyses each life experience rather than allowing themselves the appropriate feeling: a sophisticated denial of the emotional impact that events can have on us all.

It is possible to find a hint or flavour of all of the above in the emotional lives of Aquarian people. The healthy balance for Aquarians is to harness the positive qualities of vision and higher compassion while learning to connect to emotions in their raw, irrational state. Aquarian logic is brilliant but it needs a little irrational water to provide some substance, sensuality and fun.

LOVE AND ROMANCE

Romantic involvement can be both tantalisingly seductive and unnerving for Aquarian people. The Aquarian mind is stimulated by the opportunity to interact with another person and enjoys the thrill of a new relationship. What is more, Aquarians love friendship and sharing so they are constantly on the lookout for an interesting new companion.

When companionship turns into romance Aquarians can feel excited and be filled with positive anticipation. At the same time they may experience fears or have an emotional cut-out mechanism that can make them want to run off in the opposite direction. Aquarians often yearn for or desire love; it is just that romantic involvements may challenge them to get out of their heads and into their hearts and this can leave them in uncertain territory.

Aquarians value their freedom and independence and one anxiety may be that in becoming emotionally involved they will forfeit their right to be free or unencumbered. Some may also fear that their choice of one person or one situation may limit all other future choices. The desire for constant change can be so strong that they need to choose a partner who is going to fulfil their shifting expectations or aspirations. Perhaps for this reason many Aquarians opt for periods in their life when they do not have a romantic involvement of any kind and many will actively enjoy this.

Others may choose to live alone while enjoying short-term relationships and superficial romantic contact. Aquarians can be very self-contained and have a love affair with life that can be as fulfilling as any love affair with another person. The choice to marry or have a long-term loving involvement may inevitably come from the Aquarian need and aptitude for sharing.

The ideal partner for Aquarius will be someone with their own desire for independence and freedom. Aquarians often appreciate someone with a spark of fire who is self-contained and able to match up to their own changing expectations. Even more ideal would be a partner who is able to balance their ability to rise to the challenge of change with an underlying stability that will keep the partnership anchored and safe.

Aquarians, while radical or independent, can often be

quite conventional in their choice of partner, reflecting the fixed nature of their sign. When they do commit to a relationship they can be very loyal and keen to do the right thing even as they strive to rebel against real or perceived limitations and conventional expectations.

For Aquarians to develop healthy relationships it helps to follow some basic guidelines. Fall in love with the person as they really are and not as you ideally hope that they will become in the future. Notice any qualities in your partner to which you aspire, and take time to acknowledge and develop those qualities within yourself. Regularly discuss and renegotiate a balance of commitment and independence that will suit you both as you continue to change. Allow yourself to get in touch with your emotions and learn to demonstrate your feelings to your partner.

Aquarians make stimulating partners who can fulfil many of the romantic needs of the people they love through their enthusiasm, fun and an exciting repertoire of new ideas and adventurous possibilities. Their relationships work because of their wonderful companionship skills. They are able to maintain a good friendship in spite of the daily ups and downs of emotional situations. They will often remain loyal to their partner even when there are some areas of disagreement. Aquarians express a wealth of care by defending the needs or rights of their partner; they are highly protective of their loved ones.

Water Affirmations for Aquarius

I carry my emotions with joy.

I am served by my heart as well as my head.

It is safe for me to fall in love.

I flow with the currents of higher compassion.

I create a healthy balance between intimacy and independence.

I open up to a positive vision of my future.

Water Visualisation: The Water-Carrier

Breathe and relax. Picture yourself as a water-carrier, tall and elegant. Your image can be male or female. See yourself bearing a jug of crystal-clear water that sparkles and bubbles with magical healing powers.

As you breathe, visualise yourself pouring water from the jug gently over your head and see it trickling down over your body to cleanse away any tensions and heal any physical pain. Imagine your stresses gently washing away from you and dispersing, leaving you clear, open and relaxed.

In your mind's eye, steady and level the jug. As you do, see it miraculously refill itself with more crystal water. This time the water is imbued with the creative power and self-healing potential of your emotions. Imagine all of your emotions as positive and transformative; love, anger, joy, sadness, passion, even pain when acknowledged and expressed can be healing. Pour the water once again and bathe in the aliveness and the healing qualities of your feelings.

Steady the jug once more and see it refill itself. This time the water is imbued with your dreams, visions, power of prophecy and higher compassion. Shower your-

self with the waters of your highest potential and awareness. See your image beginning to change, becoming
more beautiful, more wise and more intuitive. Imagine
yourself as cleansed and balanced; ready to experience
your life in new and better ways. Your higher spiritual
qualities radiating from you to cleanse and heal all of
your relationships too.

Think of anyone in your life that you need to express
your feelings to now and in your mind imagine yourself
telling them what you feel; hear your inner voice express
it word for word. 'I am angry,' 'You bring me joy,' 'I
appreciate you,' 'You make me sad,' 'I love you' – whatever is appropriate at this time. When you complete,
imagine any excess feelings gently and safely being
released.

THE SPIRITUAL PURPOSE OF AQUARIUS

Aquarians are here to learn and teach new directions of
thought; they lead the way to revolutionary life paths and
fresh approaches. The spiritual purpose of Aquarius includes
learning new ways of relating to oneself that are going to have
a bearing on humanity as a whole. Aquarius or not, when we
begin to view ourselves differently and begin to live our lives
according to new principles of freedom, understanding,
equality and compassion, then we can have a positive, knock-
on effect on the people that surround us.

Aquarians need to explore the higher principles of
sisterhood and brotherhood. If you are born of this sign, you
will need to recognise and act upon the similarities between

yourself and other people rather than react to perceived differences. When we begin to view others as an extension or reflection of ourselves then we can find ways of understanding the motivations and lives of everyone around us. This, in turn, brings us to a greater awareness of our own human nature.

The purpose of Aquarius is also to explore the fun of the new in all of its forms. New science, new technology, new lifestyles, new forms of energy and new ways to relate to other people. Aquarians are often at their happiest when they are at the forefront of discovery in whatever fields they have chosen to explore. Aquarians need to keep their lives on the leading edge of exploration, evolution and personal development.

Perhaps above everything else, Aquarian people need to learn to find some stability within the constant changes that they initiate and create. When you are compelled to break down the structures of your life on a regular basis and you are constantly reassessing what you believe to be true, there is a necessity to discover an inner core of security that can keep you balanced. The trick is to keep yourself from holding on to external, material things that can only provide temporary stability and instead learn to listen to your inner voice, your own guiding star of intuition.

THE AQUARIAN GIFT TO THE WORLD

The energy of Aquarius brings us to an age where we can begin to see ourselves as a global community. Through the Aquarian technologies that we have created such as electricity, radio, television, computers and satellites we are able to be in touch with the culture, politics, economics and needs of the entire planet. This allows us the opportunity to come to a new understanding of others. Bit by bit, Aquarius teaches us that to thrive we need to live in harmony and unity with other people as well as with the planet itself and all living things.

Aquarians often find their greatest self-healing through exploring lives dedicated to social change; the well-being of the group rather than the individual is a concern that can bring them much joy and fulfilment. Aquarians help to create environments where everyone wins, knowing that true success is a success that everyone can enjoy.

It is not surprising that Aquarians can be found in the forefront of new technologies and political change. Aquarians can be scientists, computer wizards, electricians, aviators, writers, broadcasters, social workers, politicians, psychologists, photographers or astrologers. They can also be found in the forefront of complementary therapies like homoeopathy, acupuncture and cranial osteopathy.

Aquarians bring to us all the fresh air of hope, high ideals and the potential for many new, positive, healing changes. Aquarius reminds us that healing ourselves comes with healing others too. As a world society, when we learn to take care of everyone then we too are automatically taken care of.

Healing with Water

DELVING INTO THE DEPTHS WITH THE
WATER SIGNS

Water is the element of the emotions and intuition. It is adaptable, nurturing, deeply feeling and concerned with the cleansing of the past. The people born into the element of water are perceptive, supportive, sensitive and psychic.

The three water signs are:

CANCER – CARDINAL WATER
23 JUNE – 23 JULY

KEY QUALITIES:
NURTURING, LOVING, MATERNAL, RHYTHMIC, RESPONSIVE, EMBRACING.

SCORPIO – FIXED WATER
23 OCTOBER – 22 NOVEMBER

KEY QUALITIES:
TRANSFORMATIONAL, PASSIONATE, SEXUAL, PENETRATING, POWERFUL, INTENSE.

PISCES – MUTABLE WATER
21 FEBRUARY – 21 MARCH

KEY QUALITIES:
MERGING, ETHEREAL, PERCEPTIVE, COSMIC, POETIC, PSYCHIC.

CHAPTER TEN

CANCER

23 June - 23 July
CARDINAL WATER

Cancer is the sign of the nurturing mother goddess. Both women and men of this sign can display strong maternal powers and a gifted capacity to embrace and cherish others. Extremely emotional, Cancerians are able to channel their sensitivity through practical skills, the support or guidance of other people, home-making and numerous creative outlets.

Picture a coastal scene, where craggy rocks drop away to a beach of silvery white sand and the moon sends its subtle illuminations of femininity, more mysterious than the golden male brilliance of the sun, to illuminate the tidal waters. The tides are teeming with life, the shifting, shallow expanses of water acting as a cradle for the many life forms that rock back and forth with the movement of the waves. This is the realm of Cancer, sea shallows, rock pools, spray and sand.

The symbol for Cancer is the adaptable crab, able to live in the briny waters and scuttle out onto land and into the air when the waves retreat. Like crabs, Cancerian people often appear to be hard-shelled, self-protective and impenetrable, but inside there pulses a soft centre, sensitive, vulnerable and open-hearted. This combination of sensitivity and protection often makes Cancer highly protective of other people too, particularly their family and close friends, but strangers can also find themselves guarded by a Cancerian who has detected their emotional need and felt moved to respond.

The glyph, or shorthand notation, for Cancer is made up of two curved lines, each enfolding a circular loop at the end (♋). The overall shape is reminiscent of a crab. Highly cautious in their approach to life, Cancerians tend to react to the world in a crablike manner. Crabs are generally sideways moving; advancing forward by sidestepping to and fro. They feel out their environment before taking action, rarely taking a direct path.

Cancerians can be loyal, subtle, moody and strong. They find strength through their adaptability and power through irrational thought or expression, rather than through logic. They can be tenacious and stand their ground when they need to. When on a path they rarely give up; instead they alter their approach. Why walk through a brick wall when you can walk around it?

The ruler of Cancer is the Moon. Its close proximity to the earth gives it a potent influence on human lives, rhythms, sexuality, fertility, dreams and creativity. The Moon influences the tides, atmospheric pressures and the subtle energies of the earth. Within us all it directs the feminine, receptive, intuitive drives, our bodily fluids and our latent powers.

Within each Cancerian the influence of the Moon conducts a symphony of passions, pleasures and the qualities of parenthood. The lives and the self-healing abilities of Cancer are often cyclical, returning again and again to the same emotional issues to heal, resolve, forgive and accept. Returning to the past, the inner treasures buried in the sands of time can be unearthed, addressed and washed clean.

CANCER IN ITS ELEMENT

The waters of Cancer are the foetal waters of the planet earth
containing infinite potential for new life, new growth and
evolution. All life crawled out of the sea and all land
creatures were amphibious in nature before breaking the
connection to the maternal oceans to become reptilian,
feathered or mammalian.

The element of water rules the emotions and intuition.
Cancer nurtures the inner creative pulses, irrational drives,
feelings, concealed powers and the ability to conceive new
forms of expression. Through their emotions and their inner
expansiveness, Cancerian people are able to instigate many
new ways of living. They can develop projects or schemes
with loving care, making gentle adjustments internally before
releasing their projects to the world.

Cancerian people can sometimes appear to be moody,
caught up in an inner world that defies logic. Successful
Cancerians discover health and joy by entering their powerful
inner feelings and discovering each of them to be a jewelled
treasure. We all bring forth creative and healing gifts when
we enter into our emotions rather than judging them.

Cancerians generally make wonderful parents, able to
nurture and inspire their offspring to create fulfilling lives
while protecting them as they develop. Some Cancers will
even dedicate their lives to the care of children, not only
their own but also choosing careers or interests that enable
them to care for the children of others.

Those Cancerians who do not choose to focus on children
will often express strong parental drives in other ways. They
may find themselves nurturing partners, lovers, friends,
colleagues and even their own parents at some time in their

lives. The need to nurture can be so strong that the healthiest Cancerians will often be those who have found a rewarding outlet for this special gift.

Like a crab dealing with the continual force of the waves as they advance and retreat, Cancerian people can hold on tight to their position, tenaciously guarding what is theirs against shifting external forces. Cancers will always keep a foothold on security, keeping the family together, the home going and food on the table as best they can regardless of changing fortunes.

Cancers are wonderful home-makers, providing a safe environment for themselves and their loved ones. They can be highly creative in making their home comfortable and warm, needing the constancy and familiarity of a home for themselves as much as needing to provide a stable home-life for others. The Cancerian home can even be a little womb-like or shell-like in nature, a peaceful retreat, snug and enfolding, where emotional batteries can be recharged and physical stamina conserved.

The home life of a Cancer will strongly influence their emotional, physical and mental health. Even in their home environment Cancerians need a safe space within which to withdraw, rest and contemplate their next move. This could be a room, or even part of a room, adorned with a few precious sentimental possessions where other people are forbidden to come unless on special invitation. Cancers need to maintain their sacred space.

CANCERIAN ZONES OF THE BODY

Cancer rules the breasts, the stomach and the alimentary system of digestive organs. Simply put, any part of the body that is involved in the nourishment or nurturing of the self or of another is Cancer's domain. For Cancerian women the breasts can be a strong expression of feminine power whether or not they are used to feed and comfort children. Cancerian men, too, can express much of their emotional or nurturing qualities through the chest, drawing children, partners and loved ones close to the heart.

Cancerians who are feeling particularly vulnerable emotionally tend to contract the chest area as a way of withdrawing themselves from harm. This can be particularly marked in Cancerians who have felt unprotected or criticised by their parents. All exercise that strengthens and expands the chest will be of benefit, relieving physical tensions and brightening emotional resilience.

Cancer needs to be encouraged to talk about their emotions and get things off their chest in a safe, supportive atmosphere. Every emotional ripple or current can be easily taken to heart by sensitive Cancer, so regular communication and expression is essential for harmlessly dispersing fears or resentments before they develop. The added bonus is that the physical body will stay healthier and lighter too.

The Cancerian influence in parts of the digestive system indicates that the healthy intake of food is crucial for the overall physical, mental and emotional health of the Cancerian soul. The benefits of a balanced diet and of eating meals at regular intervals are widely known; more and more we are discovering that fresh, unrefined food is the best medicine for many ailments and minor ills. Preventative medicine of all kinds requires the integration of a correct dietary approach.

Cancer could be encouraged to experiment with wholefoods, plenty of fresh fruit and vegetables, unrefined grains and foodstuffs free of preservatives. As many Cancerians love cooking, this could be an enjoyable and imaginative process of creating new dishes at home. Some Cancerians may even be drawn to explore macrobiotic cookery, which places emphasis on eating food that is indigenous to the part of the world where you live and preparing it according to seasonal rhythms.

After meals, Cancer needs to take time to relax and digest. The modern tendency to snatch a bite to eat while on the move is quite unsuitable for Cancerians, whose health depends on gentle assimilation. Taking time to refuel and recharge will bring heightened energy and balanced moods, easing the passage through the day.

In a similar way, Cancer benefits from taking time to assimilate and digest new ideas or feelings. Knowing when to slow down can ultimately save time, struggle and stress later on. For Cancer the stomach can be quite a nervous area, where unexpressed tensions or unspoken fears can be held. Gentle care of the intake and absorption of the new can bring calmness and well-being.

EXERCISE AND THERAPIES

All forms of swimming suit Cancer, from solitary, meditative glides to the competitive excitement of swimming galas. Swimming is an excellent way of building overall physical stamina and expanding the chest. Breast stroke would be ideal, particularly when emphasis is placed on correct movement rather than speed. Gentle floating on the back would be wonderful, allowing the Cancerian to feel the subtle rhythms of the water and relax into the buoyant support below, releasing physical and emotional tensions. Cancerians who enjoy swimming could also enjoy teaching others to swim, particularly children.

Sporting Cancerians will generally enjoy the comradeship and fun of team games. These provide a good balance of human contact, exercise and mental stimulation. However, as Cancerians are more likely to be drawn to group activities than to individual pursuits, it would be good to balance out the team games with some more solitary physical ventures such as mountain-climbing or a gentle jog along the beach. Regular exercise is important to help Cancerians in the elimination of excess fluid from their bodies and the breaking down of fatty tissue.

All forms of rhythmic movement would be fun and healing for Cancerians too. When alone, playing some music and swaying from side to side in time with the beat can be calming or invigorating. Cancer may also enjoy circle dancing, a form of dance or moving meditation that has seen a re-emergence in recent years.

Cancer can respond well to drumming of all kinds, either by listening to and dancing to percussive music or by playing the drums themselves. Drumming can build up arm, shoulder and chest muscles, develop Cancerian confidence and put Cancer in touch with their internal rhythms and drives. Drumming has been used for centuries in shamanic or natural medicine traditions to induce meditative states of awareness and inner peace.

Cancerians will benefit from the subtle nurturing therapies of hands-on and spiritual healing. In Western traditions there have long been gentle practices of the laying on of hands, healing through touch and healing directed through the subtle energetic fields, or aura, that surrounds or encompasses the physical body. Some of the most wonderful healers are mothers whose children have grown up and flown the nest leaving them free to develop their spiritual or psychic awareness and use those skills to help other people.

Spiritual healing can bring love, reassurance and release at the deepest levels. Cancer will always benefit from the compassionate, reassuring attentions of another person, particularly from someone with a motherly touch that nourishes the inner child of the Cancerian soul. Emotionally there is always a part of our personality that is still a beautiful little child that craves nourishment and comfort. Healing can help to take care of that need.

LOVE AND ROMANCE

Cancerians are emotional and tender lovers, and highly protective of their partners. They will often instigate the first move in relationships, even if that move is subtle or covert – a glance of an eye perhaps that draws an approach from the object of Cancerian desires. Once the other person has been attracted though, Cancer can appear to be evasive as they size up their new catch and assess them for suitability.

Perhaps because of this elusive guile, partners can find themselves drawn in to the Cancerian world of domestic bliss before they realise how involved they have become. If they are assessed as suitable then they could find themselves becoming the focus for waves of affection or nurturing that can be powerfully disarming. Cancer really knows how to bolster the ego of their mate when they choose to. They can often fall over themselves to meet the needs of those they love, showering them with blessings and providing an atmosphere of security that many will find appealing.

The ideal partner for a Cancerian will be someone who is in touch with their own feelings while being able to maintain a sense of logic or objectivity within the tides of irrational expression that is typical of Cancerian love. Cancer needs people who can keep a level perspective on life and who can balance their home-loving tendencies with a touch of exploration and adventure.

Cancerians are often happiest when in long-term, involved relationships, preferring the security of an ongoing commitment to the uncertainty of shorter affairs and flirtations. Most of them need regularity and familiarity to maintain a sense of well-being and they will scout around for a partner who can provide this. They also love to be needed and they will want to settle down with someone who values the nourishment and nurturing that they can give.

At times, Cancer can have a tendency to over-nurture or over-protect their partners. This is a path that can bring about mutual frustration and disharmony. It is generally caused by the Cancerian person losing their own inner balance in some way. The partner can find themselves swamped or smothered with attention while Cancer can feel needy, unacknowledged and resentful. To maintain healthy relationships, Cancers need to learn to direct their nurturing abilities to themselves, taking time out for their own needs, peace and quiet or creative expression.

When making love, Cancer can be sensuous, seductive and stimulating, drawing lovers into their hidden, mysterious world of feeling, fantasy and imagination. They will be attentive lovers, wishing to give pleasure and nourishment during sex but sometimes needing to be encouraged to express their own desires. Cancerians sometimes need to remind themselves that healthy, intimate relationships require a two-way communication or involvement. The better they become at communicating their own needs, the more pleasurable the experience will be for their partner, who will then feel able to give as well as receive.

Cancerians need to direct their creative energies into their own careers or vocational development rather than becoming so nurturing that they begin to live through other people. The Cancerian imagination can be powerfully vivid, and it often requires an additional, separate form of expression to that of doting partner, parent or lover.

Cancerians who can find and maintain the right balance between nurturing others and nurturing themselves can awaken a deep inner joy that will radiate out to enhance all of their relationships and have a healing impact upon the world around them. The ebb and flow of Cancerian love teaches us that loving our neighbour as ourselves is an equation; the more we love ourselves, the more love we will have to give to others.

Water Affirmations for Cancer

I trust my inner feelings.

I am always secure in the currents of life.

I easily nurture and protect myself.

My cycles are healthy and flowing.

I have the perfect balance of vulnerability and strength.

My relationships are always nourishing and supportive.

My home is a safe harbour for me to return to.

My needs are always met.

I create the perfect balance of stability and change.

I experience healing ripples of joy and peace washing through me.

Water Visualisation: Waves of Emotion

Find a quiet, comfortable place and relax, preferably lying down or sitting with your back properly supported and your body open.

Breathe deeply. As you do, picture a deserted coast-line with the waves washing in and out, extending up the beach and retreating again. Co-ordinate your breathing with the image of the waves.

As you take a long, slow, deep breath in, picture the waves rising up the sand. As you slowly and gently exhale, picture the waves falling back again. Repeat this a few times until you develop a peaceful rhythm in and out.

Imagine your emotions moving in time and rhythm with the waves and with your breath. Each in-breath brings forth a wave of emotional, creative energy to be felt for a moment before being released with the out-breath. Imagine yourself feeling full and then empty before refilling once again and continuing the pattern.

It is not important to be aware of any particular feel-ings; the idea will be enough to create an inner emo-tional balance. If you are feeling highly emotional perhaps visualise the release of the emotions bringing you positive experiences, creative opportunities, loving relationships and peace. You could see the waves casting beautiful pebbles, jewels, flowers or crystals onto the beach.

When you have completed you may choose to write down or record any feelings or impressions that you had.

CLAMBERING INTO THE AIR

The element of air is the realm of the mind. For Cancer, air brings forth the mental agility of dreams and the stirrings of the unconscious mind. Thought for Cancerians is essentially irrational and mysterious, filled with half-remembered pleasures and the stirrings of consciousness prior to physical birth and incarnation.

Cancer's highly emotional inner world does not naturally lend itself to logic and objectivity. For a healthy balance it would help Cancerians to learn to be as objective as possible. Mental and emotional well-being can more easily be maintained when the carelessness or unconsciousness of others is not taken too personally. Cancer can be so sensitive that the actions or words of other people can easily be taken to heart; a little objectivity provides a safe distance for Cancer to keep their hearts safely protected.

Objective thought can also help Cancer to stay with what is real and be aware of what is illusory. Sometimes Cancers can get so wrapped up in their own dreams and drives that they lose touch with what is really happening. In relationships, particularly, Cancer can tend to take on board the shortcomings of the other person and blame themselves for them. A little rationality can give a clear perspective on what belongs to another person and what is our own responsibility. To blame ourselves, or another, never achieves anything. Rationally assessing our choices and taking responsibility for negotiating or creating what we really want is a much healthier recipe for peace of mind and success.

Cancer can use the objectivity of the mind to find stillness and calm in an ever-changing world. Quieting the mind through chanting would be one way of achieving this. A pleasing sound, phrase or affirmation is repeated, over and over again, giving the mind a focus for stillness. The repetition can be silent and internal or sung and spoken aloud. Words like 'relax' or 'peace' may be chanted in this way to provide a pause in the tidal flow of Cancerian thought.

Many visions, impressions and ideas will come to Cancerians at night-time, when they are asleep. Dreams yielding powerful memories of childhood and of states of awareness that are beyond normal human reality give birth to new thoughts. In the morning Cancerians will be able to write up their night-time inspirations and act on them. In some cases it can benefit Cancerians to get up in the middle of the night to work, write their impressions in a dream-log or plan the day or week ahead.

Sleep is a wonderful time for Cancerians to digest new ideas and put the activities of daily life into a deeper context. For their health and well-being it is important to have regular sleep patterns and ideally as little noise or distraction as possible. Rather, it is better for Cancer to be interrupted by their own inner creative drives calling for conscious recognition and expression.

For Cancer the imagination is an essential mental tool, providing the resources to bridge all of those inner impulses to the intellect and ultimately to the outside world.

Cancerians who have neglected or rejected their imagination need to put aside their limited thinking and rediscover this resource, for it unlocks the full power of the Cancerian mind.

Air Affirmations for Cancer

I trust my imagination.

I nurture my new thoughts and ideas.

My memories of the past inspire me to a happy, healthy present.

I easily communicate my impressions as ideas.

I picture myself in full, abundant health.

I sleep easily, peacefully and creatively.

Air Visualisation: Breezes of New Thought

Find a quiet, comfortable space and relax. Breathe deeply and imagine your ideal home environment, safe and secure. The picture in your mind may be of your current home or an ideal fantasy of how you would like your home to be. Fill this home with the physical things that would help you to feel secure and comfortable. This could include photographs of loved ones, familiar objects, possessions that invoke happy memories, soft, warm furnishings, or natural things like plants or family pets.

Wherever you may physically be, imagine yourself sitting in the most peaceful spot within your home. See yourself getting relaxed and settled, able to be in a dreamy, receptive state.

If you have pictured yourself indoors, now visualise a new window, close to where you are sitting and imagine it beginning to open a little. As it does, feel soft currents of air caressing your face and filling your lungs with freshness.

If you have pictured yourself outdoors, imagine a magical breeze easing its way into your secure spot to touch and refresh you in the same way.

Either way, as the gentle air makes contact with you, imagine a fresh wave of new ideas flowing into your mind. You do not need to know what they are and even if you do, there is no need to analyse or judge them at this stage. Just visualise wave upon wave of new ideas, inspirations and impressions entering your mind at a pace that is comfortable for you – one that maintains the security of your quiet home space while bringing clarity and vigour to your mind.

In your mind ask the air to bring you any thoughts or ideas that would aid your healing at this time. For example you may think of an exercise, activity or treatment that may be of benefit for you. When you have completed this visualisation you could choose to write down or record any ideas that you had.

THE NOCTURNAL FIRES OF CANCER

The fires of Cancer are soft, subtle lights of nurturing guidance and inspiration. They can be likened to the glow of burning embers that appear to be fading away and yet underneath are vibrantly alive, filled with the potential to warm, transform and inspire. Cancerian fires are also the subtle, silvery lights of the moon, piercing the darkness to aid nocturnal travellers, drawing them home.

Cancerian people often appear to be motivated by some inner, guiding force that is mysteriously out of grasp and infinitely compelling. This inner flame drives Cancer to arrange, decorate and nourish their environment with warmth. Cancerian creativity can be expressed through gardening, interior design, home-making, soft furnishings, acting and the visual arts. Whatever form of expression they choose, Cancers will apply themselves to the task in hand with commitment and dedication, glowing with a soft inner light of inspiration.

Cancerians will be passionately motivated by the objects of their love and desire. Normally home-loving Cancerian parents can get fired up to travel great distances if their children call out in need from another part of the world. Cancerian lovers can keep an inner flame burning for absent sweethearts – one that will direct life choices and behaviour on all levels despite being subtle enough to be hidden from view. In some cases even the Cancerian themselves will not recognise that they are still carrying a candle for this cherished soul. The Cancerian flame can light the way home for many who have become blessed by these loving attentions.

Being watery in nature, Cancerians do not naturally have overtly fiery traits and are not able to go about their life's purpose in an extrovert, demonstrative way unless their Cancer Sun is complemented by more fiery placements in their birth chart. For a healthy balance it would benefit Cancer to express those subtle inner lights in a more obvious way occasionally, to tell people about the passionate nature within and spontaneously leap into the new experiences of life.

CANCERIAN INSPIRATION AND CREATIVITY

Inspiration for Cancer comes in waves or cycles. Whether focused on career projects, creative endeavours or domestic tasks, Cancerians find themselves becoming full with inspiration, a bit like ripe fruit ready to burst open, spilling an abundance of seeds into the world. Sometimes this feeling of fullness can be overwhelming, bringing with it an intensity of feelings that have to find their outlet.

At these times of fullness Cancerians will find themselves brimming with ideas, having an excess of energy and perhaps feeling like they want to do everything at once. Generally this is a time of glowing positivity, although some Cancerians become frustrated when people around them fail to respond to the urgency of this creative inspiration.

Gradually this ripe energy will find creative expression, be used and begin to wane. The ideas and inspiration will appear to retreat leaving Cancerians with a feeling of emptiness and receptivity. Motivational energy may well be low and there can even be feelings of apathy or fatigue. This is the time to be silent, take stock of life, digest recent experiences and meditate. Some Cancerians can get frustrated at this stage of the cycle because it appears that nothing is happening.

These times of low energy are an essential part of the creative pattern, and as such they need to be seen in a positive light and entered into fully. They are the times when new inspirations are received on a subtle level. There is a need for silence, sleep, entering into dreams and listening to the inner rhythms before building up again to fullness. It is the feminine part of the creative cycle without which the full, male time would not find its potency.

To some extent we all experience these cycles regardless of our Sun sign, but for Cancerian people this is a fundamental part of their nature. The times of silence, devoid of external energy and activity fire the Cancerian soul with the light and fuel needed to maximise the nurturing, creative impact that only a Cancer can make.

For women this cycle may be inextricably linked with their menstrual cycle, rising and falling with their monthly rhythms. For men the cycles of creativity may be similar or alternatively there may be a longer rhythm of ebb and flow more linked with seasonal changes. For both men and women there will also be a greater cycle of inspirational light that ebbs and flows over a period of years. Some years will be overflowing with activity while others will seem barren by comparison.

Fire Affirmations for Cancer

I heal and harness my inner flame.

I hold a light for the people I love.

I am fired with the cycles of inspiration.

I create the perfect balance of rhythm and spontaneity.

My shining creativity brings inspiration to the world.

I create new space to be filled by fresh passions.

Fire Visualisation: Silver Pathway

Breathe and relax. Picture yourself, comfortably dressed, standing alone on a beautiful, deserted beach. The sun is going down and you watch it disappear below the horizon, its golden light melting into the waves.

See the image of the moon emerging in the night sky, piercing the newly fallen darkness with its clarity but sending out beams that are soft, like a cool silvery fire. The moon shines a pathway of silver light across the water, stretching out over the waves and onto the beach.

Visualise yourself stepping into a patch of moonlight and instantly being transported across the waves on this pathway of cool moon fire. Imagine the light safely transporting you towards the horizon and towards new possibilities. In your mind's eye imagine yourself heading for a glorious future filled with health, well-being, prosperity and joy. See yourself smiling, happy, contented and surrounded by the people you love. Linger there for a while, bathing in the light and the images of your future self.

After a time allow the moonlight to bring you back from your glorious possibilities. All of those abundant eventualities are left intact for you to grow into and collect at the appropriate moment. With the light bring the strong essence of health, love and contentment back to the present to start developing in your life right now. See the moonlight shimmer around and within your body to nurture and inspire your special creativity; fuelling your rhythmic journey through life.

If you had any inspirations for the future that you

would like to set in motion right now, make sure that you write them down or record them on completing this visualisation.

CANCER ON DRY LAND

Dry land, the realm of earth, is a comfortable second home for Cancer. The adaptable crab is destined to bridge the impulses of the tidal waters to the practical solidity of the earth. Cancerian people are urged to bring the flowing impressions of their dreams into physical form, focusing at least half of their attention on worldly concerns.

Much of Cancer's earth energy goes into being a provider and protector. Cancer will be drawn to make money to keep the family and the home together; taking care of the practicalities that will maintain stability and nourishment in their lives. If money can be made from a career that provides a service or creates nourishment for other people then Cancerians may derive great satisfaction, particularly if this service puts their intense creative potential to use.

Even when times are lean, Cancer displays an extraordinary ability to make sure that basic needs are taken care of; keeping food on the table and a roof overhead. It is as if Cancer becomes magnetic to the financial or material resources needed to carry them through. Cancer knows how to adapt to times when careful budgeting is necessary as well as relaxing into relative extravagance when the coffers are full. However, there will always be something kept to one side for a rainy day.

A great deal of emotional healing is available for

Cancerians through their day-to-day world of work. The inner emotional restlessness that Cancerians may sometimes feel will find form and foundation through material ambitions and creative aspirations. Cancer will take practical responsibilities seriously but usually not so seriously that they deny themselves the joy and peace of mind that inner personal responsibility can bring.

Cancerians most easily experience the element of earth through their opposite sign, the earth sign of Capricorn. Through the Capricornian influence Cancer often becomes dedicated to ambition, taking a persistent, step-by-step approach that will ultimately bring success. The difference is that Capricorn takes a direct route upwards towards inevitable achievement, whereas Cancer will move indirectly upwards, reaping unexpected bonuses along the way.

PARTNERSHIPS, BUSINESS AND SUCCESS

Cancerians will provide the roots and stability of any partnership or business team. They will be the home base that colleagues and clients alike return to for guidance and support. For this reason Cancerians often make good co-ordinators, synthesising the skills and interests of others for the success of group projects. Cancerians can combine their nurturing skills with business acumen in personnel departments, employment agencies and branches of the caring professions, such as child care or social work.

Cancerians are able to instigate new projects because they see the needs of others so clearly. Being able to perceive what is needed in a business or domestic setting, Cancer is often able to respond easily and effectively. The Cancerian will often be able to avert a crisis or make the most of new opportunities.

This tendency can make Cancerians highly inventive, able to find alternative routes to achieving a goal that appears to be unavailable to a more direct approach. However, it is often other colleagues who will follow through these initiatives, as Cancer will be too intent on holding together the basic stability of a project to follow every new route themselves, despite their own ambition.

Cancerians benefit from working with partners and colleagues who are willing to be the travelling representatives, field workers or researchers doing the exploratory work. Cancerians will particularly enjoy colleagues that they can train or guide in some way; providing the encouragement, nurturing and emotional support that will keep everyone happy and working at maximum, creative capacity.

Cancerians are often successful where others fail purely because of their ability to hang on tightly to a goal or a prize, refusing to let go until victory is in their grasp. More dynamic competitors, rivals, or in some cases colleagues, will often get tired and give up their claim long before Cancer even considers letting go.

Cancerians can appear to have wonderful successes just drop into their laps. Colleagues can marvel at how Cancer can be magnetic to the glittering prizes that have eluded others for long periods of time. The secret of Cancer's success is often a willingness to hang in there; remaining in one place long enough to be available when opportunity knocks.

Earth Affirmations for Cancer

I deserve to have successes that easily drop into my lap.

I balance my stability with my ability to take risks.

I am credited for all of my good ideas.

My willingness to receive attracts money to me in abundance.

I manifest all that I need and all that my family needs.

I am rooted in well-being, stability and joy.

Earth Visualisation: Waves of Abundance

Breathe and relax. Picture yourself as a beachcomber walking barefoot along warm, satin sands and watching the waves washing in and out.

Feel the sun on your back and the support of the earth beneath you as you walk up and down, searching for the treasures that the sea has cast out onto land to be discovered and enjoyed. Perhaps you visualise yourself finding beautiful pieces of polished wood or pretty pieces of coloured glass that have been worn smooth by the waves and sand.

You could see yourself collecting colourful bottles, each with a special creative message or prosperous idea written on parchment that is curled up inside. Imagine yourself placing these bottles to one side so that you can read their contents when you most need them. See the parchments ready to unravel themselves in your dreams or when they can be of most use during your working day.

Visualise yourself collecting a bright, shining coin made from solid silver. Imagine how it would feel in your hands before casting it into the water and allowing the waves to carry it away. When the waves rush up the beach once again, see them depositing a pile of silver coins at your feet.

Repeat this process, keeping some coins and casting others back into the water. Again, visualise the waves depositing a pile of silver at your feet, this time bigger than before. Each time you repeat the image, see your wealth increasing and imagine yourself tapping into your own ability to attract infinite abundance.

Imagine yourself collecting together all the objects that you have collected, coins, glass, bottles, stones, wood, or perhaps even gems or pieces of sculptured metal. Picture them all dissolving into the silvery light of Cancerian prosperity, abundance and healing. In your thoughts have this light surround and fill your body, making you magnetic to the love, health, money or joy you wish to attract. See the light enhancing your ability to manifest whatever you need, materially or otherwise.

THE SPIRITUAL PURPOSE OF CANCER

The energy of Cancer fills the world with love, care, stability and nurturing for us all, increased by the powers of creativity and physical manifestation. Cancerian people greatly enhance the lives of all who come into contact with them, and this needs to be balanced by them learning to enhance their own lives.

Cancerians need to learn to bring love and care to themselves; providing themselves with gentle encouragement, creative and material nourishment and positive self-parenting at all times. In doing so, they can extend their ability to love and care for their families, friends and colleagues.

When Cancer becomes so involved in the nourishment of others to the point when they neglect their own needs, they can build up underlying resentments and create disharmony within their relationships. They can also create for themselves patterns of weariness that could develop into deep fatigue.

This can be like a parent who has for too long been the first to work and the last to sit down to eat, burning the candle at both ends and not properly refuelling in an effort to care for everyone else in the family. Without rest and nourishment this parent is likely to get sick and be unable to provide for anyone else. What is more, the emotional atmosphere of the family may also sour.

The spiritual purpose of Cancer requires that Cancerians maintain their own emotional and material well-being first so that they may better serve others. Cancer needs to give to the world from a state of being replenished, full-hearted and having abundant resources on which to draw. In this way the quality and quantity of their gifts to others can be maximised.

Spiritually, Cancerians need to learn about physical manifestation, channelling formless abstract inspirations into physically tangible events and creations. Being a Cancer is an ongoing lesson in how to bring peace and love of the highest quality into daily life, and using the imagination to bring into the world the kind of healing that is as far-reaching as parental love.

While doing this, Cancerians need to become the most

tender, loving parents to themselves. As adults we all carry an inner child within us that has the joys, fears, strengths and insecurities that we had when we were small. Cancer or not, the benefits of taking time to listen to our inner child and respond to our own deepest needs are enormous.

THE CANCERIAN GIFT TO THE WORLD

The energy of Cancer provides us all with many of the nurturing and healing qualities needed for us to bring comfort to each other. We need the Cancerian influence in the world to provide us with a sense of home, roots, family and security, both externally through our relationships to other people and internally through the discovery of our own rhythms and cycles.

Cancerian people can be found in many nurturing roles such as those associated with child care, nursing, healing, gardening or situations where a nurturing service can be provided like hotel management and some branches of catering. Creative Cancerians are also drawn to many aspects of the visual or performing arts as well as the art of home-making. Cancerian ambition is often channelled into the many skills required to accomplish domestic success and family harmony. Cancerians can be historians, archaeologists, estate agents or sailors, expressing strong interests in the past, property and navigation.

Cancerians remind the world of the power of dreams, helping us to look beyond what is logical and conscious to find answers to the mysteries of life. Dreams bring with them many inspirations that will instigate new approaches to the adventure of being alive.

Perhaps above all, Cancer is the healing power of the mother touch. Strong, capable, forgiving and unconditionally loving. The people of this sign truly are a gift to the world.

CHAPTER ELEVEN

SCORPIO

23 October - 22 November

FIXED WATER

Scorpio people are perceptive, intuitive, sexual and seductively intense. They have gifted minds that can penetrate and solve the mysteries of the universe, teamed with a lustful desire to seek out and uncover all that is hidden.

Scorpio is the sign of constant transformation. Scorpios are the phoenix rising from their own ashes, emerging triumphant from the past into a better life. Scorpionic people experience within themselves a continual process of death and rebirth; in so doing they are the catalysts of much change, healing and self-discovery for us all.

Scorpio is compelled to discover and bring to light many secret inner powers. This compulsion facilitates healing on all levels, physical, emotional, mental and spiritual. A Scorpio person who is able to harness these healing gifts can create for themselves many miracles, large and small.

The most popular symbol for Scorpio is the Scorpion, tail poised to sting others or even herself. In many branches of medicine, conventional or complementary, drugs and herbal remedies that can be used as deadly poison can also provide life-giving cures. In the same way Scorpio can take the challenges of life and turn them into wonderful opportunities or confront the darker side of their personality, converting it into lightness and positivity. The glyph, or shorthand notation, for Scorpio is like an 'M' with an arrow on the end; the arrow perhaps being reminiscent of the Scorpion's tail: ♏ .

In many cultures around the world there have been shamanic or folk-healing traditions passed down from ancient times that have viewed the endurance of poisons, whether physical, mental, emotional or psychic, as a rite of initiation. Individuals who were able to look upon their fears, insecurities, negativities or limitations and turn them all into strengths would have earned the right to greater personal power. That power included the development of wisdom and the gifts of inner peace. Scorpio has the potential to do this, moving towards greater and greater illumination.

For a water sign, Scorpio also contains a strong burst of energy from the other elements. This is partly due to the influence of its two ruling planets, Mars and Pluto. The fiery planet Mars lends Scorpionic emotions a passionate intensity, while the earth connection comes through Pluto, god of the underworld, who leads Scorpio into its hidden depths. Both have a powerful influence that can help Scorpios to experience the ecstasy of their own creative drives and psychic potential.

Scorpio people who have mastered their Scorpionic selves can be piercingly wise; those that have not can be clouded in seductive dramas or disturbances. All have mystery and magic.

SCORPIO IN ITS ELEMENT

The element of water courses with the emotional and psychic depths of Scorpionic expression. Scorpio nature is intensely feeling and most Scorpios experience a rich and dramatic range of emotions. They revel in the passionate sensuality of being alive. This can mean extreme highs and lows with powerful swings from one to the other.

The waters of Scorpio can be likened to the deeper caverns of the sea, many of which still remain uncharted territory, or to underground courses rushing through hidden tunnels of rock miles below the surface of the earth. Scorpio feels very deeply about life, love, intimate relationships, sex and the issues of the world. A Scorpio person will often experience a powerful attraction to the objects of their desire and they will want to experience an intense unfolding of their relationships with hot-blooded drama.

Water cannot be easily contained. A hole through which water leaks will often grow rapidly as more and more water escapes. Similarly, Scorpio emotions defy restriction and Scorpios can be carried away by the blissful flood of their own love or desires. It is not surprising, then, that Scorpio very often makes decisions that are more motivated by feelings than reason. Relationships can be plunged into with an astonishing intensity of courage, compulsion, lustful glee and foolhardiness.

Much healing is available for Scorpios through the exploration of the psychic, mystical or esoteric. The Scorpio soul certainly contains an innate psychic potential which some may choose to develop. Even for those Scorpios who do not elect to explore their own psychic gifts, books, television programmes or lectures on psychic phenomena may hold some fascination.

Scorpios can use the symbolism of esoteric or spiritually based philosophies to give focus and meaning to their inner world. Divination tools like the Tarot, Nordic rune stones and the I Ching could be helpful, not necessarily as a means of divination but to promote understanding of the self and the deeper drives of the personality. All of these systems have a visual component to their use, particularly the Tarot, which would help Scorpio to externalise deeper impulses and feelings, learning to see themselves with greater objectivity.

Scorpio nature is always probing for the inner spiritual source. The contemplation of the mystical or the meditative is a useful way of putting aside the business or busy-ness of daily life and finding a place of inner silence that can provide a multitude of healings. Being around a Scorpio can be a stimulating experience; many have a compelling personality or appearance and an air of potent danger, spirituality or sexuality. The sense of secrets and deep feelings that Scorpio has can be very seductive.

SCORPIO ZONES OF THE BODY

Scorpio rules the genitals, bladder, urethra, colon and rectum. Those parts of the body concerned with sexuality, reproduction and elimination. The comfort and health of these areas can be an excellent barometer for the overall physical or emotional state of the Scorpionic soul.

Elimination on many levels is the key to maintaining good health for Scorpio people; care needs to be taken to ensure that the diet is rich in water and fibre as well as a good natural balance of vitamins and minerals. Fresh fruits with a high water content are excellent for flushing through the system and cleansing the Scorpio physique of toxins. Melon is particularly good as it has the highest water content of any fruit and moves very quickly through the stomach. Fruit is perhaps best eaten in the morning when the body is involved with the elimination part of the digestive cycle.

It does not serve Scorpionic health, physical, emotional or psychological, to hold onto anything that is outworn, outmoded or complete. The healthiest Scorpio is the one who has learned to flow with life, realising that each experience needs to be embraced and then released, making way for new and better areas of growth and stimulation. This can be like a snake shedding a skin that has become old, and restrictive, allowing a new, healthy skin to emerge. Scorpios often feel lighter, freer and more expanded after one of their many life transitions, almost as if they had bathed and put on newer, more comfortable clothing. They feel cleansed from the inside out and they carry a feeling of having grown into themselves a little more.

Bowel and bladder movements provide an indication of the Scorpionic state of mind or state of being. Diet aside, a Scorpio person who is fearful of life or resistant to change may notice that their body reflects this by becoming constipated or irregular, or by retaining fluid. If this is the case then the Scorpio may need to ask themselves, 'What am I holding onto that no longer serves me?' 'What am I scared of?' Very often, the simple acknowledgement of the fear or resistance itself is enough to get things moving again.

Scorpios need to encourage themselves to move forward constantly, letting go of the familiar and moving into the wonderful mysteries of the unknown. Fears can be channelled into positive motivational energy rather than being seen as a disabling force. It just takes some practice and patience with oneself to plunge into the adventure of life despite the churning in the pit of the stomach. Transformation is so fundamental to the basic nature and purpose of Scorpio that it needs to be entered into as fully as possible. For those Scorpios who rise to the challenges and opportunities of their lives the benefits are endless.

The genito-sexual areas of the body and the psyche need care and attention. Usually these areas stay vibrantly healthy unless a Scorpio person is experiencing some mental or emotional stress. In sexual relationships the libido is mostly vibrantly active and to the fore except when there has been some area of disagreement or misunderstanding that has upset the Scorpionic sensibilities.

It can sometimes take a heated discussion or even a row for the mood to shift and the sex drive to be back at full throttle. Any underlying anger or resentment needs to be talked about and acknowledged for sexual healing to occur fully. It would help for Scorpio to develop a positive attitude to their own sexuality, free of guilt and full of self-acceptance. For many of us the embarrassment and uncertainty around sexual or emotional issues that we learnt from our parents, and which they in turn learnt from their parents, needs to be talked about and broken down so that we can take full pleasure in our bodies without guilt, fear or shame.

A Scorpio deprived of full sexual or emotional expression either through a strictly prudish upbringing or in relationships with overly cool partners can feel restricted and frustrated. For some there could be a pressure-cooker build-up of their sexual and creative energies that may be unbalancing. Sooner or later all of this energy will have to find some kind of outlet; it would serve Scorpio to handle all pent-up feelings positively and constructively rather than becoming stressed, sick or explosive.

Creative pursuits of all kinds are good for Scorpio and provide a safe and healthy release for some of that sexual power. It may also help to have some individual counselling sessions to discard old, sexual guilt and fear or relationship counselling for both partners in any relationship that has become stuck within sexual or emotional frustrations.

EXERCISE AND THERAPIES

As for all of the water signs, swimming is wonderful for relaxation, general toning and for reminding Scorpios of their uncontainable watery nature. More active Scorpios may consider taking up diving as a direct physical expression of the Scorpionic ability to dive deep into the self and into the mysteries of life. Some may enjoy building up their muscles and strengthening their lungs with bursts of underwater swimming or perhaps learning life-saving skills.

Massage of all kinds is excellent for Scorpios, helping them to become attuned to the sensuality of the whole body rather than being overly focused on the genital area. As well as utilising the skills of massage therapists, Scorpio would be well advised to take themselves and their partners off on a basic massage course so that they can broaden their repertoire of intimate physical expression, giving and receiving in ways that are mutually pleasurable and fun.

One of the best massage therapies for Scorpio is the oriental practice of Shiatsu. Like Scorpio itself, this discipline is deeply penetrating as pressure points around the body are stimulated by the therapist's fingers, elbows and sometimes feet. This opens up or unblocks invisible energetic meridians that run throughout the body, allowing for a healthy flow of the body's chemical or electrical impulses.

The practice of rolfing is another deeply penetrating

physical therapy that could be beneficial for Scorpio. A rolfer works by straightening out and realigning the deep tissue of the body that is called the fascia. This is both helpful in correcting the nuts and bolts of the posture and in facilitating an emotional release of old, pent-up feelings.

For the Scorpion who is plagued by vague nervous complaints, fatigue or toxicity, a course of colonic cleansing might be considered. This involves the colon being flushed out with water to remove the build-up of undigested food and other substances that the body has been unable to eliminate. This is not suitable for everyone and needs to be undertaken by a trained colonic therapist who is aware of the physical comfort and the sensibilities of the client. After cleansing, the therapist sometimes inserts a herbal mixture that acts as a tonic for future elimination.

Scorpios seeking deep emotional or psychological release may consider a course in rebirthing. This is a guided therapy that uses deep breath work to access and liberate deeply held emotional memories. The name 'rebirthing' comes from the experience that many people have had of reliving and healing birth traumas. A recent variant on these techniques is 'vivation', in which there is less emphasis placed on birth trauma and more emphasis on the release of tension.

All exercise programmes that focus on the region of the groin, anus and base of the spine will benefit Scorpio. A course in belly-dancing would be fun and will stimulate these areas. Alternatively, gently tensing and relaxing the muscles of the anus, lower stomach and genital area on a regular basis can aid relaxation. Any form of spiritual healing or chakra balancing could also be best focused on these areas of the body. The bottom of the spine is the location of the base chakra which is the lowest of the seven main subtle energy centres of Indian yogic tradition. The other six follow the line of the spinal column upwards to a point above the head. This base energy centre relates to the basic survival issues within us all and as such it often needs a great deal of love and attention.

LOVE AND ROMANCE

An ideal partner for Scorpio will be someone who is willing to explore the deeper mysteries of love and romance. A relationship with a Scorpio will often prove to be a richly penetrating experience that delves into the depths of the soul. It would be helpful if a prospective partner could also bring some lightness to balance Scorpio's depths and a little rational thought to balance the emotional intensity.

Scorpio people possess gifts that bring them and their partners much joy. One such gift is an intense sexuality. Through sexual expression Scorpios are able to surrender to their passionate feeling nature, giving and receiving much pleasure. A sexual involvement with a Scorpio can be profoundly spiritual, perhaps meditational in essence at the same time as being steamy, lusty and deliciously sensual, such is the range of Scorpionic expression.

Once in a romantic or sexual relationship Scorpio can be both extremely giving and demanding. Scorpio instantly forms deep connections, often longing for a profound, transformative, lasting union with the other person. This can be beautifully stimulating and thrilling for both parties. It is quite a disarming adventure to enjoy the company of someone who feels so intensely for you and many are drawn into the mysterious inner world of a Scorpionic union.

Some Scorpios can, however, be so desirous of this connection that on occasion they become possessive, jealous or even suspicious of their loved one's attentions. Scorpio often expects their own intense desires to be matched by their partner and can be disappointed if this is not so. Some Scorpios may even require passionate or dramatic demonstrations of love on a regular basis and can even feel a little frustrated by partnerships that do not give them this.

It is important for Scorpios to remember that some of their desires for a deep soul connection with another person really spring from their basic need to connect deep within themselves to their own spiritual and creative source. By focusing inward on their feelings, motivations and drives, Scorpios can find great healing, emotional and otherwise. When Scorpios are willing to do the inner work that facilitates their own personal development then their relationships too will undergo a positive transformation. A little quiet time away from their partner to meditate and contemplate, or even to have a long relaxing bath, could see some Scorpios claiming their birthright of inner ecstasy and bringing a greater level of bliss to the relationship.

When entering and exploring relationships, even the intense friendships that Scorpio can enjoy, it helps the Scorpio person to remember that all relationships are healing ones, all are transformative, and all have their benefits regardless of the outcome. The healthiest Scorpios are those that have learnt to weather the quieter, less demonstrative moments of any union and can enjoy the stillness as much as they enjoy the passionate activity that they often revel in. Sometimes in the silence and peace, deeper feelings of love, joy and passion can be discovered and strengthened.

Water Affirmations for Scorpio

My feelings are my power.

I am safe with my desires.

I swim to the source of my peace and my power.

I enjoy the full range of my sexual and emotional expression.

I experience and enjoy my inner ecstasy.

I let go of the old and embrace the new.

There is always more to love within myself.

I am safe with all of my feelings.

I dive into the magical mysteries of life.

I penetrate the wisdom of the world.

Water Visualisation: Charting the Depths

Find a quiet, comfortable place and relax, preferably lying down or sitting with your back properly supported and your body open rather than curled up.

Close your eyes and breathe deeply, imagining that you are able to breathe right the way down to the base of your spine and into the area of your groin, bladder and rectum. As you do, picture yourself diving deep into an inviting blue ocean. Discover that it is easy to breathe down there; you do not need special equipment and you feel safe as you plunge downwards. See yourself moving easily and fluidly, a lantern clasped in one hand that brightly illuminates the waters over a wide area around you.

When you reach the ocean bed, picture yourself finding an underwater cave. With your light you easily locate the entrance and go inside. In your vision, find that the cave is filled with fresh air and space; see yourself beginning to explore.

Taking your light, seek out the treasures of this underwater cavern. You may discover gemstones, sunken treasures like golden caskets, or coins and beautiful pieces of coral. Ask your mind to present you with symbols or images of the buried treasures within yourself and be aware of any ideas that you have, even if they seem incongruous or out of place. What special talents, powers or inspirations have you hidden from yourself? What does your deeper self need to tell you or show you? Imagine collecting your treasures together before finding your way out of the cavern and ascending easily to the surface of the ocean. Take your inner treasures to the air and the light, and, as you do, picture them transforming every area of your life. See your relationships, your health, your home and your career healing and becoming more positive, touched by your newfound qualities as they emerge.

On completing this visualisation you may choose to write down or record any insights or inspirations that you have had about your deep inner world.

THE FIERY PASSIONS OF SCORPIO

Scorpio has a strong relationship to the element of fire through its ruling planet Mars. Mars gives Scorpionic people a great deal of will, courage and determination. Mars can also provide Scorpio with physical strength and resilience; most Scorpios can find some reserves of energy to help with the process of healing when needed.

The deep red lights of Mars can endow an individual with a good bodily resistance to disease and can be called upon to dissolve survival fears, real or imaginary. Within Scorpio, Mars provides a driving energy to fuel Pluto's transformative power; the two forces complement each other very well and both are necessary for Scorpionic evolution.

Fire energy is the source of human and spiritual desire, so it is no surprise that Scorpio is one of the most passionate signs of the zodiac, not just sexually but through all avenues of expression. Scorpios can be passionately committed to projects, relationships, ideologies, deep feelings and the challenges of life itself.

This passionate nature can lead Scorpios to be pioneering, vigorous, brave and strong even at times when they are not feeling it. Fired up by a quest for power, Scorpios are determined to make their mark in the world. In some cases Scorpios become too driven by their desire to succeed and can become headstrong, jealous or ill-tempered. Fiery Scorpionic drives can just as easily be used as a powerful force for positivity.

It is wonderful to have a strong will that can take you to the top of your chosen field, but it needs to be kept in balance with other physical, emotional and mental needs. True success comes with listening to all of your inner voices and

taking loving care of all aspects of your personality, not just
the one that wants to win no matter what the consequences.

SCORPIONIC INSPIRATION AND CREATIVITY

The fiery passions of Scorpio need to be channelled creatively
if health and balance are to be maintained; their purpose is to
be the creative part of the transformation cycle. Regardless of
the energies that a Scorpio person directs into their work or
relationships it is important to reserve certain avenues of
creativity that are purely for the self and not for the approval,
benefit or whim of others.

Any Scorpio person who finds themselves resentful of the
time and energy that they channel into others would be well
advised to open their diary and book themselves time for
their own expression. 'Thursday, 2.00 p.m. – dancing' or
'Saturday morning – gardening' perhaps. It is amazing how
much additional, positive energy can be created to deal with
the million and one things that always need doing when you
firmly say 'stop' and take some time out for yourself.

Scorpios often benefit from an involvement with sensual
art forms that require them to roll up their sleeves and plunge
in their hands. Scorpios may enjoy working with clay, thick
paints, sand or highly textured cloth. Scorpios love to be
tactile and fully involved with their medium. Visual or
performing arts for Scorpio need to be highly sensual,
passionate, full-blooded and rich in images. This is true of
both the art forms they create themselves and those created
by other people; many Scorpios love to have their emotions
stirred by powerful symbolism.

A source of light or inspiration for Scorpio could be

naturally formed crystals. Crystals are Scorpionic in nature being created by intense underground pressure (Pluto) and in many cases being able to reflect or channel energy and light (Mars). Experts in Feng shui, the Japanese art of healing the environment, often advise people to hang crystals in windows to bring vital energy, called *chi*, into rooms that are lacking in balance and prosperity.

Crystals hung in this manner in a Scorpionic household could well bring in much-needed light, particularly in the winter months. Any Scorpio person residing in a part of the world where the winters are dark and grey could well benefit from acquiring a light box as a way of making up for the deficiency of natural sunlight. These special electrical lamps are proving to be invaluable for many people, not just Scorpios, who suffer midwinter depressions through lack of light.

Scorpionic fire can also be likened to a forest fire, dramatically clearing away the old, dead wood and making space for new growth. A Scorpio person entering a new job or environment can often bring this forest fire tendency with them, proving to be a catalyst for transformation. This is a highly positive Scorpionic quality although it isn't always appreciated by those who fear or resist change.

Scorpio can be like a phoenix rising from the ashes, building a fire of passions within themselves to clear away all real or perceived limitations before rising triumphant to reap the rewards of transformation. Scorpio has an incredible capacity to transcend their situation. Faced with a lack of time, money or energy, or feeling scared, Scorpionic fire can often find a way to push through and succeed, becoming renewed, recharged and enlightened.

Some Scorpios may be unsure of how to use or channel

their fiery passions; sometimes the most available way of expressing fiery energy is through sex, conception and birth. This is one reason why Scorpio is such a sexually focused sign. However, there are many other wonderful possibilities for passionate expression. One only needs to think of the exquisite beauty of sunlight shining or bouncing off the surface of a deep lake to realise that Scorpionic energy has infinitely beautiful possibilities.

Fire Affirmations for Scorpio

I am a shining crystal of light.

I am filled with enthusiasm for life.

My inner lights guide me to greater peace and joy.

My path through life is illuminated with love.

I am the pioneer of my life's adventures.

I tap into my courage and vitality.

Fire Visualisation: Jewelled Flower

Sit with your back properly supported or lie down so that your spine is as straight as possible.

Imagine that at the base of your spine there is a beautiful deep red crystal, pulsing with its own inner light. Place your attention in this part of your body and breathe deeply, picturing the light from within the crystal glowing brighter and brighter.

Next, imagine that at the area of your solar plexus or

the centre point at the base of your ribs, there is a small golden sun shining brilliantly and as you breathe picture the light building in this area too.

See this sun send rays of light and warmth throughout your body, touching and healing all parts of you. Imagine the light moving into your emotions to heal and balance them too. Perhaps see light moving into your mind to brighten your thoughts with positivity.

As the light touches the base of your spine and the ruby red crystal, picture the crystal beginning to open out and expand into a beautiful jewelled flower that glistens with magical properties.

Imagine that your sun and your jewelled flower shine light into your immediate environment and into the world around you.

If you choose you can visualise the flower closing up again into a crystal, to keep all of your creative potential safely protected.

THE FERTILE DEPTHS OF SCORPIO

The element of earth brings form to Scorpionic transformation and additional sensuality to Scorpio's sexual drive. Scorpio forges its link to the earth in two ways. The first is through a relationship to its opposite sign, the earth sign of Taurus. The second earth connection is probably the more profound. It is the influence of Scorpio's ruling planet Pluto.

In ancient mythology Pluto was the god of the underworld who carried off the beautiful goddess Persephone into Hades to live there as his queen. Persephone's mother, the goddess Demeter, ruler of the crops and the harvest, was consumed by grief for the loss of her daughter and took revenge by putting a blight on the earth.

Zeus, father of the gods, fearing the starvation of humanity, persuaded Pluto to let Persephone go. However, as Persephone had eaten some seeds from a pomegranate that Pluto had offered her, a fruit that symbolised sexual consummation and death, she was only allowed to return to the surface of the earth for what became the fertile months of the year and forever bound to return to the underworld for the winter.

The story symbolises the seasonal cycles of death and rebirth, with seeds and plants resting for the winter months only to come to life again, flourishing in the summer. It is quite common for Scorpios to be both drawn to and fearful of the element of earth, earthly images or activities. At the extreme some Scorpios can fear periods of depression or entering a dark night of the soul where aspects of the personality that are normally submerged need to be faced.

In most cases Scorpios find that their times of inner reflection or soul-searching are filled with gifts. The healthiest and most successful Scorpios are the ones who are willing to embrace and enter into the hidden aspects of themselves. This is like a child venturing into a darkened room, night light in hand, to discover that there is truly nothing to fear. On the contrary there is usually an abundance of things in the room for that child to enjoy.

Rather than deny underlying feelings, impulses or drives and leave them to create imbalance within the body or mind, it is better to look deeply into oneself with a light in hand. The light is a willingness to explore all aspects of the personality and develop self-acceptance. This is a powerful key to healing for us all, the true essence of preventative medicine. What is more, the healing nature of Scorpio brings with it many positive opportunities for growth, enlightenment, creative expression and material gain.

Death of the old self always gives birth to the new as night gives birth to day. A good exercise in grounding, to be repeated at intervals, is the process of going through drawers and cupboards to clear out, throw away or give away anything that no longer serves you. This can be anything from old papers to clothes that no longer fit. Clearing away the old and outworn always leaves space for newer, better things. Scorpio can always benefit from using practical tasks to symbolise their mental or emotional healing process.

Scorpio's search for inner peace can be aided by the natural world. Gardens and gardening can be particularly beneficial for Scorpio health. It benefits Scorpio to stay in touch with the rhythms and pulses of the changing seasons and therefore the positive side of their Plutonic nature. Preparing a garden for winter by pruning and disposing of dead leaves can be therapeutic, and planning the garden for the spring, planting bulbs and choosing colours, will keep Scorpio focused on a positive future vision.

PARTNERSHIPS, BUSINESS AND SUCCESS

Pure Scorpio energy can bring a thrilling intensity into work or business settings. Scorpio people often find within themselves the drive and determination to handle the details of a project that others are unable to grasp, particularly if those details involve deep research and analysis.

Scorpio will always be able to do the detective work that brings forth the information needed to make all of the pieces of the jigsaw fit together; if some useful nugget of information is hidden from them they will leave no stone unturned until they find it. This makes Scorpio an excellent research person to have in any team.

Scorpios are often good at completing a task, having a fixidity of purpose, and finding resources within themselves to bring projects to a climactic conclusion. They are best served by colleagues who are able to build upon their input and follow through the flow of activity into the next new scheme, keeping things on an even keel when the Scorpionic temperament has taken a major mood shift.

Through its opposite Sun sign of Taurus, Scorpio has an innate awareness of the sensual delights of the material world. Scorpios certainly have the capacity to make and handle money if they choose to, although this is not always their first priority. Scorpios love to be powerful and the money may only be as good as its ability to extend Scorpionic ambitions and influence.

A Scorpio who is ambitious may well be more concerned with doing something that has impact and meaning rather than with pure material gain. Scorpio often seeks work that is as intensely involving as their intimate relationships, giving them penetrating contact with others, whether colleagues or clients. When material gain presents itself, most Scorpios are certainly capable of enjoying the benefits to the full. Scorpios appreciate sensual pleasures. However, many may be tempted to plough the money back into the latest project or scheme.

Success for Scorpio is often equated with coming to a state of inner peace and discovering the part of themselves that is always stable regardless of the powerful transformations or intense transitions through which they are moving. If you think of Scorpio as being like a butterfly going through its phases – egg, caterpillar, chrysalis, finally attaining its full winged splendour, then the healthiest Scorpios are those who have come to terms with and are at peace with each stage of the cycle. Success comes with self-acceptance, and stability comes with a willingness to trust the changing process of life.

Earth Affirmations for Scorpio

I am in harmony with the seasons of my life.

Fertile prosperity is everywhere for me.

My transformational purpose is funded with love.

It is safe for me to be earthed and grounded.

I unearth many powerful inspirations.

I steadily maintain myself in health and comfort.

Earth Visualisation: Seasonal Rhythms

Place your body in a relaxed, open position and breathe deeply. Imagine yourself standing next to a tree with its branches and twigs full of leaves, bright and green. See yourself placing your hands on the trunk and feeling the bark; imagine, too, that you can feel the pulse of life vibrating within the tree and in your mind have yourself attune to the strength and stability of this elegant being.

Next, picture yourself merging with the tree, becoming the tree, feeling what the tree feels, knowing what it knows. Feel your roots connecting you safely and power-fully to the earth. Allow the seasons to change and see your tree-self shedding leaves as the weather becomes colder. Think about the thoughts, beliefs, life experiences, relationships and possessions that you need to let go of from your life and see them falling away with the leaves.

Imagine yourself in the void of winter and see yourself becoming comfortable with that void. See your branches bare and your energy drawn in as you recharge your powers and receive new inspirations from your creative source. Know yourself to be rested fully in this intro-verted state.

Picture spring coming and see your tree-self growing new leaves that are even more beautiful than before. Think about the new thoughts, beliefs, relationships, life experiences and possessions that you would like to create.

When you have completed this visualisation, make a note of any changes that you would now like to make in your life. Take any practical steps that you may need to implement these changes.

ASCENDING TO THE AIR

Air is the element of the mind and of the higher mind. Scorpio's mental powers are most attuned to probing the mysteries of the universe; in doing so Scorpio is often able to connect to a higher awareness or a bigger picture of life. This is a useful tendency for Scorpios to nurture within themselves as it could prevent an over-intense involvement with their own feelings.

Scorpio will always benefit from taking time in the open air both physically and metaphorically. Physically it is very helpful for Scorpio to feel the air massaging their skin, particularly when it is warm enough to shed clothing. Mentally the positive exploration of ideas will give Scorpios a healthy perspective of their lives.

Historically the Sun sign of Scorpio has had several symbols attributed to it other than the Scorpion image that is now generally recognised. Two of the other symbols are birds – the eagle and the dove. The image of the eagle can be viewed as the soaring spirit of Scorpio that balances the desire to plumb the depths. In some traditions, particularly those of native Americans, the eagle is seen to bring illumination and clarity. The air currents that support the eagle's wings are seen as the breath of the great spirit, the higher mind and the higher streams of consciousness.

The eagle of Scorpio carries with it a refreshing air of objectivity that can oversee and put into perspective the many shifts of mood involved in Scorpionic transformation. The endless cycles of change in the inner and outer worlds of the Scorpio person can seem disorientating at times, so it is good to have a higher vision or a greater perspective of life to act as a guiding force. Scorpios who are willing to accept the challenge of a flight through the element of air could be blessed with the clarity needed to make sense of all of those creative, deeply passionate, irrational drives.

The dove is a universal symbol of peace and for Scorpio it symbolises the higher realms of transformation or ascension. Peace is perhaps the highest purpose for the Scorpionic soul and the mind is often the bridge or the vehicle to create it.

We all benefit from choosing peaceful thoughts and Scorpios may find that calming affirmations can keep them from burning out through nervous exhaustion when feelings become particularly intense.

Air Affirmations for Scorpio

It is safe for me to see the bigger picture of my life.

My thoughts are always peaceful.

I soar to the highest levels of inspiration and joy.

I enjoy and explore the powers of my mind.

My higher vision always guides me.

I breathe in the positive and breathe out the negative.

Air Visualisation: Fly with the Eagle

Breathe and relax, making sure that you have a good circulation of air available to you. Close your eyes and imagine yourself going about your life, at home, at work and socially; review your activities, feelings, thoughts and relationships at this time. Be aware of any worries or concerns that you may have.

Next, imagine your arms becoming wings, richly feathered, and your body becoming the majestically beautiful body of an eagle. See yourself take flight, leaving behind your normal everyday environment and earthly concerns; imagine the air currents gently moving upwards to support your wings as you ascend.

See yourself flying higher and higher, all burdens or responsibilities dropping away from you. As you soar, imagine yourself seeing the bigger picture of your life. Looking down upon everything, see yourself able to put all of your day-to-day concerns into perspective. Ask your eagle-self to give you any visions, ideas or inspirations for the future and make a mental note of any thoughts that you have.

Still with this sense of freedom and perspective intact, imagine yourself returning to earth and becoming human again. You may want to write down or record any ideas that you had.

THE SPIRITUAL PURPOSE OF SCORPIO

The continual thread of transformation that guides the lives of Scorpio people carries with it a multi-faceted spiritual purpose. Firstly Scorpios need to learn to master the process of transformation in itself for this can bring them to a state of acceptance. Scorpio learns to embrace change and healing as the universal order of things, becoming comfortable with the shifting rhythms of life. There is also an acceptance of all aspects of the self, light and dark, male and female, positive and negative.

Through transformation Scorpio learns to transmute any pain, fear or limitation within the psyche and transcend all self-created demons; expanding into a limitless potential of light, creativity and joy. With this comes the realisation of how powerful, magical and divine we truly are.

Scorpios need to build an awareness of what is constant

within themselves and learn to find their own innate stability rather than leaning too heavily on some external, illusory crutch. Being a Scorpio is a life lesson in the correct use of intention and energy. When any mental or emotional approach to life comes to the end of its usefulness then Scorpios will be given powerful signals that they need to make adjustments. When signs are ignored then they come back again and again until the message is understood and acted upon.

Scorpio or not, when we embrace change then life has a tendency to present us with an abundance of fun, joy and support. If we resist change then we can sometimes create events that propel us forward anyway. This is not because we are being a victim to some strange outside force; rather, it is our own higher awareness pulling out all the stops to let us know that there is a better path to follow. The mastery of Scorpio comes with recognising the signs early on and acting upon them. Even with all of its challenges, life can be simple and easy; it is we who may choose to make it hard for ourselves.

Each transformation takes Scorpios closer and closer to home, putting them in touch with their own divine spark and the realisation that it is they who are the source of their own power. Connecting to that source brings the discovery and the expansion of peace. Scorpios may well experience an extraordinary amount of self-healing in their lives. An in-built awareness of the cycles of life and death when properly utilised can bring about a desire to live life to the full and an appreciation of the limitless colour and magic of the world.

SCORPIO'S GIFT TO THE WORLD

Scorpio energy creates much healing within the world. On a global scale it is the higher vibration of Scorpio that penetrates and brings to the light all of the intrigues and dark secrets that need exorcising so that we may all live in freedom. Scorpio is a force that guides us towards the attainment of peace even if in some cases it acts as a catalyst for conflict. It brings to the surface whatever is present so that it may be released.

It is no surprise then that some Scorpios are drawn to military careers. The combination of Mars and Pluto can create effective soldiers. More often, though, Scorpios are drawn to jobs that involve them in healing or penetrative thought and action. Many surgeons are Scorpios, as are psychologists, spiritual healers, psychics and mediums.

Scorpios' skills in deep analysis can lead them to be excellent detectives, researchers or physicists. Scorpios' ability to penetrate the mysteries of the universe leads us all from ignorance to greater and greater enlightenment. The world needs constant transformation and rebirth; movement is healthy, stagnation is not. Scorpio, through the influence of Pluto, can bring about change at a deep cellular level. It is part of the force of human evolution that is helping to guide us to a new level of awareness and a new age of self-understanding.

CHAPTER TWELVE

PISCES

21 February - 21 March

MUTABLE WATER

Picture in your mind a water-colour painting, vividly tinted and yet diffuse as if the pigments are almost evaporating from the paper. Perhaps this painting is of a seascape, created in abstract and ethereal in quality. Looking into it for too long could have you drifting away into a dreamy fantasy world of sensual splendours. These are the realms of mysterious Pisces.

Pisces is the sign that completes the astrological cycle. The people of this beautifully imaginative Sun sign carry within them an aspect of each of the other eleven signs plus some very special qualities of their own. This is like a mature man or woman who has lived through all of the stages or cycles of life and who is enjoying the wisdom that maturity now brings.

Pisceans seem to have a wealth of knowledge that comes only with experience and yet they radiate a childlike innocence too. This is Pisces, infinitely old while being only one step away from a rebirth into extraordinary unknown dimensions.

Pure Pisces energy is that of the hermit, the wise man or woman, the healer, the mystic or the shaman. Look into the compelling eyes of a Piscean and you will see a soul with an innate awareness of all things universal. Look at the actions of a Piscean and you may see a person with a vulnerability and an innocence of all things worldly.

Pisces is symbolised by two fishes swimming in seemingly opposite directions whilst being bound by a cord of unifying mutual purpose. The fishes represent the polarities of Piscean worldliness and otherworldliness, extroversion and introversion, youth and age. The glyph, or shorthand notation, for Pisces is of two curved lines joined by a single straight line or thread that crosses them horizontally (♓). The two curved lines are the two fishes, perhaps representing the spiritual and physical nature of humankind that is joined yet separate.

The full symbol of Pisces is not unlike the ancient yin and yang symbol of Chinese philosophy. The bodies of the two fishes balance each other in a similar way to the black and white curved shapes of yin and yang. A single eye of each fish is like the single dots of black and white placed within the contrasting areas; black on white, white on black. Perhaps Pisces teaches us the point of understanding to which we all must come – one of divine balance and unity within ourselves and within all of creation.

The ruling planet of Pisces is Neptune, legendary king of the oceans and bringer of illusions. More than two-thirds of the earth's surface is covered in water; leagues of it still remain uncharted. Neptune is a nebulous, irrational ruler that endows Pisces with mystery, imagination and depth. The influence of this watery planet is vast and stretches into areas that are beyond human comprehension. Pisces is an expansive energy that pervades all things with a subtlety and a power that is beyond the grasp of many. Pisceans can travel into poetic states of consciousness that others have yet to reach.

PISCES IN ITS ELEMENT

The element of water is the realm of emotional expression, love, romance, intuition and psychic awareness. The waters of Pisces teem with life, activity and energy. There are a myriad of colours, forms and shapes to be found in the oceans and the Piscean personality reflects this by finding expression in an infinite number of ways.

Pisces can be a kind of shape-shifter or chameleon, adapting their personality to suit different relationships, environments or needs. This comes from an acute sensitivity both to other people's feelings and to atmospheres. This is like a fish that can detect a change of current before it happens and alter the direction in which it is swimming to utilise the energy of its surroundings accordingly.

Sometimes the real personality of a Piscean is tricky to detect as they have already adapted their behaviour, outlook and rhythms to mirror those of the people around them before anyone has managed to take a closer look at what is truly there. The reasons for this are manifold. Piscean energy is so infinite and all-pervading that it really can be everything or express anything.

Pisces has an innate awareness of the unity of all things and knows that we are all part of a collective consciousness or a group mind. When we peel away the surface layers of belief, attitude and behaviour we often discover that all people are essentially the same. We are all doing the best we can with the knowledge and awareness available to us. What is more, we all need to be loved.

Piscean people are so sensitive that they often do not see any separation between themselves and others. Fish do have separate physical bodies but the waters that they inhabit connect them sensually with all other life forms over a wide area. Changes in atmosphere, feeding conditions and potential dangers are all detected. Subtle messages are rippled through the oceans and are acted upon immediately. In the same way, Pisces has detected a shift of mood and made the appropriate change in themselves without always being consciously aware of what they are doing. This is a great survival technique that keeps Pisces safe in most situations, able to fit in and be accepted.

The challenge for Pisces is to maintain a sense of stability and not get swamped by the unconscious feelings and desires of others. Pisces can sometimes feel pressurised to express the unacknowledged emotions of people around them. It is essential therefore that Piscean people have periods of solitude where they are totally free to rest, be with themselves and discover the harmony of their own emotions.

The healthiest Pisceans are those who are willing to love and accept their open, sensitive nature while being prepared to create some boundaries in their lives and in their relationships. Empathising easily with other people, some Pisceans may tend to put the needs of others above their own needs a little too often and this can become tiring or draining after a while. A Pisces who is sick or fatigued would benefit from examining their emotional environment and curtailing the relationships that are depleting for them.

Many Pisceans need to learn to say no to the whims or desires of other people and say yes to their own need for peace and quiet more often. In some cases, the only way for Pisces to do this effectively is to withdraw completely by going home and closing the door, moving to another room or unplugging the telephone. Most Pisceans are too sociable and caring to detach from other people for too long but a strategic

withdrawal at the right moment can help them to re-emerge
with new vitality, positivity and love.

PISCEAN ZONES OF THE BODY

Pisces rules the feet, the lymphatic system and the pituitary
gland. A great deal of physical relaxation and healing can be
achieved through foot massage of all kinds although some
Pisceans may initially be a little sensitive or resistant to
having their feet touched.

Reflexology would be particularly beneficial. This is the
therapy of stimulating the pressure points on or around the
feet that relate to the zones and organs of the body. The two
feet together can be seen as a map of the entire human system
and any imbalance can be detected and in some cases
corrected. At the very least reflexology can bring about a deep
release of tension that could be of help with the management
of pain and other symptoms.

The feet are a good barometer for the level of stress that
Pisceans are dealing with. If the feet are tense, tight, sore or
unyielding, then a dose of peace and quiet in a tranquil
environment would be the first step towards healing. Often
this is enough to have Pisces people back in the swim of life
again, feeling relaxed and able to be their fully expressive
selves.

Dance of all kinds can be healing for Pisces, particularly
when an emphasis is placed on the movements, flexibility and
suppleness of the feet. The discipline of ballet would be good,
especially for children, although prolonged balletic training
may distress the feet. Perhaps the freer forms of contemporary
dance would be even more ideal and the sensuality of Indian

dance forms would appeal to Pisceans' poetic nature. Pisces is too free-flowing to be rigidly imposed upon by a system or discipline of any kind although some structure would help them to give shape to their limitless creativity.

The health and comfort of the feet will always need to be checked and monitored. Pisceans would be well advised to wear shoes that fit correctly and support the foot as this assists psychological balance as well as physical health. Plenty of time spent walking barefoot, allowing the toes to spread out fully on grass, soft sand or warm earth would also be wonderful. This is a safe way for us all to discharge stress or negative energies.

EXERCISE AND THERAPIES

In addition to foot massage, full body massage can also be very healing; perhaps, too, a lymphatic massage that is carefully administered to stimulate and drain the lymphatic system. The lymphatic system circulates lymph around the body and is keyed to the circulation of the immune system; it requires physical movement to keep it active as it is not pumped internally in the way that the blood circulation is pumped by the heart.

Another way to stimulate lymphatic circulation is through regular skin brushing. Good bristle brushes are available from health or beauty shops and can be used to brush the full body before bathing. Care needs to be taken to avoid the face, neck and genitals and to brush upwards or downwards in the direction of the heart.

An aromatherapy massage would be particularly good as Pisceans respond quite readily to the aromatic or vibrational qualities of plant, fruit and flower oils as they are gently applied to the skin. Smell evokes powerful memories and can aid in the healing of past traumas by bringing unexpressed feelings to the surface to be released. On a physiological level some oils are also wonderful for stimulating the immune system.

Water play and swimming benefit Pisces, especially if Pisces has the time, space and quiet of a pool on their own to stretch and flex their limbs through the water. Perhaps even a spot of water ballet when no one else is looking would free the Piscean body and soul. For socially minded Pisceans, joining a water aerobics class could be fun. The more athletic Pisces could consider synchronised swimming or water polo.

Yoga is excellent for Pisces as it combines fluidity with strength and stamina. It is also a form of exercise that can be enjoyed as a solitary activity or with a group, giving Pisces the option to experience it as a quiet meditation or as a collective celebration. Yoga will help the Piscean circulation, balance and immune system. It will also strengthen the subtle electrical impulses that run throughout and around the physical body.

All forms of art therapy would aid psychological and emotional health, giving Pisces a vehicle for expressing underlying fears, tensions, powers and knowledge. When working with a therapist it would be helpful to use paintings or drawings as a focus for making sense of the world and putting the mind in order.

Solitary time spent on artwork could place a greater emphasis on the process of creativity in itself. Expression brings with it its own healing; not everything needs to be analysed to be therapeutic.

Many Pisceans find release through drama and theatre,

whether therapeutic role-playing or amateur dramatics. Pisces is a born actor and the quietest of Piscean people will amaze family members or close friends by becoming the extrovert on stage, expressing humour, pathos and passion in abundance.

An excellent psychological, emotional and spiritual therapy for Pisces is the practice of regression. Many illnesses, physical tensions or negatively repeating patterns of behaviour in the present can be healed by tracing the original emotional, mental or psychic trauma from the past; expressing it and releasing it. Pisceans can be particularly good at healing themselves through an exploration of the past and these techniques tap into that ability.

Regression is becoming increasingly popular and comes in many forms. It can be practised by psychologists, spiritual healers or psychics and covers anything from childhood experiences to altered states of awareness most easily described as past lives. In some cases people are able to access their higher awareness and wisely guide themselves through their own process of healing. The beauty of good regression is that it moves people into their emotional body and spiritual awareness, expanding them beyond the limitations of their intellect. Some Pisceans may find this kind of therapy invaluable for reawakening their intuition, perceptiveness and self-confidence.

LOVE AND ROMANCE

Most Pisceans make tender, romantic lovers and friends, sensitive to the needs of the other person and sensual within intimacy. Pisceans are open-hearted people who fall in love very deeply, often letting their heart rule their head and romance win out over the practicalities of life.

A healthy partner for a Piscean would be one who can provide a few boundaries to balance out the nebulous, Neptunian nature and help Pisces keep their feet on the ground, at least for some of the time. Pisceans will tend to choose more worldly partners who are able to deal with the material aspects of life. This can be a constructive partnership although it is important for Pisces to develop a worldly side to their personality rather than always relying on someone else to act on their behalf.

Pisceans are perfectly capable of forming good, happy marriages and long-term relationships. They are often able to keep the romance and mystique alive, finding freshness within each cycle of life to share with their partner. However, most Pisceans will require a certain amount of solitude for health, balance and peace of mind, retreating into their own inner world of imagination and illusion.

For this reason some will choose to spend periods of their lives without a relationship. It is as if Pisces needs to return to their own rhythms, away from the influence of even their nearest and dearest, to tap into their extraordinary flow of creativity and inner healing. Sooner or later, though, Pisces will find themselves being drawn into another relationship. The adventure of merging with another human being is a little too compelling to resist.

Pisceans can be flirtatious, even when in a committed relationship. In most cases this does not come from a need for conquest or even from a desire to play games, although if there are other people involved then games can often ensue, rather it comes from an endless capacity to see the beauty in another person and fall in love. Some Pisceans can even develop an addiction to the romantic feelings themselves, falling in love with love.

Once committed, Pisces will usually do their best to remain faithful. They would rarely set out to deliberately hurt someone, particularly not someone that they have chosen as a long-term partner. In some cases they just get a little carried away. Pisceans will often find a safe romantic outlet through books, poetry, romantic movies and beautiful music. Pisces will be touched and inspired by aesthetic good taste and escapist sentimentality alike; all can provide a safe and pleasurable release for romantic feelings.

When choosing partners Pisces would do well to bring their minds back from escapism and fantasy long enough to make clear, calculated choices. Some Pisceans have found themselves in ill-matched relationships because they have been too willing to see the beauty within another person and not willing enough to check out compatibility or suitability. When you have as much love to give as Pisces has, you owe it to yourself to choose the object of your affections wisely.

Water Affirmations for Pisces

Peace and beauty are always available to me.

I swim through the sensuous oceans of life.

I see beauty within myself as well as in others.

I flow with my own inner rhythms.

I love and accept my emotions fully.

Love flows to me, through me and around me.

I easily adapt to the many changes of life.

I swim towards my highest joy and greatest healing.

I listen with love to my instincts and intuition.

I bathe in the oceans of love and well-being.

Water Visualisation: The Ocean of Life

Find a quiet comfortable place and relax, preferably lying down or sitting with your back properly supported and your body open.

Breathe deeply and, as you do, imagine yourself as a brightly coloured fish swimming in a tropical ocean. With each breath imagine your fish's mouth and gills ingesting and eliminating the fresh seawater as you glide through the shimmering expanses that are lit by the tropical sunshine.

See yourself as exquisitely beautiful, being both delicate and robust, as you swim with the currents, changing direction or adjusting your course with every subtle change in oceanic pressure. In your mind, paint a watercolour picture of this under-sea world with its muted, subtle shades highlighted by brightly coloured corals or other fish that pass you.

Feel your connection to all other life forms through the movements, vibrations or mineral balance of the water. Although you see yourself as this one fish, imagine that you are able to feel the sensations of this whole oceanic universe.

The currents of life wash your fish self and your human self with wave upon wave of loving acceptance. Feel yourself fully loved and appreciated by all living things. Check through your body for any stress, tensions, disease or disharmony. Picture the currents of love and acceptance dissolving all of this, releasing any pent-up negativity or held-in emotions.

The luxuriant waters cleanse and heal every part of you, correcting any mineral or fluid imbalance within your body. See yourself moving through life with the flexibility of the fish, adapting beautifully to changes of environment and able to indulge in safe and free emotional expression.

Within your human body, as you breathe, imagine yourself experiencing a state of oneness with all life, plants, trees, animals, human beings – perhaps you even imagine the whole ocean as being a single life form that you can connect with.

THE EARTH AT THE OCEAN BED

The element of earth provides a supportive foundation for the watery realms of Pisces. It is through earth that Pisces can find some boundaries and form for all of that boundless creativity, imagination, fantasy and dreaminess.

Pisces will often resist earthy restrictions and disciplines, wanting to swim clear of practicalities, financial responsibilities or routines. Some Pisceans never seem to be able to develop a healthy dose of worldliness to balance their ethereal qualities but for those who do, the rewards are great.

The symbol of two fishes swimming in opposite directions gives us a picture of the Piscean dilemma. One fish is half of the Piscean psyche wanting to swim away from all worldliness and live in a state of spiritual retreat or peaceful sanctuary. This aspect of Pisces longs to feel the higher currents of the universe and explore the mysterious depths of the soul. The second fish is the other half of the Piscean psyche that wants to swim with the world, taking an active part in life, developing a career, having a family or exercising a healing influence on the environment.

A classic Piscean would be the artist, musician or poet able to express a great deal of creativity but being unsure of how to market the fruits of their endeavours. To swim with the worldly side of Piscean nature it helps to view marketing, presentation, packaging and business acumen as part of the creative process rather than as a necessary chore.

Pisceans who do turn their hands to the practicalities of life often attract a great deal of success. Imagination when properly channelled tends to attract money, recognition and greater opportunities.

PARTNERSHIPS, BUSINESS AND SUCCESS

When given the choice, Pisces will team themselves up with partners or colleagues who can deal with the earthy activities of accounting or administration and the airiness of public relations or promotion while they get on with being the creative genius. However, Piscean flexibility could see them taking up any role within an organisation, at least until the creative opportunities come their way.

Pisceans will often become self-employed or freelance at some time in their lives. They are often not suited to regular routines or a rigid work environment and can be at their most productive when they are able to work at their own rhythm and pace. It helps to be free of noisy distractions too.

Pisces people need to find an inner discipline rather than having an external discipline imposed upon them. This inner discipline often comes with the discovery of a vocation that Pisces can feel passionately inspired by. When Pisceans find their heart's desire they will be willing to work day and night if necessary for their beloved project or cause. However, some may have to risk a swim through periods of self-delusion and a lack of motivation in order to discover and tap this sense of purpose.

Pisces best experiences the element of earth through its opposite Sun sign, the earth sign of Virgo. Through Virgo, Pisces can often find its place in the world by making a commitment to the service of others. Pisces may find fulfilment through some form of social service, care work or the healing professions.

Through serving other people, Pisces can develop a strong sense of self and a state of peace. In situations of emergency, disaster or stress, Pisces can even become an island of peace and stability within the stormy ocean. A temporary steeliness can become enmeshed within all of that watery compassion and the Piscean expansiveness can be complemented by Virgoan attention to detail.

Pisces provides a safe harbour for many shipwrecked souls. It is only when the storm is over and the urgency of the situation wanes that the steeliness dissolves. Pisces disappears home to have a pause for thought and a good cry – in some cases aided by a stiff drink and followed by a full night's sleep, the latter being of greater benefit for Pisces than the former.

In most situations Pisces will be a well-liked member of the team, being flexible enough to adapt to changing circumstances and the personality traits of colleagues.

Pisceans do also have an earthy ability to roll up their sleeves and get their hands dirty if necessary, particularly when the job involves caring for others.

Pisceans will only create friction or lose direction in work or business environments by being too caught up in their own fantasy worlds. To make a living, ground all of that creativity and fulfil all of their commitments, Pisces needs to remember to stay with what is real; not allowing themselves to get caught up in self-delusion or be over-sensitive and take everything too personally.

When Pisceans discover what they truly love doing and allow themselves to rise to the challenges of the material world, they can be highly successful financially. Piscean creativity really can be channelled into business acumen when the desire is there. However, Pisces has the gift of being able to see beyond the illusions of materialism and as such tends not to take the acquisition of wealth too seriously.

It may take practice or experimentation over a long period of time for Pisces to find the balance between being the unworldly mystic and putting food in their stomach. Pisceans who make the commitment to find that balance can be very happy indeed. When they follow the currents of their own self-healing and learn to love themselves fully, they often come to the realisation that there is no conflict between the two.

Earth Affirmations for Pisces

My imagination brings me prosperity and joy.

My opportunities are infinite and tangible.

Money flows to me with ease and fluidity.

I am clear, firm, businesslike and strong.

I make decisions that support me in peace and prosperity.

I trust my intuition.

Earth Visualisation: Magic Coral

Find yourself a quiet, peaceful place to stretch out and relax. Breathe deeply, picture yourself snorkelling or swimming in a warm blue, tropical sea. Above you, the sun gently warms and relaxes your back. Even if you are not a swimmer in real life, see yourself swimming along beautifully and easily in your mind's eye.

As you peer through the transparent, blue waters below you, imagine that you see the most beautiful corals. Their colours are vivid and their shapes have a mysterious intricacy. Picture yourself reaching down and picking up small pieces of coral; the water is shallow and it is easy to do. In your thoughts place these pretty pieces in a net or pouch by your side.

As you collect your coral, notice that for each piece you take, more grows in its place; within your imagination there is truly unlimited abundance. Once your net or pouch is full, swim to shore with your bounty and see yourself walking across the beach to the fertile earth beyond.

In your thoughts find a patch of particularly rich, fertile soil and think about the material things that you would like to create in your life right now. This could be sums of money, a new place to live, a healthier body or specific creative opportunities.

For everything that you desire, plant a piece of coral in the earth and instantly see it grow into a symbol of material success. This could be a beautiful tree, a pot of gold, a picture of your new home or anything else that could represent physical attainment for you.

Think about any practical steps you could take to help create these things in your life and when you complete, make a note of them. In the days or weeks that follow write the letters, make the telephone calls or follow through any other plans that you have to make your visions a reality.

SWIMMING WITH THE CURRENTS OF AIR

The element of air represents the realms of the mind and the higher mind, filled with ideas and inspirations. Pisces loves ideas and can dreamily imagine numerous possibilities, images and ideal scenarios when required to add their thoughts to any discussion. Pisces is truly aware of the fluidity and expansiveness of choice that is available to us all; there are no limits to the imagination and no limits to what we can create through the use of imaginative thought.

Piscean thought springs from intuition and the irrational meanderings of the mind rather than from the intellect and the harder lines of logic. This is why Pisceans can often arrive at a correct answer or an effective solution to a problem without knowing or being able to explain how they got there. This approach is very free and resists the mental rigidity that hinders some zodiac signs.

To stay healthy Pisces needs to be able to allow themselves the pleasure and joy of their free-flowing imagination while learning to create a level of discernment. Having a wonderful idea is no guarantee that it is workable and practical or that it will be automatically understood by others. Discernment can bring a healthy and balanced communication of creative thought.

Some Pisceans may forget to take care of themselves, particularly in matters of health; they can become so carried away with their creativity and illusions that they do not pay attention to their physical well-being. Pisceans with health problems can often learn to float off mentally and detach from physical pain or discomfort. This is quite a gift, allowing Pisces to stay as comfortable as possible during trauma or the stresses of medical treatments. There is a need, however, to come back from the voyages of the mind for long enough to attend to the cause of the illness rather than just escaping from its symptoms.

The Piscean vision of the world is often a psychic vision; many Pisceans are so open-minded and without boundaries that they are able to perceive and receive information that is extrasensory in nature. Pisceans often have a heightened form of the perceptiveness and intuition that we all have, only for Pisces these abilities are more likely to be more fully developed. These gifts include spiritual healing, clairvoyance (clear sight), clairaudience (clear hearing) and a heightened feeling awareness.

Even for the many Pisceans who would not consider themselves to be psychically gifted there will be a spark of vision that seems to come from beyond the person themselves. This vision may come in the form of creative ideas or be expressed through a desire to bring healing comfort to others and peace to the world. Pisceans who are able to use these visionary gifts can expect to experience a greater sense of satisfaction, joy and well-being in their lives.

The Pisces mind loves to find escape from the daily routines or challenges of the world; escapism of all kinds can be sought and enjoyed. Pisces dives delightedly into science fiction, fantasy, romance and poetry. Some Pisces people may even make careers or hobbies out of creating escapism for others to enjoy. Pisces can bring its poetry to all forms of the entertainment industry, most often through writing, an activity that allows Pisceans some solitude in their work while having the potential to touch many people.

A certain amount of escapism is essential for the mental, emotional and physical health of many Pisceans but it needs to be balanced with a willingness to deal with life or a desire to engage with other people. Even without a focus for escapism Pisces can so easily float off into the expansive realms of the mind, finding this a safer place to be than what many would consider to be 'the real world'. For this reason it is no surprise that Pisces is the Sun sign that is linked to the anaesthetic influence of drugs used in surgical medicine.

Pisces' escapist and anaesthetic tendencies come from the influence of its ruling planet of Neptune. Neptune also has a powerful relationship to hallucinogenic drugs and alcohol. Some Pisceans can be drawn to use drugs or alcohol as a means of escape but this will rarely benefit them. Being the most sensitive sign of the zodiac they tend to react quickly to even small amounts of any drug.

Piscean health would be greatly enhanced by keeping the use of recreational drugs to a minimum. It would also benefit Pisces to question doctors and complementary practitioners alike about the properties and possible side-effects of prescribed substances. Pisceans are often more sensitive to drugs or remedies of every kind.

A healthy, natural escape for Pisces would be through a regular meditation practice. Meditation can help Pisces to clarify thoughts, release negative thinking and expand into the higher mind or higher awareness. Linked with a commitment to take care of the practicalities of life, a meditative approach can help to create very healthy, happy and balanced Pisceans indeed.

Air Affirmations for Pisces

I expand my intuition and build my objectivity.

My thoughts are positive, perceptive and practical.

I dream myself to greater health and positive awareness.

I swim to the realms of higher thought.

My imagination is limitless and focused.

My fantasies inspire me to act in the world.

Air Visualisation: A Breath of Sea Air

Place your body in a relaxed, open position and breathe deeply. As you breathe, imagine yourself inhaling lung-fulls of sea air filled with ozone and tasting of salt. Imagine your lungs being safely cleared of any tightness, congestion or toxins.

Next, imagine yourself becoming one with the currents of air skimming over the surface of the water. Feel yourself light and free, travelling over a wide distance.

Have an image of a school of flying fish bobbing in and out of the water and for a moment see yourself as one of those magical fish, with its wing-like fins shimmering in the sunlight, as it appears above the waves. Imagine yourself moving freely from your emotions into your mind and back into your emotions again.

Picture a porpoise or small dolphin moving playfully through the water and in your mind allow yourself to be that creature, living in the water but coming to the surface for air. Breathe very deeply and relax.

Imagine yourself becoming the currents of sea air once again; moving across the waves. Perhaps see yourself supporting the wings of seabirds as they fly or filling the sails of a yacht to give it motion and speed.

Allow this airiness to bring you any ideas, inspirations or gems of wisdom that would aid your healing, creativity and success at this time. When you complete this visualisation, write down or record any ideas that you had.

FIRE IN THE SOUL

The element of fire brings the realms of positive expansion, enthusiasm and energy to Pisces. Before the planet Neptune was discovered the ancient ruler of Pisces was the planet Jupiter. Neptune and Jupiter have some similarities, both being expansive in nature and having an influence that is spiritually opening. Neptune is essentially watery whereas Jupiter is associated with the element of fire.

It is perhaps through Jupiter that Pisces can best experience the realms of fire. This influence often motivates Pisces with a spiritual passion or religious fervour. Pisceans can sometimes be said to have fire in the soul, spiritual convictions and a heart filled with true compassion.

The symbol of the fish has long been associated with Christianity and some Pisceans can appear to be a little saintly or angelic, but Pisces can be found on many other spiritual paths too, committed to any one of the many branches of faith. Having an extraordinary awareness and sensitivity, Pisceans can feel that there is more to life than that which can be tangibly seen or felt. Faith in a divine purpose or higher path is less of a stretch of the imagination for them than it might be for others.

Pisceans have often been drawn to a spiritual ministry of some kind. Many become priests, vicars, rabbis, swamis or imams. Many more choose monastic lifestyles both as spiritual hermits and as women or men of God, working in the world. Other Pisceans express a fiery spirit as healers, shamans, mystics or teachers of New Age thought and philosophy.

Pisceans with faith are generally healthier than those without. This does not mean that all Pisceans need to be religious in order to be healthy. Piscean atheists who display faith in their convictions will also benefit. It is the feeling and experience of having faith in itself that fires Pisces with enthusiasm and acts as a source of healing.

PISCEAN INSPIRATION AND CREATIVITY

Pisceans are often fired with passion to express their creativity through painting and all forms of the visual arts; some may be fascinated with light, whether depicting the movements of light on water or the diffusion and refraction of light through the atmosphere. Light has always been the essential inspiration and motivating force for the artist; art studios are often chosen to provide as much natural light as possible during the daytime.

An actor on stage or on film becomes more special, more captivating, when properly lit. This focuses the attention of the audience and highlights the drama of the piece. The mood of a ballet, a concert, or a recital can owe much to the effects of lighting too. Light brings magic, mystery, whimsy and suspense. The lights of performance attract many Pisceans to develop and share their special creative gifts.

Light for Pisces is the divine spark of creativity that shimmers within each Piscean soul. Pisceans are so creative that they are often able to turn their hands to a number of different creative mediums, providing the world with inspiration, entertainment and beauty with everything that they do.

Having your Sun in Pisces fires the imagination in a way that is so compelling that sooner or later appropriate creative outlets will need to be found. Piscean health and happiness is often linked to the expression of the imagination; failure to express can be a little like an eclipse of the Piscean life force that restricts the expansion of joy and well-being.

Creativity does not necessarily have to be channelled through activities that have been traditionally labelled as artistic or literary. Many people think that they are not creative because they do not paint pictures, write or dance but we all express creativity through everything that we do.

The way we dress and present ourselves is an expression of our unique creativity. We express ourselves in the way we decorate our home and through the ornaments or pictures that we choose to adorn it with. Creativity can be expressed through even the simplest business or domestic tasks. For Pisces the light of creativity shines into every corner of their world.

Fire Affirmations for Pisces

I expand into a greater lightness of being.

My soul is fired with enthusiasm.

I surrender to the flow of my creative power.

My creativity lights the way to my success.

I am a shining inspiration for myself and for others.

My body shimmers with healing light.

Fire Visualisation: Reflections

Find a peaceful place to sit or lie down, with your back supported and your body open and relaxed.

Breathe deeply and imagine yourself sitting, looking at the golden sunlight reflected off the surface of an expanse of water; perhaps the sea, or a large pond.

See the light shimmer on the rippling water, and reflect for a moment on your physical health, emotional well-being, state of mind or spiritual development.

What is it about yourself that you would like to change? Do you need some physical healing or would you like to feel differently about yourself inside? Would you like to enter a greater state of peace and progress fully onto your spiritual path?

In your mind's eye watch the light on the water and see images begin to form through the shimmering haze. Picture your ideal future self, physically healthy and with a bright, alert, mind, filled with positive thoughts. See your future self as smiling and happy, filled with inner peace and spiritually aware. Add any qualities or details to this image that you choose, painting it as vividly as you can.

Imagine your present self now being floated upwards and out across the water to meet with this image of the future. See your present self touch and merge with your future self, the two images becoming one. See yourself floating in the light across the water and back to dry land, your feet touching solid earth.

See that you have become your ideal future self, the light still rippling through you and around you to help create the healing transformation necessary to bring you closer to these changes in physical reality.

Reflect on any practical steps that you might need to take to help facilitate these changes and when you have completed, write down or record any ideas that you had.

THE SPIRITUAL PURPOSE OF PISCES

Pisces has the ability to hold up a mirror to the world, reflecting back the dramas, intrigues and beauty of life for us all to look at and enjoy. So much of the pleasure that we obtain from the cinema, television, theatre or visual arts comes from the ability that these art forms have to whisk us off from the day-to-day reality of our lives while reminding us of ourselves and the world we live in.

Perhaps the most successful forms of art or entertainment are those that seduce us into getting emotionally involved. A single picture can invoke powerful feelings from love, joy and sadness to shock or sexual excitement. This is Pisces reflecting our deepest feelings back to us and bringing them to the surface for us all to see.

Pisces rules dreams, giving us a vivid inner world that can seem as real as waking reality. Without Pisces we would lack the source of our creativity and inspiration for the journey that we take through life. Dreams build empires; imagination provides us with a bridge towards high achievement.

The highest spiritual purpose for Pisceans is perhaps in coming to an understanding of unity with all things. Pisceans tend to merge with the people or the environment around them; feeling the emotions, aspirations and drives of others. In this way they are able to come to an understanding that we are all essentially the same, regardless of age, sex, colour or religion.

Similarly Pisceans can come to an understanding of unity with all forms of life, able to connect to all living things. When we become sensitive to the feelings of the animals and plants with which we share this planet, and perhaps with planet earth herself, it becomes more compelling to take care of our environment and learn to foster an atmosphere of peaceful co-existence.

THE PISCEAN GIFT TO THE WORLD

We all need Piscean energy to bring a little magic or poetry into our lives. What would life be without illusion, romance, intrigue and inspiration? Pisces entices us away from the rigid routines of life into the realms of dreaminess, glamour and innocence. At its highest vibration Pisces wakens us all to our spiritual purpose.

Piscean people can be found in creative professions of all kinds. They can be poets, actors, musicians, artists, dancers, film makers or photographers. Many others are drawn to the healing arts and can be doctors, nurses, spiritual healers, complementary therapists, counsellors or psychics. Some are called to positions of spiritual ministry in all branches of religion.

Pisces is a force in the world that takes care of human need. The waters of Pisces bring comfort, compassion and joy to us all. Pisces opens the heart and feeds the soul with infinite love.

Astrology and Beyond

In this book we have offered many thoughts and suggestions for self-empowerment that we trust will be fun and beneficial for you to use. There are an infinite number of ways that we can develop ourselves and heal our lives; it is important that we all maintain a willingness to explore new things without becoming fixed on one approach.

As we delve into the realms of astrology we each need to decide on the ideas that are positive and supportive for us to adopt while discarding any concepts that do not serve our growth or development. We are constantly changing and the beliefs or techniques that we use need to remain flexible enough to reflect our changing nature.

Astrology provides us with a useful guide to our personality; it is not intended as a set of hard and fast rules that we have to follow. Whatever an astrologer or an astrology column in a magazine may predict for us, we can still influence the events and developments of our own lives. No one is at the mercy of planetary forces, unless, of course, they choose to believe otherwise. All movements of the stars can be acted upon positively for health, joy, peace and success.

The same movement of the planets that can be interpreted as bringing challenges could also be interpreted as providing exciting new opportunities for transformation, healing and growth. Astrology can help us to see the trends; it is our choice to act upon those trends in ways that will benefit us. We are the authors of our own fate; we create all of the healings, the miracles and the successes of our lives.

By maintaining a positive approach to everything that we do we are able to respond to the higher vibrations of our personality and tune into the beneficial influences that are available to us. Perhaps having explored astrology for the tools of healing and transformation that are appropriate for us we may begin to focus our attention beyond the influence of the stars and planets into the higher wisdom and mysteries of the universe. Self-healing and spiritual growth is meant to be fun. The higher currents of healing delight in carrying us to the realms of greater joy and bliss. We just need to be willing to play.